W9-CZR-250

TILL

From the Library of
Eric

August '39

August '39

The last four weeks of peace in Europe

Stephen Howarth

A John Curtis Book
Hodder & Stoughton
LONDON SYDNEY AUCKLAND TORONTO

British Library Cataloguing in Publication Data

Howarth, Stephen, *1953* –
August '39:
the last four weeks of peace in Europe
1. Europe, 1939–1945
I. Title
940.53

ISBN 0-340-42902-X

Published by Hodder and Stoughton,
a division of Hodder and Stoughton Limited,
Mill Road, Dunton Green, Sevenoaks, Kent TN13 2YE.
Editorial Office: 47 Bedford Square, London WC1B 3DP.

Photoset by Rowland Phototypesetting Limited,
Bury St Edmunds, Suffolk.

Printed in Great Britain by
St Edmundsbury Press Limited,
Bury St Edmunds, Suffolk.

For my beloved sons
Christopher and Liam
with the hope that, like me,
they will be
fortunate enough to
grow up in peace

Contents

Illustrations

(between pages 96 and 97)

Endpapers: 2 September: the crowd awaits outside Downing Street *(Imperial War Museum)*

The newspaper headlines reproduced in the text were supplied by the John Frost Newspaper Library and the *Daily Telegraph*.

Picture research by Julia Brown.

Preface

This is not so much a history as a story: a story of a time which for many people, including myself, *is* history – and yet which for millions of others is an unforgettable part of their lives. Because of that, I have been particularly concerned to convey an accurate sense of the moods, as much as the objective facts, of the period. In this I have been greatly helped by interviews, either in person or by letter, with many 'witnesses' of August 1939. Conducting these interviews was both a privilege and an enormous pleasure for me; my only regrets are that time prevented me from carrying on the process *ad infinitum*, and that space has prevented me from using all the personal information I was given so freely and kindly.

Very little in this book is invented, and where invention has been necessary it is always closely based on factual authority. Scenes and conversations between private individuals are reconstructed from their memories, supplemented by diaries, letters and personal photographs. Others in public life, now dead, left copious diaries and correspondence which have provided me with further sources of authentic thought and dialogue. The same is true for those many private people (some certainly dead, some perhaps still living) whose diaries form the core of the Mass-Observation Archive in the University of Sussex. I am very grateful to Curtis Brown Ltd and to the Trustees of the Mass-Observation Archive for permission to use extracts from these unpublished diaries; to Shepheard-Walwyn (Publishers) Ltd and to Janine Phillips for permission to use extracts from her diary of a Polish childhood; to William Collins, Sons and Co., for permission to use extracts from the diaries of Harold Nicolson, edited by Nigel Nicolson; to C & T Publications Ltd, copyright holders, and to William Heinemann Ltd, publishers, for their permission to reprint extracts from 'The Companion', Part 3, to Volume V of Martin Gilbert's biography of Churchill; to Ernest Kroll, poet, for permission to use parts of his written notes; to William Heinemann Ltd, and to Malcom Muggeridge, editor, for permission to use passages from the diaries of Count Ciano, Mussolini's Foreign Minister; to Macmillan Inc., and to the Executors of the Estate of Sir Alexander Cadogan, for permission to use extracts from his diaries; and to Opera Mundi, Editions Robert Laffont, for permission to use passages from the memoirs of Paul Schmidt, *Hitler's Interpreter*. I regret that some copyright holders have been untraceable. I am also indebted to the London Library, for their long loans of various crucial volumes; and to the Meteorological Office, Bracknell, for their patience concerning an extremely long loan of the weather records of the period, and to the Royal Greenwich Observatory, Herstmonceux, for settling a question of time: in August 1939, Great Britain was working on British Summer Time, an hour ahead of GMT, while Germany was operating on its own standard time, also an hour ahead of GMT. Thus, for example, 9 a.m. in Britain was also 9 a.m. in Germany, a small but important factor in a story of this sort.

Notes at the end of the book indicate the major published sources for each chapter. Without those, this would have been a very different kind of book; but I cannot help feeling that its most important sources are the living witnesses of August 1939. On request, some of their names have been changed, and sadly, I have not been able to make use of all the memories I have been given. However, among those included in this book are Oscar Baker; Molly Brown (née McAndrew); Catherine (Kit) Clifton (née Dennis) and her husband Joseph; Tom Elliott; Dorothy Emanuel (née Williams); Barkeley Goodrich, his wife Libby (née Tufts) and her mother Mrs Annie H. Tufts; Colonel Denis Harding and his brother Frank; my father, David Howarth; Mrs Eleanor Kennerley; John Landells; Revd Professor Robert Leaney and his wife Elizabeth; Dr and Mrs Michael Haigh; Zofya Olscholwska and her late husband Taddeus; Reginald Panting; James ('Sandy') Powell; Richard Richter; John Scott and his wife Elspeth (née Harmes); Mrs Stella Sutherland (née Smith), and her sisters Nanette (my mother) and Jessamine; Lionel Tomlinson; my father-in-law Francis Vanek; and Mike Warbreck-Howell. I am grateful to them all, and to all those I could not include.

For some mysterious reason it is conventional for authors to relegate thanks to their immediate families to the very end. Considering that without their support few books would be written, this seems odd; certainly without my darling wife Marianne I would get little done, and without our beautiful boys Christopher and Liam I would have little reason for doing it. Yet in this case it may be appropriate to leave them all to the end. The others named above are from the past, and are owed an unrepayable debt by my generation for the chance to grow up in peace; but my wife and sons are the present and future.

S. H.

Prologue

No one who heard the Prime Minister's speech ever forgot it, or where they were and what they were doing at the time. He spoke carefully and deliberately; there could be no mistake about his words.

> This morning the British Ambassador in Berlin handed the German Government a final note, stating that, unless the British Government heard from them by 11 o'clock that they were prepared at once to withdraw their troops from Poland, a state of war would exist between us. I have to tell you now that no such undertaking has been received, and that consequently this country is at war with Germany.

In parlours and kitchens and drawing-rooms throughout Britain the moment crystallised – quarter past eleven in the morning, 3 September 1939, a bright, warm day, placid and tranquil. Because it was a Sunday, many people were told the news in church. There, the interruption of the service heightened the sense of unreality, so that afterwards it seemed to have happened in slow motion; someone coming in and whispering to the vicar, the hymns fading and the congregation stock-still, then the awful announcement from the pulpit that war had come.

In church or at home, it was a moment which seemed to last an eternity. Some people, after the weeks and months of uncertainty, felt a relief so intense it was almost thrilling; some felt nauseous and dizzy with a depth of horror they had never known before; and others, stunned into emotional numbness, felt nothing.

The time of real fear had been twelve months earlier, during the Munich crisis. Ever since the Prime Minister, Neville Chamberlain, had returned in triumph from his negotiations with Hitler, there had indeed been evacuation exercises in Britain; in various parts gas masks had been issued and blackout practised; and especially in the cities there had been endless debates over different types of air raid shelter. But throughout the twelve months many British people honestly believed there would be unbroken peace in their time; and now, after a week of humid, thundery weather, August 1939 – the last four weeks of peace in Europe – had become a summer to remember. Brilliant

sunshine; temperatures comfortably in the high 70s Fahrenheit; daily work for some, but summer holidays for others and a Bank Holiday for all. Seeing walls of sandbags growing outside public buildings had been unsettling, but watching searchlights being hauled into position was interesting, and trying on gas masks comical and embarrassing: they made a nasty farting noise if they did not fit. Now, though, it felt as if these preparations had been only half-serious, tiresome additions to the daily round, innocent diversions of children playing inadequately with the idea of war. Now no one could predict what would happen; war was a reality, and the sunshine, the breezes and the birdsong seemed unreal, as though they belonged to another era.

They did. As the weight of the Prime Minister's message sank in, men and women began to wonder if they would live to see such a splendid summer again, and understood that nothing they had known would be the same again; for in that moment the world had been altered for ever.

This story is an echo of the world which had vanished.

The first week

2–8 August 1939

The Daily Telegraph

and Morning Post

TODAY'S WEATHER: Bright intervals; local showers.   LONDON, WEDNESDAY, AUGUST 2, 1939   BROADCASTING—Page Six   ONE PENNY

PETROL AND OIL TO BE RATIONED IN WAR

ANGLO-FRENCH STAFF TALKS

MISSIONS TO MOSCOW TO MEET IN PARIS

A VITAL POINT IN 3-POWER PACT

A.R.P. WORKERS AT A LONDON BANK

M.P.S' PRAISE FOR PROGRESS IN A.R.P. WORK

OFFICIALS ALREADY APPOINTED: 35,000,000 COUPONS PRINTED

SUPPLIES FOR MOTORISTS ON HORSE-POWER BASIS

PRICES AND DISTRIBUTION TO BE CONTROLLED

STANDARD HIGHER THAN ABROAD

SIR J. ANDERSON & RESPONSE

1,906,000 PERSONS ENROLLED

COUNTRY SWEPT BY STORMS

HALF-INCH OF RAIN IN TEN MINUTES

NEW BRANCH OF THE R.A.F.

Technical Section to be Formed

ARMAMENTS AND ENGINEERING

JAPAN MOVING HER TROOPS FROM CENTRAL CHINA

RESTRICTIONS ON LUXURY MOTORING

I

Take your gas mask with you

NEAR PLYMOUTH in Devon, in the orchard at the back of Winsor Farm, a half-grown lamb stared up at an open bedroom window and bleated restlessly. There was no reply. A lean-to roof reached from just under the window nearly down to the ground. The lamb was impatient to start the day, so it trotted away from the house, turned, ran, and leaped on to the lean-to roof. Picking its way carefully up the gentle slope, it reached the window and looked in. Inside all was neat and tidy in the bedroom: rugs on the lino-covered floor, a couple of wooden chairs, a small fireplace and a big wardrobe, a chest of drawers with a china basin and a ewer of water on top; and two beds, each with a young woman asleep in it – everything just as the lamb expected. It put its front legs on the window-sill, pulled itself up and jumped lightly in. Its small hooves, clicking on the lino, were silent on the rug next to Catherine's bed. She had not heard it come in; and so, as it did every morning when the weather was fine and her window open, the lamb reached up to waken her, and very softly nibbled her cheek. The time was a quarter to seven and the morning was humid and cloudy, almost windless, with only a hint of a breeze from the west. Wednesday, 2 August 1939, was beginning.

Kit Dennis (she was called Catherine only if someone was annoyed with her) was twenty-one years old, the youngest of six children, and had been born and brought up on Winsor Farm. Many would have said it was an idyllic place, and most of the time Kit would have agreed with them. The 300-acre farm was tucked away down a narrow winding lane outside the village of Yealmpton. To the north rose the brown wild hills of Dartmoor; to the south lay Winsor's own fields and woods and streams in the valley below the house; and past that the English Channel, hidden from view by the far side of the valley where the protecting hills came up again. Plymouth, seven miles west, was another world, busy, crowded, noisy and visited only for farm business or for trips to the theatre and cinema. A crow flying eastwards across the orchard would pass over eighteen miles of gentle hills and valleys, many farms and a few villages, before arriving at Dartmouth, too far away for Kit to consider. Isolated but self-contained, Winsor, like much of agricultural Britain, supplied almost everything the family needed.

As the nation awakened, people of every condition made ready to face the day. On his own dairy farm at Plympton, seven miles from Winsor, Joseph Clifton had been up for an hour and a half, and with two men to help him had almost finished the milking, coaxing the warm frothy liquid by hand from the udders of fifty cows. In South Wales the members of Swansea Amateur Football Club were looking forward to an outing: they were to go 50 miles by road to the pretty seaside resort of Tenby, on the other side of Carmarthen Bay. Near the centre of England, at 102 Southwell Road East in the Nottinghamshire village of Rainsworth, Oscar Baker heard his father's alarm clock ring at seven sharp and the immediate daily reaction: thump, clatter, a burst of cheerful whistling, energetic footsteps rattling down the stairs, the sound of the kettle going on and tea being made. Across the ridge of the Pennines in Cheshire, while the kitchen of a house named Westgate also came to life, Mike Warbreck-Howell slumbered contentedly upstairs, knowing that breakfast would be ready when he felt like it; the maids Hetty and Sarah would see to that. At 54 Falton Street in Byker, a suburb of the north-eastern shipbuilding city of Newcastle, Molly McAndrew came into the kitchen from the bedroom she shared with her mother – the only other room they had – and began to make porridge, using water from the setpot; its fire had gone out, but the bricks kept the heat in quite well, so it saved on gas. In Northern Ireland, alone in a cottage called The Porter's Lodge, 12 miles outside Belfast and half a mile from Strangford Lough, David Howarth began shaving, and wondered who he would get to talk about what today. As head of the Talks Department of BBC Belfast he had to have new ideas all the time. In the most distant north of Great Britain, on the island of Bressay in the treeless Shetlands, Lollie Anderson, one of the island's three postmen, looked out from the Old Manse across the Sound, to see if the ferry had started over; and, far south in the leafy Weald of Kent, punctually at eight o'clock Winston Churchill, Member of Parliament for Epping, sat upright in bed, pulled his black sleeping mask from his eyes and rang for his valet.

This Great Britain is a long thin country: many of its people, having travelled very little, never think how long and thin it is. But from Winsor Farm in Devon to the Old Manse in Bressay is something more than 700 miles. Draw a circle of that radius around Winsor Farm, and it shows some curious things. Norway, neutral Sweden and most of Denmark lie outside the circle. Inside, however, the Republic of Ireland is encompassed and nearly the whole of France and Switzerland; while Belgium, Luxembourg and the Netherlands are comfortably included. The entire North Sea, a slice of the Atlantic, the Bay of Biscay and even the Mediterranean Gulf of Lions all fall within its range. And with its northern arc dividing the Shetlands, its southern arc touches Oporto in Portugal and Madrid, the Spanish capital. To the south-east it comes close to Milan in Italy; and its eastern arc runs through the centre of Germany. In 1939, on a steep hill called Obersalzburg in the Bavarian Alps, not far beyond the limit of that line, stood a house called the Berghof. In English the name means the Mountain Court. As Britain awoke on the morning of 2 August, so did the Berghof's builder, owner and main occupant, Adolf Hitler. The leader of Nazi Germany was recently back from a flying visit to Berlin. Whatever else the day brought for the millions of people within the circle, for Hitler, just outside it, it was to be a day of pleasure; he was on holiday, and already keenly anticipating the evening. By then he would be in Bayreuth's elaborate Festspielhaus, the opera theatre, enjoying the final performance of that year's Wagner Festival. Like Bressay, Oporto and Madrid, Bayreuth lies exactly on the line, 700 miles from Devon. Kit Dennis would have been amazed, and amused, to realise that Winsor Farm, the centre of her world, was also the centre geographically, at least, of such an extraordinary ring.

'It may look like a lamb,' said her mother with mock disapproval, 'but it thinks it's a dog.' Kit giggled, and held out another rasher for Mary. Its duty as alarm clock done, the lamb had skittered back down the lean-to roof, and at breakfast stood by the kitchen window, poking its head through the bars, eagerly gobbling fried bacon and potatoes. Far from the centre of public life, Kit was one of the few of these ordinary people to keep a daily record of her private life. Somehow she lost her diary; but she was blessed with a good memory, and August 1939 was a month which stuck fast, as much for the small events as the great public ones.

Life on Winsor Farm was not hectic but always busy; and never more so than during August, the harvest month. Her eldest brother John had joined the Royal Navy; his visits home were rare now. William, the second brother, was married and ran his own farm less than five miles away; Alice too, the eldest sister, had married a farmer and lived five miles in the other direction. Apart from Kit, that left at home her parents; one more brother, Henry; and one more sister, Margaret. With three labourers to help, it was a pretty small group for 300 acres.

Kit's first jobs of the day were light. First, she had gone down to feed the hens and the calves, then while Henry and two of the men did the morning milking she went to the dairy and skimmed the cream from last night's milking. The dairy was designed to be as naturally cool as possible: facing north, its single window was shaded by a high hedge; its floor and wide slab shelves were all of slate. Skimming was simple, but effective; the fresh milk was poured into wide stone troughs, like shallow sinks, and left for twelve hours. During that time the cream rose to the surface, until the milk below could be drained off directly into the churns. A thick layer of sweet yellow cream remained, to be ladled into butter-churns. But then the easy part of the day was over; after breakfast the hard work began.

In Kent as in Devon it was a stuffy, oppressive sort of day. While Kit Dennis rode out to harvest, leading a team of four heavy horses harnessed to a binder, Winston Churchill was being driven from Chartwell, his country home, to London. At the same time, from all parts of the capital and country, nearly four hundred other members of the House of Commons were heading towards Westminster. The sky was overcast, with low, ragged clouds foretelling bad weather, and the afternoon debate promised little better. A year ago, acting as his own Foreign Secretary, Prime Minister Neville Chamberlain had brought out of Munich Hitler's signed promise of lifetime peace: 'symbolic', said the note, 'of the desire of our two peoples never to go to war with one another again.' The British nation, in more pacifist mood than ever before in its history, had hailed Chamberlain as a great statesman. But since then much had changed. Now war seemed imminent; yet this afternoon he was going to propose that Parliament should adjourn at the end of the week for two months' summer holiday.

Churchill, for one, was convinced it should not: three weeks was the maximum he felt should be allowed. He had prepared his speech saying why in detail, and had tried it out at home the day before on a friend and fellow Conservative, General Edward (Louis) Spears, the Member for Carlisle. He had also written to another friend, Viscount 'Top' Wolmer, the Member for Aldershot, asking him to be sure and vote against the motion, or at least to abstain. Wolmer felt it was a waste of time; Chamberlain's majority was so big, he would be able to follow whatever policy he chose. Nothing daunted, after lunch on 2 August Churchill took his habitual corner seat in the lofty Commons chamber; and it was recorded in Hansard, the official account of proceedings in Parliament, that 'the House met at a Quarter before Three of the Clock, Mr SPEAKER in the Chair'.

First for this afternoon there were some routine home affairs: the third readings of the London Gas Undertakings (Regulations) Bill and the Hamilton Burgh Order Confirmation Bill. Such things were the bread and butter of the Commons, and always would be, as long as the House and nation retained their independence. But in 1939, 'third year of the reign of His Majesty King George VI', much of Parliament's time was spent in a way which would soon be only a memory. The Prime Minister himself put it in a roundabout fashion: 'There is a special responsibility resting upon Parliament, acting through the Secretary of State, for the welfare and progress of

22

the British Colonies and Dependencies.' Another member was more forth-right: 'We are Members of Parliament for the Colonial Empire.' And empha-sising the Empire, next on the agenda after domestic topics were matters relating to the West Indies, Cyprus, Sierra Leone, Ceylon, Trinidad, Jamaica, East Africa, Guiana, Honduras, Barbados, Gambia and South Africa, every one a British territory. The South Africans in particular were being much irritated by a German radio station broadcasting what they called 'fictitious statements' about them, and the question was 'whether all statements of this kind are brought to the notice of the BBC to ensure that proper corrections are made in the Empire broadcasts'. The Prime Minister skirted smoothly round that one: the BBC was not an organ of government, but he was confident that the Corporation's policy was appropriate. With that, at 3.46 p.m. he opened the debate that all had come to hear: should Parliament adjourn, and if so, for how long? He proposed until 3 October. Home and imperial business had been despatched in a single hour; the adjournment debate took nearly six hours more.

In peace and solitude, Paul Schmidt was on holiday. The island of Norder-ney suited him ideally: it was small, sparsely populated, and very, very quiet. Just nine miles long and a mile and a half wide, it was one of the East Frisian chain that stretched like vertebrae for 150 miles around the north coasts of Holland and Germany, from Den Helder to the mouth of the Jade. It was not far from the naval port of Wilhelmshaven, but without actually going outside Germany, it was just about as far from the Berghof as possible. Wherever Schmidt went on the island, the only sounds were the seabirds, the seabreezes and the constant sigh of the sea itself. He could swim, walk, or simply sit and reflect, without being obliged to talk to anyone at all. For Paul Schmidt, the silence of Norderney was perfection; as he sometimes explained to people, his work as Hitler's interpreter involved an incredible amount of talking.

Schmidt had been in the German Foreign Office since 1923 and had worked for almost every Chancellor and Foreign Minister. For the past four years he had been the Foreign Office's senior interpreter. Four hectic years, unlike anything he had known. Very exciting, but very wearing. The first time he had interpreted for Hitler, 25 March 1935, had been a time of crisis; and overall since then the crisis had done nothing but escalate. Schmidt neither liked Hitler nor approved of his politics; despite pressure, he had not joined the Nazi Party, though the time would come when he could no longer avoid it. As a German he could understand (and sometimes share) his countrymen's common resentment of the terms imposed on them by the Allies in 1919. But as an interpreter he was far better able than most Germans to understand other countries' thinking; and he could see that from foreign points of view

23

the mounting crises of the past four years looked as though they were mostly the fault of the three Fascist states of Europe, Spain, Italy and Germany.

After an hour of debate in the Commons, that was exactly what Churchill was telling the House. 'If you wish to check this by examination,' he observed, 'see how oddly they have timed various strokes . . .' It seemed to him that something nasty always happened when Parliament was in recess. 'Take the latest of all, the Albanian outrage at Easter.' That was when Italian forces had seized independent Albania: 'nicely timed', said Churchill, 'for the moment when it was known that Parliament was scattered, when the Ministers were scattered – and when the Mediterranean Fleet, unfortunately, was scattered too.' Recalling the previous year, he pointed out that when Parliament adjourned, large troop movements had begun in Germany; that there were now two million men under arms in Germany; that by the end of the month this would have increased by half a million; and that German troops were massed all along the Polish border. 'This is an odd moment for the House to declare that it will go on a two months' holiday. It is only an accident that our summer holidays coincide with the danger months in Europe, when the harvests have been gathered, and,' he added ominously, 'when the powers of evil are at their strongest.'

Standing on an empty beach, Paul Schmidt gazed out over the grey North Sea. Somewhere out there, only two or three hundred miles away, was the coast of England. It occurred to him that just then, he was probably physically closer to Chamberlain, whose words he had translated so often, than he was to the Führer. For a moment he wondered what they might both be doing, and then thrust the thought away: he had an uneasy feeling that, much sooner than he wanted, he would be extremely busy, and would know the answer in detail. Before then, he was determined to savour every moment of his holiday. He sat down on the sand, lit his pipe, and listened to the sea.

'It is a very hard thing,' Churchill continued, 'for the Government to say to the House, "Begone! Run off and play. Take your gas masks with you . . ."' That made the Members laugh. 'Take your gas mask with you' had been a constant refrain in newspapers, on posters and on the wireless for the past year. They were glad enough of a reason to laugh.

Teatime. At Winsor Farm it was only a short pause in the exhausting afternoon; harvesting had to carry on as long as the light lasted. Pasties and orange squash made up Kit's lunch; now it was time for sandwiches and a flask of tea. Her father did not stop. He drank quantities of strong cider throughout the day, but never got drunk. Once, when she had asked, he laughed and said, 'I sweat it out, girl.' Not everyone could do the same: last year a farmhand who had had too much had fallen headlong from the top of a wagon and broken his arm.

As Kit rested briefly and her father sweated on, a more decorous tea took place in London. With fine china and sweet biscuits between them, Herbert von Dirksen and Lord Kemsley had much to talk about. Von Dirksen was Germany's Ambassador to Britain; Kemsley was a newspaper baron, proprietor of the *Sunday Chronicle* and *Sunday Empire News*, proprietor and editor-in-chief of the *Sunday Times*, recently ennobled, and just back from a visit to Germany. It had been, he felt, most instructive and enjoyable, and he was pleased to tell the Ambassador his impressions. After a day in Berlin he had motored to Bayreuth via Leipzig, visiting a labour camp on the way. It was most impressive how keen and enthusiastic all the German public men were, even down to the minor officials, Gauleiter Waechtler in particular, who had shown him new construction work at Nuremburg. Lord and Lady Kemsley had attended a performance of *Parsifal*, and during the interval were introduced to the Führer, who looked very vigorous and healthy, and with whom Kemsley had subsequently had an hour's conversation. Both agreed that a dangerous state of tension prevailed, and that something had to be done to break it. Reichsleiter Rosenberg (a charming personality, said Kemsley) had been much struck by his lordship's remark that Chamberlain was the Führer of England, similar to Hitler and Mussolini; Kemsley in turn could not avoid feeling that Joseph Goebbels, the Minister for Propaganda, was a clever and broadly educated man. Naturally he had spent a long time with the Reich Press Chief, Otto Dietrich, discussing a proposed exchange of newspaper articles; they had in fact agreed that it was not the proper political moment, but that no doubt a more favourable opportunity would come soon. With a little luck, Kemsley might be able to accept an invitation to the Party Congress; he hoped so, but he was a very busy man. Indeed, said von Dirksen amiably, wishing his lordship luck. Kemsley then departed, amid mutual expressions of esteem; the tea-things were removed; and the Ambassador, left alone, wrote the conversation down. One could never completely rely on memory.

In the House of Commons the debate continued in a courteous, even a courtly manner; yet underneath its purpose was deeply serious, perhaps deadly serious. There was some strong support for Churchill. 'Today,' said Vyvyan Adams, 'Parliament is being invited to suspend completely its animation for two months, which the blindest and most deaf of individuals knows beyond question are going to be the two most critical months for a quarter of a century,' and he warned that 'at any moment this war of nerves, of which the dictator countries are boasting, may develop into a war of guns'. Talking to the German Ambassador, Lord Kemsley had been right in one thing: in his own way, Chamberlain could be as autocratic as any European ruler. The debate had begun on a non-party basis. However, around a quarter past seven, he said bluntly: 'The question is whether you trust the Government or distrust the Government. If you distrust them, and show it by your vote, very well; it is a vote of no confidence in the Government, and no confidence in the Prime Minister in particular.' That changed the debate's whole foundation. It had already been going on for three and a half hours, and members were tired, frustrated and cross. Like Churchill, Ronald Cartland was a member of the ruling Conservative Party who found himself in deep disagreement with Chamberlain. He could not understand why the Prime Minister would not agree to an earlier recall – no one was suggesting that the House should stay in permanent session – and with sudden passion he jumped up and shouted, 'We are in the situation that within a month we may be going to fight, and we may be going to *die!*' Sir Patrick Hannon, Conservative, could not take him seriously, and burst out laughing. Flaming with indignation, Cartland turned on him: 'It's all very well for you to laugh – there are thousands of young men at this moment in training in camps . . .' He sat down bitterly. The House was galvanised. In a moment, Cartland's acid rebuke conjured up the horrors of the Great War, of old generals far behind the lines sending the young, in wave on wave, to their deaths.

Hours pass before the decision is made. From some point high above the turning world, it can all be seen clearly. Over the British army camp at Mingaladon in Burma, deep night has settled: it is already into the early hours, 4 a.m. on 3 August. Apart from the pacing and shuffling of duty guards, the barracks are quiet. Reg Panting, twenty-six-year-old lance corporal in the 1st Battalion of the Gloucester Regiment, sleeps, but no longer dreams of home, five and a half thousand miles distant in the Forest of Dean; or if he does after nearly seven years in the army he has learned to forget those dreams before he awakes. The regiment is his family now and he knows that a good soldier is a man who can keep his kit clean. Only two or three hundred yards away, but infinitely separated from the other ranks, Lieutenant Denis Harding sighs in his sleep and turns over. The mosquito net twitches. For him too the regiment is becoming his family, but it is less than a year since he last saw England and Biddy, the girl he loves. The lieutenant is twenty-four years old and must wait six years before the army will allow him to marry. Meanwhile Biddy's letters arrive regularly, and a young, contented officer in love has good reason to dream.

At the same time, far westwards, the European night of 2 August is beginning. On the shores of the Baltic in the port of Gdynia, close to the northernmost point of the Polish Corridor, it is half past ten in the evening, and Taddeus Olscholwski is at home in the Villa Sadyba with his wife Zofya.

He is just thirty-two; she will soon be thirty. Their fifth wedding anniversary is only two months off. From the bedrooms comes the tranquil, rhythmic breathing of their two sons, Stefan, aged three, and Andrew, just a year old. Taddeus has no brothers, and though he and Zofya would have been content whether God sent them a boy or a girl, to the young parents the sound of their sons is still a special joy, by night or day. The Olscholwskis have many sources of pride: their family, their work, their nation. Like all parents they are proud of their children; like all Poles of gentle birth, they are proud of their backgrounds. Both come from landowning families, the top one per cent of the population, with large estates in central Poland; Taddeus's uncle was a diplomat, and took part in the negotiations at Versailles in 1919 when Poland gained its corridor to the Baltic Sea. Given such ancestors, Taddeus's own work is a particular satisfaction: less than a year ago, with six partners, he formed the Baltic Shipping Company, the first private shipping company in the country, and it is a success. In 1930 when he announced to his mother that he was going into ship-broking, she had been shocked. 'Is that an honest career?' she asked. Zofya's family had felt the same; landowners had always married landowners. To them, entrepreneurs – 2 per cent of the people – are slightly suspect. But the business has prospered, and the Olscholwskis have a right to be proud.

In fact there is no such thing as a humble Pole. A census in 1921 showed that nearly two-thirds of the population were still peasants; yet whatever their individual circumstances, everyone who calls himself Polish does so with a fierce affection and prickly pride, deeply conscious that the nation is simultaneously one of the oldest and one of the youngest in Europe. Some Poles, say that it is easier for an Englishman to understand Japan than Poland. There is much truth in that, for in 1939 the conditions of Britain and Poland could hardly be more different: Britain, the island mistress of the largest empire the world has ever known, its language spoken all around the globe: Poland, landlocked except for the artificial corridor, without any natural frontier, its language barely pronounceable by anyone else, even in Europe. Britain has known no serious invasion for the better part of 900 years; the last time Poles had to fight to secure their borders was in 1920, against Bolshevik Russian incursions from the east.

It is true that there are some similarities between Britain and Poland, including a love of legend. Thirty-nine years into the twentieth century, British people still sometimes think fondly of Alfred the Great as the founder, in the ninth century, of their kingdom; Poles give the same honour to Alfred's contemporary, Piast, whose dynasty lasted 500 years. Both nations also look back to the sixteenth century as a golden age: Britain's Tudor era was, for Poland too, the time of renaissance and religious reformation; it was then that Mikotaj Kopernik, the Pole whom people in the West call Copernicus, shook the heavens, and stated that the Earth moved round the Sun. Others muddle his nationality and think he was Italian or Danish; Poles never forget he was Polish. But after that time, the histories of Poland and Britain took very different tracks. While England fought its civil war and laid the basis of parliamentary democracy, Poland called itself 'the Noble Republic', and for more than 200 years was ruled by elected kings. It was a system which, ever after, seemed to Poles to have been an ideal; yet in 1795 the country ceased to exist. By 1939 only the most educated Poles knew all the reasons for that catastrophe, but even the simplest knew the effect. Russia, Prussia and Austria had divided Poland between them; the nation's very name was scrubbed from the map, its use forbidden anywhere; and for five generations the ancient cities, the towns and villages, and the vast beautiful plains surrounding them were ruled by foreigners.

Every Pole knows all this, even if only in a vague way; they have all grown up with it. British people might know it too, but only as an idea, a piece of information. Except for those prepared to try a prodigious leap of imagination, it does not and cannot form part of their emotional world; and there is no particular reason why it should. For them the time when there was no Poland, the nineteenth century, had brought to Britain the great flowering of the Empire abroad, and at home, the wonder and squalor of the Industrial Revolution. Britain was and is great: even its name says so. Every Briton knows that. By 1939 the contrast is enormous: since the war of 1914–18 the Republic of Poland has been remade, re-identified, almost as an afterthought. Once it was great; perhaps it can be again. Twenty years of new-found freedom is a blink in history. But it is all Poland has, apart from proud memories and a deep-seated, bred-in-the-bone distrust of Russia and Germany. And Poland will not easily let go of its memories, its distrust or its freedom.

This is the kind of mental background which has helped shape the lives of Taddeus and Zofya Olscholwski. It is a background of absolute insecurity only recently made secure, of complete foreign domination only recently overcome; a background where, in little more than twenty years, national identity has changed from a romantic remembered idea to a reality – or at least the start of a reality. And in that short time, so much has been done, so much is promised. Taddeus, Zofya and their millions of compatriots will not easily give it up. Even so, as August 1939 begins, they have little reason to feel either content or safe. The Olscholwskis do not need reminding, but if they walk out for some fresh air by the sea-shore this evening and look south, they will see, only ten miles beyond the lights of Gdynia, the glow of the lights of Gdansk.

Albert Förster lives there. He is not the direct cause of the Poles' fear, but he stands for that cause. As proud as any Pole of the history and achievements of his race, and of his personal achievements, Albert Förster is German, and has become district political leader of the National Socialist Party: the Nazi Gauleiter of Danzig. As Hitler's representative in one of the most sensitive areas of the political world, his is a key position, and he carries out his responsibilities in a commendably vigorous, thorough and conscientious manner. He has already had the honour of several personal meetings with his Führer, and in two days he must travel again to the Berghof, Hitler's Mountain Court. Tonight, therefore, Gauleiter Förster is busy making ready; and as he does so, Hitler himself is sitting in the opera house in Bayreuth, gazing raptly at the stage as Wagner's heroic masterpiece approaches its climax: *Götterdämmerung*, the Twilight of the Gods.

Thus at one moment the Far East slept soundly; Europe prepared for sleep; and in London, lights glittered on the Thames as, at last, the House of Commons voted on the Prime Minister's motion: 40 Members abstained; 129 said no; 245 said yes. So on Friday next, the House would adjourn. It could be summoned at forty-eight hours' notice if necessary; otherwise it would not meet again until 3 October. The little group of Conservatives who had supported Churchill shuffled out disconsolately. The lobbies were humming with conversation. 'Ronnie Cartland's ruined his chances with the Party,' said one Liberal member to a Conservative friend, 'but he's made his Parliamentary reputation.' Cartland himself felt utterly depressed. Turning to Churchill, he said with a sigh, 'Well, we can do no more.' A glint came into Churchill's eye: he had not given up. 'Do no more, my boy?' he echoed. 'There is a lot more we can do. This is the time to fight – to speak – to attack!'

It has been a long day. But evening in London is afternoon on America's east coast, and on the way across the wide Atlantic one may pass through the sunset towards a place where 2 August is far from finished – Long Island, and in particular Nassau Point, languidly stretched under the afternoon sun that shines on Great Peconic Bay. Here, with concern and some reluctance, the most famous scientist in the world is preparing to write a letter to the President of America.

Albert Förster and Albert Einstein have only two things in common: the coincidence of their first names and the fact that both were born German. Otherwise, even if they stood side by side, they could not be further apart. Förster delights in being German; his self-esteem increases each time he

29

thinks of the journey he will make to the Berghof next weekend. He cannot understand the theory of relativity which made Einstein an international celebrity; he certainly never gives Copernicus a second thought – Polish intellectuals, past or present, do not interest him. But he does grasp that Einstein could have brought great intellectual lustre to Germany, and he would have been glad of that, if only because other nations respect intellectuals. However, Einstein, now fifty years old, found their native country's way of life, 'the over-emphasised military mentality of the German State', so repressive that as a teenager he decided he would change his nationality and become Swiss. The deed was done as soon as he reached adulthood. Worse, for many years thereafter he was an outspoken pacifist. Either that or his change of nationality would have been enough to make him contemptible to a man like Förster. But worse still: after much soul-searching, Einstein has renounced pacifism to speak publicly against Hitler and Nazism, the man and the system which have given Förster his pride and position. And worst of all Einstein is, of course, Jewish, *Untermensch*, subhuman. For Albert Förster that explains everything about Albert Einstein.

In the middle of Long Island, Great Peconic Bay covers 35 square miles or so. Shelter Island protects it from the Atlantic swell and makes it a wonderful place for leisurely sailing, which is why Einstein has come here for his vacation from Princeton University: he loves sailing, and at Nassau Point can also practise the violin in peace. But this afternoon, instead of sailing or playing, he is sitting, pensive and worried, on the veranda of his holiday home. He and his companion Leo Szilard have been friends for many years; in 1921, in Berlin, they jointly invented and patented a refrigerator. The two scientists are strikingly different in appearance. On one side of a small slatted table, Szilard, a stocky, heavy-looking man, is upright, neat and trim, clean-shaven, with short dark hair, wearing a long-sleeved shirt with collar and tie; as a concession to the weather he has taken his jacket off. Opposite him, leaning forward, Einstein sits in short sleeves with his collar open, and puffs on a very long-stemmed pipe; the smoke circles his familiar lined face, his wild white hair and woolly moustache. With his elbow on his thigh, resting his head on his fist, he gazes at the papers in Szilard's hand, at the bottle of ink, the pen and the other papers scattered on the table.

Four miles away across Great Peconic, easily visible from Nassau Point, is Conscience Point. It is an apt name for the scene. Over the past few years, through experiments in England, France, Denmark, Germany and Italy, the international scientific community has learnt how to split atoms, and found that doing so released astoundingly large bursts of energy. Hungarian-born Szilard was the first to suggest that a chain reaction might occur, and early in 1939, working with the Italian Enrico Fermi at Columbia University, he had come close to an experimental proof. He and Fermi are refugees from the politics of Europe; Fermi's wife is Jewish, and in September 1938 anti-Semitic laws had been introduced in Italy. Now both men have realised that the work they left behind could be developed by the dictatorships they had fled. Perhaps it was an outside possibility – but the Fascists might succeed in building an atomic bomb.

An odd sequence of events first brought Szilard out to Nassau Point. Like Albert Einstein, Queen Elizabeth the Queen Mother of Belgium loved the violin. Because of that shared love, they had become firm friends. At Columbia, Szilard and Fermi had conducted their experiments with uranium, since its atoms contained the heaviest and most highly charged nuclei known; and by chance, most of the world's uranium ore came from the Belgian Congo. Szilard began his mission to Nassau Point by hoping that Einstein would agree to find out if, somehow, the queen could prevent Nazi Germany buying ore from the Congo. It seemed an unlikely chain, but the chance of a chain reaction of uranium nuclei had seemed unlikely too. Nevertheless Szilard was profoundly worried. The stakes were inestimably high. The idea of Hitler as master of a nuclear bomb was an unthinkable nightmare. To rely on Einstein's friendship with the Belgian Queen Mother was too weak a defence, and Szilard thought of another approach, more certain of success. Einstein should write direct to President Roosevelt and warn him of what might happen.

This is what they are discussing as they sit on the shady veranda, and it has placed Einstein in a serious ethical dilemma. What, he wondered, could the President do? He could hardly prevent any German experiments; at best he could authorise a research programme which might beat them to the goal. And if so, what kind of a goal was this for a humane pacifist to recommend? It would create a danger which no one had ever conceived. And again, understanding the kind of power which success could give to the Nazis, can Einstein ignore Szilard, pat him on the back with a regretful refusal, send him away and sail peacefully over Great Peconic? Conscience Point has come to Nassau.

At last Einstein agrees to Szilard's request, and together they draft the letter, to be sent to the President over Einstein's signature:

> Some recent work by E. Fermi and L. Szilard, which has been communi-cated to me in manuscript, leads me to expect that the element uranium may be turned into a new and important source of energy in the immediate future. Certain aspects of the situation seem to call for watchfulness and, if necessary, quick action on the part of the Adminis-tration.

Nothing but Einstein's conviction that Nazism is more evil than war itself could persuade him to write this letter. In it, he explains the sense of duty that impels him, and warns that 'extremely powerful bombs of a new type' may be constructed – 'A single bomb of this type, carried by boat or exploded in a port, might very well destroy the whole port together with some of the surrounding territory.' And he adds:

> I understand that Germany has actually stopped the sale of uranium from the Czechoslovakian mines which she has taken over. That she should have taken such early action might perhaps be understood on the ground that the son of the German Under-Secretary of State, von Weizsäcker, is attached to the Kaiser Wilhelm Institute in Berlin, where some of the American work on uranium is now being repeated.

The letter is signed, the ink blotted; the two scientists shake hands, and just before he leaves, Szilard, satisfied and much happier than when he arrived, reassures Einstein: he has undoubtedly done the right thing. But when Szilard has gone, it seems he has left some of his first fear and doubt behind him. Heavy-hearted, Einstein stares out over the water. It has grown too dark to see Conscience Point. Night must come, even to Great Peconic Bay, and now it is too late for any sailing. He turns sadly indoors, and picks up his violin.

2

The Earth's a good place

DIRECTLY AFTER BREAKFAST on Thursday 3 August Kit Dennis's parents clambered into their Austin 16 and set off on their regular excursion to the Corn Exchange in Plymouth. Most of the farmers of the county would gather there once a week to do business, buying and selling produce and livestock; and while their wives met for tea, the menfolk bargained, with a look at teeth and an experienced hand on ribs and legs and backsides of cattle and pigs and horses. Later, as they settled a deal over a pint in the pub, they talked of crops and workmen and mutual acquaintances: who had died, who was getting married, how the land would be joined or divided; who was doing well and who badly, who might have to sell and who might be able to buy; the cost of feed and, with petrol at ninepence a gallon, the cost of cars. They did not gossip – that was for the women – but they did enjoy a business-like chat.

About the same time that day, Kapitänleutnant Fresdorf, first staff officer of the U-boat department of Germany's Naval High Command, completed a paper for Kapitän zur See Karl Dönitz. Fresdorf – in the US Navy or the British Royal Navy, he would have been a lieutenant commander – was confident that Captain Dönitz would endorse the paper's analysis of their department's needs. Working closely together, the two officers knew each other's thinking well. Dönitz, forty-seven years old, had been in charge of the U-boat arm of the Reich navy for almost four years. His superiors described him as 'an excellent officer of iron will, goal-oriented certainty and unwearying toughness'. Tall, slim, eagle-nosed, with eyes at once alert and wary, Dönitz was a charismatic leader. With unbounded confidence in his boats and their crews, he deliberately fostered in the officers and men the sense of being an élite; and they responded with proud, fierce loyalty. Under his leadership the U-boat arm had grown rapidly, and he was committed to its continued growth, hence Fresdorf's confidence that his own paper would be welcome. In January Hitler had approved an ambitious naval staff plan, the Z Plan, which included a target figure of 249 U-boats to be built by 1947. After exercises in the spring aimed at theoretical British supply lines across the

Atlantic, Dönitz had raised that number to 300. Just a month ago, at the beginning of July, he had introduced a proposal for large 'workshop ships' to be on permanent foreign stations, so that damaged U-boats could be repaired without having to return to Germany. His proposal emphasised that 'an essential part of the war against England will fall to the U-boats in the commerce war'; and now Fresdorf had taken the analysis further. Fast long-range boats should be placed off the American coast to follow convoys on sailing; attack boats would wait in the eastern Atlantic. Milch-cow boats, acting as underwater tankers, would replenish fuel and food stocks, while smaller boats would operate in the Baltic and North Sea. The total U-boat fleet required would be around 500. Such a programme would need much money and time; but since Dönitz had taken control of the U-boat arm, money for its development had always been forthcoming, and there was plenty of time: through Admiral Raeder, Commander-in-Chief of the Navy, Dönitz had received Hitler's personal assurance that if it came, war with Britain would not come soon. 'Do not believe the Führer would bring us into such a desperate position,' Raeder had said after an inspection only twelve days ago, 'for a war with England would mean *Finis Germania!*' They were naval officers, not politicians; they accepted the Führer's word without question, and happily – it meant they could continue as they were, training, building, planning. At the moment, Dönitz was away on leave; so Fresdorf re-read the grand proposal, and with a glow of satisfaction, placed it in the captain's file to await his return.

About half past eleven in the morning, a small, slightly built man alighted from his train at Charing Cross Station in London. Walking briskly down the Strand and across Trafalgar Square, he soon came to Horse Guards Road, a pleasant approach to work, running as it did next to St James's Park. He had just broken a holiday at High Corner, his newly bought cottage in East Sussex, and come up to town in torrential rain ('a very good day to go to London', he said wryly) to catch up on events. Few people passing him in the street would have recognised him, or paid much attention to him: with his neat moustache, sober suit, rolled umbrella and soft trilby hat (which he preferred to a bowler), he looked the epitome of a pleasant, undistinguished City businessman. In some ways he was indeed quite an ordinary man, who loved his nation and its countryside; a note in his diary for April 1939, remarking on the daffodils and primroses, ended wistfully, 'The Earth's a good place, if only Hitler weren't on it!' But his noon appointment today was with Lord Halifax; and under the soft hat, taken off as he entered his office building at 11.40, was the high intelligent forehead of his aristocratic background. In this building, Sir Alexander Cadogan, youngest son of the fifth Earl Cadogan, ex-Eton, ex-Balliol, and thirty-one years in the diplomatic service, was in charge: this was the Foreign Office, and he was its Permanent Under-Secretary of State. His own Private Secretary had already briefed him on the substance of the talk between Hitler and Lord Kemsley. *Seems to me*, Cadogan had thought when he heard it, *as harmless, and as useless, as most such.*

There is quite a lot that could be said in favour of things which are harmless, even if they are useless; and there is even more in favour of things which are harmless and useful. Teaching the children; serving in shops; simply growing vegetables and delivering the post; these are hardly world-shattering occupations, but little could be done without them. Living with her widowed mother in the Welsh village of Tonna, Dorothy Williams was a teacher at Cadoxton school, working with the little ones, from four to six years old. She did not actually like it very much. Before, she had taught drama and art, which she enjoyed, in another school, which she liked, to older girls, whom she found more rewarding. The sole reason for the change to Cadoxton was that it was only twenty minutes' walk down the valley from her mother's home, and her mother, overweight, with a heart condition and a chronic cough from bronchial pneumonia, had to be looked after. So it was back to the three Rs. That was tolerable, even satisfying in its way; what made life so difficult was her colleagues in the staff room. She tried to fit in, but couldn't seem to. Little things; she hated smoking, but in the breaks everyone else puffed away happily, expecting to share each other's packets of cigarettes, so rather than seem mean or supercilious she did the same. By itself that was nothing much; but all through the summer term there had been arguments in the staff room about the prospects of war or peace, and in those she always ended up isolated. Everyone else seemed to accept the promise of Munich without reservation, because, she said, they wanted to. They did not want it to go wrong, so they would not let in the idea that it might. Keeping the peace by incantation, she called it. Of course she wanted peace as much as anyone, but she thought it was wise to prepare for the worst; and then they would call her a scaremonger, and laugh, which made them feel better, and her feel foolish. 'Dorothy, dear, I think we'd better just call you Dotty, hadn't we?'

She still flushed at the memory. She had kept back the retort that sprang to her lips: 'You're just like the Monkey People in the *Jungle Book*, "We all say so, so we must be right."' Instead she had answered, simply but finally, 'Well, I'm sticking to my ideas.' There was no point in being rude in return; and it seemed all were thankful to drop the subject.

In the village a few of the older people who had lived through the Great War believed another would come, and that it would be very different. She had listened to them, and when asked if and how she would help 'in the event of war', the phrase had both frightened and excited her. And there was one

35

thing which she could do very well, which might be useful: she could speak Welsh. Perhaps it was going a bit far to imagine a German invasion; but perhaps not. That was a chilling thought. Yet if an invasion came, there would be a resistance, and whatever the Germans spoke, it was not likely to be Welsh. 'In the event of war' then, Dorothy had a job: to take messages in a language an invader could not understand.

She could not imagine what it might be like, and in her more confident moments it seemed almost childishly cloak-and-dagger. But at least she knew that in the direst of emergencies she could help a little, and that she was ready. By itself, that calmed her, and when term ended, she embarked on the holidays with a lighter heart. Though she would not be going away, there was much to do that she enjoyed – blackberrying, jam-making, perhaps a picnic on the beach at Aberavon, dances at the Empire ballroom in Neath . . . Except when she met someone of like mind, when suddenly she would be overtaken by apprehension, thoughts of war receded. There might be no man in her life just yet, but there were many friends; she was never lonely, and August was a happy month.

So it was for Molly McAndrew as well, and not least because of Ernie Brown. She was just twenty-one, he was almost twenty-three; for two years they had been engaged to be married, and some time very soon they would decide a date. Molly had been a late and only child, born when her mother, now a widow, was already forty-seven. Like the Williamses in Wales, the McAndrews in Newcastle lived together, but without the sense of duty; it was simply convenient for everyone, until Molly and Ernie finally got married. Then the newly-weds would have a fine modern council flat, for Ernie's work as a pattern-maker brought good money, three guineas a week. Between them, Molly and her mother had less than two guineas a week coming in: Molly earned one guinea for her work at Woolworth's store, while her mother had fifteen shillings widow's pension and, to cover the rent on their two rooms, another five shillings from washer-work in a Chinese laundry.

The hours at Woolworth's were long – from nine in the morning until 7 p.m. Monday to Thursday, 8 p.m. on Friday and 9 p.m. on Saturday – but Molly enjoyed the bustle. She was a strikingly beautiful young woman, and the red zip-up uniform set off her dark hair well. She was proud of that uniform, with its motto 'FWW – I'm one of Woolworth's girls', and her appearance and liveliness made her popular with the customers. The store; Ernie and his boat, a converted lifeboat called *Monarch*; her mother and their cramped little tenement flat; these made up the major part of her life, and she was happy with them all. The world beyond Newcastle hardly intruded. Mrs Blair, who lived in the ground-floor tenement below the McAndrews, had a wireless and would sometimes come breathlessly up, summoning them to hear some news; very occasionally, if they could afford it, they bought a newspaper. On those days, or if someone else bought a paper, it would be passed from house to house up and down the streets – no point in everyone buying their own when its news would soon be old. Otherwise, all Molly knew of world events came from newsreels in the cinema, and they did not worry her at all. All that about the Germans taking over Austria last year, it was far away, unreal. They had done the same last March with Czecho-slovakia. What a name! She could barely get her tongue round it, and though she had seen the maps, she still did not really know where it was, and did not specially want to know. When she did think about it, she felt quite safe, because one thing she knew for certain was that Britain was an island. But still she could pretend to be frightened, sometimes, just for fun; then, knowing perfectly well it was only an excuse to cuddle her, Ernie would tell her not to worry: he would go out in *Monarch* and drive the Germans off, if ever they dared approach the coast. And she would say how brave he was, and they would ignore the goose-steps on the screen.

It was all a matter of how much you wanted to know, how much or how little you cared – or dared – to imagine. In Bressay, far away in the Shetlands, the Anderson family were better informed of events than was Molly in urban Newcastle. Despite its imposing name, suggesting the sprawling one-time residence of a church minister, the Old Manse was a simple croft house, typical of the islands: two rooms but and ben, the front and back of the house, with two attic bedrooms for guests. Normally Lollie, the island postman, his brother Tommy and their father were on their own there, but just now the place was full to bursting – five of the family were visiting, on holiday from the isle of Foula. There was Lizzie, one of Tommy and Lollie's sisters; her husband Willie Smith; and their three daughters, Stella, Nanette and Jessamine. Those were good names, uncommon, quickly remembered and distinguished. Often, otherwise, so many Christian names and surnames were alike, and so many of the Shetlanders were related one way or another that it became easiest to have nicknames. Three men, for example, living within two hundred yards of each other and all called Alec, were known better as Muckle Alec; Peerie Alec, his adult son; and Square Alec, unrelated to the others, very muscular, and as wide as he was high. Likewise Lollie's brother Tommy was named after their father; and always, when someone got married, some of the new relatives' names would match those of the existing family: Lizzie's man Willie, for instance. When they wed there was already another Anderson brother called Willie. He at least was away at the fishing just now, which was as well, considering the numbers crammed into the house. All, Andersons and Smiths, were true islanders; 'the mainland' for them was Shetland's major island; anywhere else in Great Britain was simply 'south'. Foula, four miles long and a mile wide, was the most westerly of the island group: after its precipitous western face, the 1200-foot vertical cliff called the Kame, there was nothing except Atlantic Ocean all the way to America. It was remote even by Shetland standards: and when the Smiths made their annual trek back to Bressay, they were always greeted with, *Well, my dears, are you come ashore again?*

In terms of money they were no better off than the McAndrews in their Newcastle slum. But at the Old Manse they were able to dig their own peat for fuel; they could raise vegetables, and they had two cows which gave good milk. It was all much smaller and far poorer than Winsor Farm in Devon, but it left a little money over, so they had a wireless, which Molly and her mother had not; they bought the *Shetland News* regularly. Above all, they were voracious readers, people of enquiring minds, curious about the world and its goings on. However, everything they heard and read about the world that summer was utterly depressing. Lollie and Tommy talked of the future, and as she listened, their fourteen-year-old niece Stella found it sinister and disturbing. This'll be the end of everything, they said, and she believed them literally. Armageddon was coming, the end of the world. But she was a stoic and sensible girl: privately refusing to let her fear show, she decided that with her mother's help, she would have time to finish the dress she was making.

Cadogan's appointment with the Foreign Secretary, Lord Halifax, had produced little new. They had met at twelve sharp, when Cadogan heard again details of Lord Kemsley's interview with Hitler. Herr Hitler was asking once more for British requirements to be put down on paper; the Foreign Secretary and Under-Secretary agreed that he, not they, should be the one to put something in writing first, and that Kemsley could be made to act as go-between again with Otto Dietrich, the German Press Bureau chief. Halifax was also much exercised about the Far East, where, for the past two years, Japanese forces had been waging undeclared war on China. Since the end of 1938 they had occupied most of northern and central China, and would have gone further but for British and American aid to China's recognised ruler, Chiang Kai-shek. Six months ago they had occupied Hainan Island, 250 miles from Hong Kong; less than three weeks ago they had begun blockading the British Concession in Tientsin, an area leased in perpetuity to the British government for trade. There was another concession in Canton. Around 600 Britons lived in Tientsin and were now more or less captive; the few who were allowed out had been humiliated by being stripped and searched in public. Two Royal Navy escort vessels sent to the area had little effect, and

Chamberlain had come very close to a *de facto* recognition of Japanese rule in China.

'We can probably go quite a long way on police, the neutrality of the Concessions and so on,' said Halifax to Cadogan. 'What about currency and silver, though? What do we do when we get on to them?'

'Stall,' Cadogan answered at once. 'We shall have to. And in the end, we can't give way.'

'I agree. I'll talk to the PM about it again. Meanwhile, there's Russia. Yes, I know – there always is,' said Halifax as Cadogan grimaced. 'We may neither of us like the idea, but it's becoming clear that a pact of some sort will have to take place; and at least Neville has stopped saying he'll resign rather than be Russia's ally. So the next step is to get the military talks going alongside the political – three men each for our mission and the French, and whoever the Russians want to put up for themselves.'

Cadogan knew the three British officers selected. 'Drax, Burnett and Heywood,' he murmured. An admiral, an air marshal and a major-general. 'Drax is . . . unstimulating, really. Burnett certainly knows air strategy, and Heywood speaks French and German. It's a pity we don't have more people who speak Russian.'

'Can't be helped. Anyway, it may be useful: so much the easier to take the conversations slowly. As for their transport, they obviously can't go by rail, since that would mean going through Germany. They could fly, but there is no suitable aircraft available. The Admiralty doesn't want to give up a cruiser, although it might impress our Bolshevik friends; so,' Halifax concluded, 'they've decided to charter a liner, *City of Exeter*, I believe. Maximum speed twelve knots.'

'That means it's bound to take them the better part of a week to get there.'

The Foreign Secretary nodded, and Cadogan noticed how tired he looked. Knowing there was nothing more to talk of in foreign affairs, he changed the subject: 'Will you be having a holiday? You could do with one.'

'Well . . .' Halifax sighed. 'I don't anticipate a real break.'

'No, you *must* have one. In fact, if I were your doctor, I'd order you to. I can't tell you how well a bit of time off has set me up again.'

'I don't doubt it,' Halifax sighed again. 'Yorkshire, Yorkshire – of course it's tempting. Well, we shall see.'

Vyacheslav Molotov, the Soviet People's Commissar for Foreign Affairs, was, just then, busy extending an unexpectedly warm welcome to Count Werner von der Schulenburg. The German Ambassador to Moscow was gratified and encouraged: when he had asked to visit Molotov the day before he had been refused. Comrade Molotov was attending the Soviet Agricultural Exhibition. It was a splendid show, covering 350 acres and dominated by two enormous statues. One, on a tower at the entrance, showed a tractor driver and a peasant woman holding on high an immense sheaf of corn; the other, in pink stone – the nearest natural colour to red – was of Stalin. Appropriately, it was even larger than the statue honouring the workers.

However, it was not because of any good mood engendered by the heavily symbolic celebration that Molotov felt ready to welcome Schulenburg; he was not a man to be swayed by moods. With a round head, thick black moustache, slightly receding hair, and, behind spectacles, eyes that seemed to understand everything and everyone he saw, he looked like the genial doctor who should have sent Halifax on holiday. He was skilled in speech, imperturbable in behaviour, and completely ruthless. All were qualities essential for survival and success under Stalin's rule. Less than three months earlier, Maxim Litvinov, Molotov's predecessor in office, had been dismissed ('sacked like a maid caught stealing', Litvinov said bitterly, 'without so much as a day's notice'). Molotov considered that Litvinov and his wife Ivy had been fortunate only to be relegated to the status of 'unpersons'; it was more usual for high officials suddenly out of favour to be equally suddenly dead. The new Commissar understood perfectly the reasons for that dismissal: Litvinov, a Jew married to an Englishwoman, was too much in favour of Britain, too much opposed to Germany, to deal in a detached manner with either. For his own part, Molotov knew that any such personal feelings in high office were to be quashed; they could damage the interests of the Party and the Motherland. Today, therefore, he would be cordial towards the count.

While Lord Halifax thought wistfully of taking time off in Yorkshire, Dr Claud Kennerley was there, doing exactly that. Except for emergency cases, Thursday afternoon was his half-day. He was a man with a pronounced sense of duty – sometimes, thought his wife Eleanor, too pronounced. Of course most general practitioners faced the same kind of draining work as Claud did, surgery twice daily, morning and evening, visits to patients' homes throughout the afternoon, and any kind of emergency from childbirth to car crashes at any time, day or night. But to that, because of his sense of duty, he added his work in the Territorial Army, as Medical Officer for the 5th Battalion of the York and Lancasters. He was a major now – he had joined in 1934, before they had married. 'Just felt I ought to be able to contribute a bit more,' he had said to her, almost apologetically. 'I mean, one never knows, of course, but one hears these things from Germany . . .' It was the year after Hitler had come to power. 'The thing is, if I'm ever needed, it would obviously be better if I had some training, at least. You do see, don't you?' She did, but she agreed with him fervently when he added, 'Of course, one hopes I'll never be needed in that way at all.' Once recently, when he was particularly tired and still had another evening at the Drill Hall to go through before what would probably be a broken night, she had asked him if he ever thought about giving it up. 'Think about it?' he had said with a wry smile, standing in front of the mirror as she brushed his uniform jacket. 'Only about five times a week.' She glanced at him with a sudden small hope. Then he added vaguely, 'But one couldn't, really – not yet, anyway . . .'

Understanding him perfectly, Eleanor knew she had not truly expected any other answer, and that she would not ask him again; and so, straightening his already straight tie, she kissed him and let him go. She helped him and protected him in many ways. Before they married, she had trained to be a dispenser (passing her exams, as she liked to tell people, when she was sickening for chickenpox, and going to a Royal Garden Party the same day. Happily, she had never heard of any of the Royal Family falling ill afterwards). Now their house on the outskirts of Rotherham was also their workplace, a square, purpose-built dwelling designed by one of her uncles, an architect, to fit their needs exactly. At 8.30 each morning the front two rooms, waiting room and surgery, were open, and the patients began arriving, farmers, miners, children, steelworkers; people who contributed to a panel fund, a simple form of insurance; unemployed people on parish relief, their medicines paid for from local funds; the poor employed, who might have to spread payment of their bill over several months at a few pence a week. They were the ones she felt sorriest for. She did not feel sorry for the private patients, the solicitors and company directors; and certainly not for their wives. Those who lived in the large houses with big gardens in Moorgate, 'the Devil's mile', had quite frightened her at first. Somehow they seemed especially fierce and powerful, all gunning for each other, competitive and ambitious. The class divisions of the community were plain and deep. Sometimes, outside Mason's, the main jewellers in Rotherham, she would see the distinctive Rolls-Royce, black and yellow with wickerwork doors, which belonged to Lord Fitzwilliam's family. She did not begrudge them the beautiful vehicle; but ever since she had been with Claud to visit a miner with pneumonia, she had wondered sadly at the gulf. That visit had taken place in winter, and the man lay visibly steaming in bed: his fever was so high, his blankets so sodden with sweat, and his house so icy cold.

Even if Eleanor and Claud went to a film of an evening, he might still be called out from the cinema, so they had quickly determined that Thursday afternoons must be sacred: absolutely no calls – instead, golf. It might, of course, be gardening or paying social visits, but Claud was as good at golf as at doctoring.

By four o'clock British time, the discussion in Moscow between Count and Commissar had ended. In London, Sir Horace Wilson, head of His Majesty's

Civil Service and one of the few men whose advice Chamberlain had sought during the Munich crisis, was just beginning an equally secret conversation with Ambassador Herbert von Dirksen. Claud Kennerley and his old friend and regular partner Bill Elmhurst were waiting at the seventh green on Thrybergh course, hoping that a rather slow pair ahead of them might let them play through. And at the same time in Haus Wahnfried, Wagner's old home in Bayreuth, two other old friends were meeting for only the second time in thirty years: August Kubizek and Adolf Hitler.

Kubizek was escorted by an SS officer. When he saw them, Hitler came forward, took Kubizek's hand in both of his, and said with real pleasure, 'Gustl!' It was the nickname he had invented in 1905. 'I am happy we have met once more on this spot – it was always the most venerable place for us both.' They had first met in their teens, when a shared passion for opera drew them together. August was a talented musician, then hoping to make his living through music; Adolf ('a pale, skinny youth', August remembered) had read him his poetry and confessed his wish to be an artist. Now one was Führer of the Third Reich; the other was town clerk of Eferding. Kubizek was so overcome with emotion, he could scarcely say a word. Very shyly, he produced some postcards depicting Hitler: would the Führer consent to sign them, for friends at home in Austria? Of course he would! Pausing only to check that no photographers were present, Hitler donned his reading glasses, sat down, and on card after card scrawled his angular autograph.

The keys of peace and war

AT THIRTY-SIX YEARS OF AGE, Galeazzo Ciano, Count of Cortellazzo, still found it easy to turn women's heads. He was vain enough to believe himself very handsome, and confident enough with the opposite sex to exploit every opportunity that arose, especially outside Italy, in spite of having been married for six years. A well-built body, brooding eyes and sensual mouth helped him in his conquests; so too did an association of power. His wife Edda was the daughter of Italy's national leader, the Duce Benito Mussolini, and since 1933 Count Ciano had been his Foreign Minister. From America came a sarcastic observation: 'The son-in-law also rises.'

Mussolini had taken power in Italy in 1922, the year he now spoke of as the first of the Fascist era. Adolf Hitler, still, then, regarded as little more than the rabble-rousing leader of a minority political party, admired the Duce's aims and methods and sought to imitate them in Germany. The attempt had landed him in gaol. But since 1933 when, legitimately, National Socialism became Germany's ruling creed, and still more since 1934 when Hitler became Führer, Reich Chancellor and supreme commander of the three armed forces of Germany, it had become more and more clear which of the two would be the senior partner, so to speak, in a Fascist Europe.

Time was, just after Hitler came to power, when Mussolini's gorgeous uniform and confident bearing could contrast embarrassingly with the German's uncertainty and shabby, ill-kempt appearance. Time was, too, when Mussolini could publicly denounce Hitler as leader of a country of murderers and pederasts, declaring that despite their superficial similarities, Italian Fascism and Nazism could not be compared. Fascism, he said in 1934, was rooted in the Italian people's cultural tradition, recognising religion, family and the rights of the individual. 'National Socialism, on the other hand, is savage barbarism: in common with barbarian hordes it allows no rights to the individual; the chieftain is lord over life and death of his people. Murder and killing, loot and pillage and blackmail are all it can produce.'

By the spring of 1939, however, that kind of rhetoric was only a memory. True, Italian forces had occupied Albania that March and Abyssinia two years earlier. The Albanian occupation had been relatively straightforward; but the Abyssinian had involved long hard fighting and much bloodshed, even though the only opposition came from Emperor Haile Selassie's small, under-armed and ill-trained army. Italians admitted privately that it had not been the smooth, spectacular display of might that they had hoped for. In contrast the Rhineland border area between France and Germany, demilitarised by the Versailles Treaty, had been occupied by German troops; Austria had been incorporated into the Reich; Czechoslovakia had been dismembered when its German-speaking area, the Sudetenland, had been taken over; and all those acquisitions had been gained without fighting. The Duce could only remark resentfully, 'Every time Hitler occupies a country, he sends me a message.'

At the beginning of August 1939 Mussolini still hoped that he might play a crucial role in the immediate future of Europe. War might not be avoided indefinitely, but it had to be staved off for at least three years if Italy was to be ready; so the Duce, who had figured in the Munich agreement between Hitler and Chamberlain, proposed a World Peace Conference. At the same time Ciano began to think that perhaps he should have another meeting with Joachim von Ribbentrop, Hitler's Foreign Minister, to try and find out exactly what was going on. Late in May they had signed an agreement with a resounding title, the Pact of Steel, which said, among other things, that each would inform the other in advance of any international events which might endanger their national interests. Since then there had been a stream of insistent messages from the Italian Ambassador in Berlin, to the effect that Hitler was planning something drastic for 15 August. But not a word had come from von Ribbentrop, and Ciano cheerfully reckoned that 'either the Ambassador had lost his head, or he sees and knows something which has completely escaped us. Appearances are in favour of the first alternative . . .'

By Friday 4 August, however, the glamorous young count was starting to feel much less optimistic. 'The situation seems obscure to me . . . The moment has come when we must really know how matters stand.'

Sixteen years previously, in 1923, King George V of Great Britain paid a state visit to the Italian King Victor Emmanuel. King George took the opportunity to create Signor Mussolini a Knight Grand Cross of the Order of the Bath, Britain's second highest order of knighthood. During the same year the Duke of York, King George's second son, married Lady Elizabeth Bowes-Lyon. Now no longer Lady Elizabeth nor Duchess of York, she would never forget the trauma of 1936: the death of the king, the accession of his eldest son as Edward VIII, the crisis when Edward would not give up his decision to marry an American divorcee. A British monarch could not marry a divorced person. The only alternative, an extraordinarily painful and shocking experience for everyone, was Edward's abdication; and unexpectedly, unwillingly, but unavoidably the Duke and Duchess of York had become Their Majesties King George VI and Queen Elizabeth.

That alone made history, and in the summer of 1939 the royal couple were the centre of another historic event: during June they visited the United States, the first king and queen of Great Britain ever to do so. At the beginning of the year, when the dates of the visit were announced, the writer H. G. Wells dismissed it as 'of very small importance', and was equally off-hand about the 'young people': 'I believe, a very charming couple, constantly smiling and bowing, but they mean absolutely nothing in the problems of today.' On both counts he was wrong. When the king decided to go, his Prime Minister Neville Chamberlain was still trying to cope with the difficulties being created by Germany through appeasement, buying the Führer off with one agreement after another. Yet in the face of those same difficulties, one of the king's principal motives in visiting the United States was to strengthen the relationship between Britain and America. Hardly the behavior of an out-of-touch young man; and the visit had been a terrific success. Of course many Americans felt suspicious – they could hardly do otherwise when their ancestors had fought for liberty against an English king – but few of them could refuse their own national instinct for giving hospitality, or resist the queen's equally instinctive charm. 'You've been here about four minutes,' Mayor La Guardia's secretary told her, 'and all New York is in love with you.' And as they drove through the city, surrounded by cheering crowds estimated at three and a half million, the mayor reckoned their coming had done more good than sending a dozen ambassadors or swapping fifty diplomatic notes. 'In fact,' he said to the king in delight, 'you've negotiated a treaty of friendship that will take many years to revoke.'

'Very kind of you to say so,' His Majesty replied – an understated answer, for he meant it deeply.

At home George and Elizabeth were becoming a very public king and queen, setting a new pattern for British royalty; but even they had their days of privacy, and 4 August was one of them. On that Friday, as Galeazzo Ciano thought uneasily about von Ribbentrop, the British royal family – father, mother and two daughters, the Princesses Elizabeth and Margaret, aged thirteen and ten – were on holiday in the peaceful seclusion of Balmoral Castle. Above the castle, to the south, Balmoral Forest's dark shades rose up the slopes of the Grampians. Below it, to the north, ran the river Dee, and beyond the river the Cairngorm Mountains began their climb four thousand feet and more into the Highland sky. Before the war was over Princess Elizabeth would be serving as a mechanic and lorry driver in the Auxiliary Territorial Service. Today, however, she and her little sister had something far more important to think about: it was their mother's thirty-ninth birthday.

In London, Parliament adjourned at four o'clock. Ministers and members dispersed; and at the same time, Nicholas Winton began considering again the likely fate of several hundred people much younger and less publicly important than the queen or any politician. With the business of the day done, he had gone directly from his office in the City of London to another one in Bloomsbury. The making of money was over for the week; work was not. Each evening – and it had been going on like this for the past eight months – he stopped only when he was too tired to make any more sense. His background was as unusual as his unpaid evening work. His family originally came from Germany, and until only a year ago had been called Wertheim, a very obviously Jewish name. But they were thoroughly British: his grandfather had become a naturalised British citizen, had converted to Christianity and served as British Consul in Moscow before the Revolution. Nevertheless during the Great War they had often been ostracised in England – by Jews because they had abandoned the faith, by Christians because they were converts, and by Britons generally because of the German ring to their name. Their decision to change their name to the more English-sounding Winton had been a direct result of Chamberlain's peace mission to Munich. There had been an upside-down logic to it: had he returned with a message of war, they would have stayed Wertheim, and put up with the same suspicion they had endured in 1914–18; they were not cowards. But all of them, especially Nicky, who worked on the Stock Exchange as a specialist in South African trade, were tired of the worn-out old jokes about Jews, and before the Prime Minister left for Germany they decided that if he brought back a promise of peace it would be as good a time as any to leave the past behind. No one could say then that they did it because they were afraid.

Nor indeed could anyone say truthfully that Nicky Winton's present work sprang from a distant Jewish ancestry. Certainly in Germany he would have been classified Jewish by race, and 85 per cent of the names on the list he was reading were Jewish; but his motive was humanitarian – to help in the evacuation of threatened children from Nazi-occupied Czechoslovakia. Late one Tuesday evening just before Christmas 1938 he had arrived in Prague, bewildered, not knowing what to expect: he should have been skiing in Switzerland. He had cancelled that at the last minute, after a phone call from a friend, Martin Blake, who merely said he was on a most interesting assignment and needed Nicky's help. Since then the 'assignment' had developed into a job filling every spare hour.

Together, Martin and Nicky had seen for themselves the crowds of refugees, Communists, Jews, gypsies, intellectuals, and many who were simply frightened, who had come from Germany, Austria and the Sudetenland.

Organisations already existed for the evacuation of adults, and Martin worked for one, the British Committee for Refugees from Czechoslovakia. But no system had been established to bring children to safety. Martin asked Nicky to set one up, and he had accepted. Ever since, he had been dazed by the size of the task he had taken on. In Prague the worst moments (and they occurred every day) were when he had to explain to distraught parents that safety for their children meant separation, with no guarantees when, or even if, they might be reunited. Trying to solve their plight was so absorbing that, until there were only four days of his 'holiday' left, he had forgotten he must go back. Thereupon he had written to his firm, asking for an extension; and now in August he still had the senior partner's reply, dated 9 January:

> Dear Winton, I have returned today to the City after a nice holiday at my new Villa in the South of France. There is very little doing in the Kaffir market; but I would sooner you were taking a rest here, rather than doing heroic work for thousands of poor devils who are suffering through no fault of their own . . . I still think Western Holdings will go lower – probably West Wits and Western Reef also. There is so much new capital required, both in South and West Africa, that there is little chance of good markets while all this fresh money has to be found.

And it ended: 'We hope you may be able to get back to the office here by next Monday. With best wishes for the New Year, and may it be more profitable for you than the last.' The letter still infuriated him. When he felt charitable, he could say the man simply had no imagination. He had not seen, as Nicky had in Prague, the unending queues of desperate families. He had not seen the map predicting the rise of Greater Germany from 1938 to 1948, detailing, step by step, the projected acquisition of Austria, Czechoslovakia, Hungary, Poland, Yugoslavia, Rumania, northern France and the Low Countries, western Russia, and at last the whole continent of Europe including Britain. He had not read the printed letter from the Commandant of Konzentrationslager Weimar-Buchenwald: 'The date when the detainee will be released has not yet been determined. Visits to the camp are forbidden. Inquiries are useless'; or the letters postmarked with the swastika and the message *Wir sind frei*, We are free.

Perhaps it was only that: perhaps the man had no imagination at all. But in his more critical moments, Nicky Winton suspected the truth was that his employer just did not care in the least: there was no money to be made in evacuating children. Nevertheless more than 500 had been brought out now, some to Sweden, most to England; some to caring guarantors, some to homes which offered little more than a roof over their heads; children of all ages from three to eighteen, the older ones knowing they might never see their natural parents again; all still frightened, confused and lonely – but at least, safe. Whatever happened to them in their foster homes, it was certainly better than the alternative, the concentration camps. Yet God only knew how many more there might be waiting to come out, how many might follow, or how much time might remain . . . Well, at any rate the weekend was beginning, and on Bank Holiday Monday the Stock Exchange would be closed. He could work in Bloomsbury House for three full days.

'A quarter of a century ago today, we were closing our first day of War.' On Saturday, 5 August the leading article in the *South Wales Evening Post* was meditative and defiant. Victory had been won in the Great War, but – all in vain, it seems – embattled as never before, the nations march and counter-march under a sky dark and sultry with thunderclouds, and lit by summer lightning. Halifax may be guarded, Inskip [the Chairman of the Committee of Imperial Defence] may be optimistic, but the British common man has long determined that there is but one man who holds the keys of peace and war, and that is Adolf Hitler, who can keep his own secrets. Recalling the Munich crisis, 'that dire week in last September, when a sense of horror surcharged the air, and there was a public instinct that we had been caught unarmoured', the article ended uncompromisingly: 'No more surrender; our backs are to the wall in European issues, and our strength is mobilised, yet far from its summit.'

What a load of nonsense, thought Tom Elliott. To him, a seventeen-year-old tinplate worker, the promise of Munich seemed perfectly secure. Turning the pages, he snorted at the photograph of 'Youth's example in ARP work', Swansea Boy Scouts helping to box up gas masks for delivery to householders. 'Look at this, Da,' he said to his father. 'Make you look like a real monster, those do. And the ones for the kiddies, with the Mickey Mouse ears, they're even worse. Wouldn't be seen dead in one myself.'

'Might be seen dead without it, boy,' his father replied. 'When we get issued with them, you'll carry yours like everyone else, and like it.'

Tom grunted disdainfully and continued flicking through the paper. Three dead, five injured in Holiday Train Smash in Saltcoats. And where was that? Somewhere in Scotland, a long way off. Inside prospects for the Denbigh National Eisteddfod: a vintage year for poetry expected. So it should be; Wales always led the world in poetry. Jazz band concert and fête this afternoon, given by the British Legion in the castle grounds at Oystermouth . . . ah, the Castle cinema: 'Boris Karloff is back in *The Mystery of Mr Wong*.'

He closed the paper. 'Right, Da, I'm off out. Going to the pictures.'

'Call in at the Town Hall on your way, if you can,' his father said. 'You might pick up a few gas masks while you're passing.'

At thirteen minutes past 2 p.m. British Summer Time, a 23½ ton Caribou flying boat belonging to Imperial Airways took off from Southampton Water, curved westwards and roared over the Solent. Inside were bags of parcels and letters. If it succeeded in its 3500 mile flight it would be the first ever British transatlantic air mail service. In Europe less than an hour later, Albert Förster, Gauleiter of Danzig, arrived at the Berghof and was in conference with Hitler; and in Danzig itself Marjan Chodacki was coming to the end of one of the most trying weeks of his life.

Danzig's positions, geographical and political, were curious in the extreme. The area designated as the Free City was about 30 miles west to east, about 25 miles north to south. Its eastern border divided it from the German province of East Prussia; its western border divided it from Poland, or at least from territory which since the end of the Great War had been Polish: the contentious Corridor. Yet only 25 miles further west was the Corridor's border with the rest of Germany. The narrow slice of land was Poland's only direct outlet to the sea; the port of Gdynia, where the Olscholwskis lived, ten miles up the coast from Danzig, was newly built for the express purpose of channelling Polish exports and imports to and from the rest of the world. Ruled by a Senate under the guardianship of the League of Nations, Danzig itself, or Gdansk, was legally neither Polish nor German. Both nations therefore maintained customs officials on their borders with the city, and diplomatic representatives in it. Marjan Chodacki was Poland's representative, but in the Free City he often felt himself to be a minority of one. Ninety per cent of its population of 400,000 were German; most, led by Albert Förster, were members of the Nazi Party; the Senate, not surprisingly, was dominated by Nazis; and since the beginning of the week they had been exchanging angry notes with Chodacki on the subject of customs barriers.

Here was the crux of all the rising European tensions of the year. Danzig was German in virtually every way except geographically, and that was an artificial separation, only twenty years old. Should it now remain a Free City or should it be re-incorporated into the Reich? In Germany and the Danzig Senate the answer was, of course, emphatically yes; in Poland, equally emphatically, no, for in practical terms Danzig's free status was inseparable from Poland's independence.

Before Hitler's annexation of the Sudetenland had taken place, the same arguments had applied on both sides, Czechoslovakian and German. The re-incorporation of the German-populated Sudetenland seemed common sense in Berlin; in Prague, it promised the destruction of the nation, which, like Poland, had only been independent for twenty years. The country's independence was guaranteed by France and Britain, if it were the subject of unprovoked aggression, and when German troops entered Prague on 15 March, war between the guarantors and Germany was only avoided because both France and Britain chose to accept that the annexation – and the immediate loss of independence for the rest of Czechoslovakia – came about from a legal Czechoslovak request. But the take-over also made absolutely plain to Chamberlain and to Édouard Daladier, the French Prime Minister, that Hitler could not be trusted one inch; for in spirit if not in the letter, he had shattered their agreement at Munich.

Had he waited, Czechoslovakia would have become German territory anyway. But though he had not used force, he had used the threat of force, thoroughly and effectively, to bully the Czech leadership into submission; and so the time of appeasement abruptly ended. British and French guarantees of independence were issued to Poland, and this time everyone accepted that they would be honoured. Everyone, that is, apart from Hitler.

In other circumstances the customs dispute in Danzig would have seemed ridiculous. When the House of Commons was debating its own adjournment, Arthur Greenwood, deputy leader of the Labour Party, had remarked: 'No one is going to pretend that Danzig at the present time is a pleasant seaside holiday resort.' In fact to outward appearances, it was swarming with tourists; at least 6000 had entered in the past few weeks. But oddly enough they were all men, they were all German, and none of them was leaving. This was because they were all stormtroopers. Theoretically the Free City was demilitarised, but arms, ammunition and military vehicles from Germany were pouring in virtually unchecked: the 'tourists' were physically preventing the Polish customs officials from carrying out their work.

In protest, Chodacki had told the Senate that if harassment did not stop, his customs officers would cease clearing the city's duty-free exports of margarine and herrings to Poland, a more potent threat than it sounded, for those two products accounted for one-sixth of Danzig's revenue. The Senate replied that, in that case, on Sunday morning they would open the border to East Prussia and stop the Polish officials from checking anything at all; whereupon Chodacki replied that if they did not withdraw that order before Saturday evening, the Polish government would commence immediate reprisals.

The Senate could work out the consequences. During Parliament's adjournment debate Arthur Greenwood had stressed Danzig's delicate balance. If 'one of the great personages of Europe' (and everyone knew who he meant) happened to be suffering from a bad liver and heard that half a dozen German subjects in the Free City had been shot, 'it only needs such a situation for the world to be at war within twenty-four hours'.

On Saturday afternoon, in the grounds of Balmoral Castle, King George and Queen Elizabeth were giving a tea-party for 200 boys from the King's Annual Boys' Camp. Each year the queen noticed how even the shyest of the boys relaxed when confronted with a table of orange squash, cake and sandwiches; and as the children were happily tucking in, the Danzig Senate (with extremely bad grace) cancelled its order, telling Chodacki he must have misunderstood, that a joke had been played on him. He knew then that, with a mixture of bluff and bravery, he had won a round. But that evening, perhaps better than anyone else, he knew too that Arthur Greenwood's remark was correct: the world had been within a day of war. If that was the Senate's idea of a joke, Chodacki could only say they had a very German sense of humour.

4

Holiday time, ladies and gentlemen!

SUNDAY, 6 AUGUST: the Feast of the Transfiguration. It was a warm dry morning in England, the sky overcast. In the church of St Philip Neri in Mansfield, Oscar Baker and his elder sister Theresa sat in reverent silence and listened to the first reading, from the first chapter of the second epistle general of St Peter: '*Carissimi: non doctas fabulas secuti fecimus vobis Domini nostri Jesu Christi . . .*'

High Mass, sung in Latin, was the most satisfying of all the services, and especially so on a day like today, marking one of the most important events in the life of Christ. There was also a practical reason for Oscar and Theresa to be glad of the rest and restoration they found in the church: this morning, as they did each Sunday, brother and sister had walked five miles from their home village of Rainworth to be there. With the best will in the world – and particularly on such a warm morning – it was tiring. As the reading continued, Oscar let his mind drift around peacefully. He liked St Philip Neri's; its services, like any in the Roman Catholic Church, gave him a sense of stability, continuity; he felt in touch with the earliest roots of Christendom, hearing the ancient words that generation on generation had spoken and sung before him. And the physical church, the building in which he sat, embodied the lasting strength of that tradition, for it was virtually brand new. Modelled on an Italian church, its design had won a special papal award; and, built in 1926, it was only thirteen years old. It occurred to Oscar that the building was just a year younger than he was, which made it all the more *his* church, spiritual and temporal.

'*Cui bene facitis attendentes*', 'you do well to attend', – the end of the reading came like a gentle rebuke followed immediately by a comfort: 'as to a light that shineth in a dark place, until the day dawn and the day star arise in your heart'.

Theresa was already on her feet for the response to the Graduale; today it was Psalm 44. Oscar stood up hastily and cleared his throat. Behind him there was a muted rumble, a heavy shuffling. Of course, he had forgotten the soldiers. For the past four or five weeks they had been turning up regularly from a camp or garrison close by. There were usually a couple of dozen, always filling the two back pews. Being closer to the front, it was easy to forget them, but there were two things he liked about them. One (he could hear it now) was how their deep male voices added beautifully to the singing; and the other was that they always left their weapons in the vestibule – a respectful thing to do, he thought.

Meanwhile the steamship *City of Exeter* was proceeding at a sedate pace across an almost calm North Sea. Ivan Maisky, Soviet Ambassador in London, had come down to Tilbury to see the combined Anglo-French delegation on its way – *almost*, thought Admiral Drax, *as if he wanted to make sure we were actually going*. Their route to Russia took them past Drax's old stamping grounds, the sites of the battle of the Dogger Bank in 1914; the battle of Heligoland Bight in 1915; and the Great War's greatest sea battle, Jutland, in 1916. He had always respected the German Navy, and had a suspicion that nowadays he should do so even more. Air Marshal Burnett certainly respected the Luftwaffe; and both agreed with Major-General Heywood that the task ahead of them would not be easy. Their instructions included the discouraging observation that 'the Russian is suspicious by nature, and a hard bargainer'; and they were disturbed to find that, while they had been told to make the slowest possible progress in the talks, their French colleagues had been told not to return without a pact.

Certainly in the *City of Exeter* the British contingent's part was being fulfilled: they never travelled at more than 12 knots. That at least gave them all, French and English, plenty of time to work out a common approach, which they did in twice daily sessions in a most incongruous setting. In the small liner there was only one room large enough for the combined delegations to meet in any comfort: the children's playroom.

In London, even close to Victoria Station the streets were quiet. Inside Westminster Cathedral, less than a quarter of a mile from the station, the air was heavy with the sultry smell of incense. As the echoes of the choir's alleluia died away, the second reading of the High Mass of the day began – Matthew 17: 1–9: 'In that time Jesus taketh unto him Peter, and James, and John his brother, and bringeth them up into a high mountain apart; and he was transfigured before them. And his face did shine as the sun, and his raiment was white as the snow.' In every Catholic community in the country, after the text had been read in Latin, the same elegant rhythms of the Douai translation were being spoken. Although he knew it almost by heart, Francis Vanek followed the service in his missal eagerly. This was one of his favourite passages: 'And as he was yet speaking, behold, a bright cloud overshadowed them, and lo, a voice came out of the cloud, saying, This is my beloved Son, in whom I am well pleased; hear ye him.' Exactly the sound of a proud father,

Francis reflected. Even a person of no faith – and his own was very strong – would recognise that. And the rest of the reading was particularly apt that day for him and the sixteen friends with him: 'Jesus came and touched them, and said, Arise, and fear not. And they, lifting up their eyes, saw no one but only Jesus.'

Parked outside the cathedral were seventeen bicycles with saddlebags and knapsacks. As soon as the service was over the St Christopher's Cycling Club would go to Victoria and board the boat train for Newhaven and Dieppe: the first stage in a 600-mile pilgrimage to Lourdes. 'As they came down from the mountain, Jesus charged them, saying, Tell the vision to no man, until the Son of man be risen again from the dead.' The inspiring words ended; and with a glorious burst of music the choir stood to sing the Credo.

At the same time, in Rome itself, Count Ciano had his mind on a different sort of glory. 'Thank you, Duce,' he said. 'Of course I shall be most honoured; and I am deeply grateful for your help.' His voice was grave. Mussolini nodded, still not entirely convinced that he had made the right decision, and Ciano tried hard to conceal his pleasure. The Collar of the Order of the Annunziata! The king had recently expressed his intention of awarding it to him. Anyone wearing the collar was deemed an honorary cousin of the king, but His Majesty wanted Mussolini's advice, and he had been doubtful: 'It might lead to compromises,' he said, 'that it would be better not to make.' However it seemed that now he was persuaded Ciano should have it: he had promised to write to the king tomorrow saying so. It was a good moment to change the subject, and Ciano cleared his throat. 'As for the Germans,' he began, 'we must find some way out.'

On the sea-front at Tynemouth Bill Hardcastle and John Landells, cub reporters on the *Shields Evening News*, were beginning to despair of finding anything to write about. Bank Holiday Mondays were generally a dead loss for news. Of course it depended on what one meant by news; usually it had to be something exciting, and there was very little going on in Tynemouth that could be called exciting, nothing but holidaymakers enjoying themselves. However, more news than anyone there could conceive was being shaped that holiday weekend: preparations in all secrecy for the making, the avoiding and the near-breaking of pacts, treaties and alliances that, soon and suddenly, would alter the face of Europe and the world. Drax and his colleagues, English and French, working towards agreement on a common approach in Moscow, hoped reluctantly that they might achieve a military agreement with their Russian counterparts. Ambassador von der Schulenburg hoped earnestly that he might have moved a step closer to achieving the same thing, and more, for Germany. Yet though Commissar Molotov had behaved towards him in a much less reserved and more friendly manner than usual,

Schulenburg remained pessimistic: it had been embarrassing, for example, trying to explain his assertion that the Anti-Comintern Pact was not aimed at Russia. Neither Mussolini nor Count Ciano knew anything of the exploratory talks between Berlin and Moscow. Indeed they decided that the next occasion Hitler and the Duce met should be, in Ciano's words, 'at some other time, when the Anglo–French–Russian negotiations have been concluded'. Moreover they agreed that in spite of the Pact of Steel – only eleven weeks old – it would be essential to renege on its obligations, if those meant following Germany into a war. And in London Ambassador von Dirksen meditated on his conversation with Chamberlain's chief adviser, Sir Horace Wilson.

This extension of earlier secret discussions made it clear that the time for negotiating was not over. Britain was prepared to increase trade with Germany, talk constructively about Germany's need for colonies, take a helpful view of Germany's need for expansion in south-east Europe, announce jointly a cooperative programme to help improve the world economic situation, look seriously at the possibility of limiting armaments (including a possible loan to Germany to offset the financial difficulties limitation would bring), and finally, agree not to intervene in matters concerning the Greater Reich, which would include Danzig. Anyone outside the diplomatic world, and many people inside it, would have been staggered at the list of possible concessions. There was only one precondition: that Germany and Britain should sign a treaty of non-aggression, in which both sides would renounce unilateral aggressive action as a policy method. Von Dirksen concluded that 'the dominant feeling was that, compared with an effective adjustment with Germany, the ties that had been formed in the last few months with other Powers were only a subsidiary means, which would cease to be operative as soon as agreement with Germany, the all-important objective worth striving for, had been really attained'.

Intrigue, conspiracy, secret international jockeying for favour, position, power; and all, with one exception, trying to work for peace at almost any price, even national humiliation or unnatural alliance. Yet not even those most closely involved could know precisely what was going on behind closed doors, or tell what the next few days and weeks would bring.

At 2.27 BST that morning – 9.27 the previous evening New York time – the Imperial Airways Caribou had landed at Manhasset Bay, one of the innermost sections of Long Island Sound. Droning in over Einstein's retreat at Nassau, it had taken more than thirty-six hours to complete its flight from England, fighting against headwinds and blinding rainstorms the whole way. That evening in southern England, however, the sunset was calm and bright. 'A good omen, I hope,' Sir Alexander Cadogan wrote in his diary for 7 August. 'The view at sunset was so peaceful and lovely: I hope it bodes that we may spend some days here in peace. Back to London tomorrow.'

And, as Francis Vanek and his sixteen fellow-pilgrims cycled innocently southwards from Rouen over the great plain of the Beauce, yellow with grain, and sighted from far away the spires of Chartres Cathedral – their first objective – Sir Alexander thanked God for his holiday, and prayed for strength to face the future.

Not all flights were as successful as the Caribou's arduous transatlantic effort; on 8 August a woman walking on Beachy Head was killed when an RAF bomber crashed three hundred yards inland, ploughed through her and plunged over the 575-foot cliff into the English Channel; its crew of three men were killed as well. At Fishguard, in the far west of Wales, a close watch was being maintained for IRA suspects attempting to enter or leave the country: from the beginning of the year there had been sporadic bombings in British stores and cities. In Scotland the Royal Family's holiday continued, with the two princesses carrying on with their Girl Guide training. Princess Elizabeth was pursuing nature studies, adding new specimens to her collection of native British wild flowers and plants, identifying each and recording them meticulously.

Three hundred and seventy-three Jewish refugees arrived that day in Haifa; and from Paris, German mobilisation was reported as being nearly complete. Claude Viviers, writing in the newspaper *Ordre*, foretold a second September crisis: press propaganda for the return of Danzig to the Reich, accentuated by moves of the German army, made the 20th seem to him the likeliest date for the next critical increase in international tension. 'The danger of war is as real as ever. At any rate, even if Germany has realised that she cannot yet risk a war, one can be convinced that she will risk a large-scale bluff.'

'This is the time to fight – to speak – to attack!' So Churchill had advised his despondent supporters when Parliament prepared to adjourn; and now he set the example, with a 15-minute radio broadcast to the United States.

'Holiday time, ladies and gentlemen! Holiday time, my friends across the Atlantic!' Taking time off from Chartwell, where he was working on his *History of the English-Speaking Peoples,* he sounded breezy and ebullient at first. But in a few moments his tone changed. Only twenty-five years had passed since the outbreak of the Great War, the war to end wars, in which more than eight-and-a-half million military people had died. In the past few days, the first week of August 1939, the anniversaries had gone by: Germany's declaration of war against France on the 3rd, Britain's declaration against Germany on the 4th. Twenty-five years: just enough time for a new generation of soldiers, sailors and airmen to come to maturity. The radio speech was bitter, heavily ironic and very powerful: 'Let me look back – let me see. How did we spend our summer holidays twenty-five years ago? Why, those were the very days when the German advance guards were breaking into Belgium and trampling down its people on their march towards Paris!'

Skilfully he drew his listeners in. 'Listen! No, listen carefully; I think I hear something – yes, there it was quite clear. Don't you hear it? It is the tramp of armies crunching the gravel of the parade-grounds, splashing through rain-soaked fields, the tramp of two million German soldiers and more than a million Italians – "going on manoeuvres" – yes, only on manoeuvres!'

America had counted 126,000 dead in the Great War. To those who had survived, his images were horribly clear, his mockery of Hitler and Mussolini simultaneously compelling and unnerving:

> Of course it's only manoeuvres – just like last year. After all, the Dictators must train their soldiers. They could scarcely do less in common prudence, when the Danes, the Dutch, the Swiss, the Albanians – and of course the Jews – may leap out upon them at any moment and rob them of their living-space . . . Besides, these German and Italian armies may have another work of liberation to perform. It was only last year they liberated Austria from the horrors of self-government. It was only in March they freed the Czechoslovak Republic from the misery of independent existence. It is only two years ago that Signor Mussolini gave the ancient kingdom of Abyssinia its Magna Charta. It is only two months ago that little Albania got its writ of Habeus Corpus . . . No wonder the armies are tramping on when there is so much work of liberation to be done.

But, he reminded his invisible audience, 'the hush of suspense . . . the hush of fear' that lay over the world was broken in one place: from China, distant, muffled but immediately distinguishable, came the dull echo of Japanese bombs, continuing to fall after two years of undeclared war.

As Churchill made his broadcast, Count Ciano received a message from the Italian Embassy in Berlin. Written in 'a rather soothing tone', he noted that it 'does not foresee any immediate aggressive intentions on the part of Germany, even though the Danzig situation is grave and dangerous.' If Churchill had been sent the same message at the same moment, he would have simply snorted and continued with his broadcast; it would take much more than an optimistic note from an Italian diplomat to soothe him. No one could truly say whether the conflicts, and threats of conflict, could be contained. So while the Chinese fought to defend their homeland and the neighbours of Italy and Germany tried to read the future, his voice came crackling out of American wireless sets; and with a grim warning he urged Americans to 'give them a cheer across the ocean – no one knows whose turn it may be next. If this habit of military dictatorships breaking into other people's lands with bomb and shell and bullet, stealing the property and killing the proprietors, spreads too widely, we may none of us be able to think of summer holidays for quite a while.'

The second week

9–17 August 1939

Sunday Express

NO. 1,076 Founded by LORD BEAVERBROOK LONDON, AUGUST 13, 1939 TWOPENCE

LATE EXTRA

This is the Gin **Gordon's** Stand Supreme

Looking Forward

COMING-OF-AGE is a milestone in the life of a business as well as in the life of an individual. It brings to the full vigour of youth a sense of stability.

To the young man of twenty-one, coming-of-age marks the dividing line between the years of preparation and the years of achievement.

The great adventure of life lies ahead. So it is with a business.

In the months the Sunday Express will be twenty-one years of age—the youngest national newspaper in Britain today.

Where do we stand at the end of these years of preparation?

A MONTH ago in our usual six-monthly statement to readers and advertisers we were able to announce

NATIONAL REGISTER MOVE

PRINCE BERNHARD SNAPS HIS NEW BABY

Towns Warned To Have Staffs Ready For Action

HITLER, CIANO, RIBBENTROP

AND

"Much Ado About Nothing"

WHILE you were yesterday Herr Hitler spent a busy day trying to take the wobble out of the Axis,

A FURTHER IM-PORTANT STEP TOWARDS COM-PILING A NATIONAL REGISTER OF THE NATION FOR WAR SERVICE WAS TAKEN LAST WEEK.

Instructions were sent from the Registrar-General to all local authorities that the enumerators who will distribute the register cards to

Yesterday's Record

More Cross Channel Than Ever Before

CONTINU

Lose Money If They Wed Again

UNDER wills published yesterday two widows will have to sacrifice a considerable part of their incomes if they remarry. Mr. Frederick Tidswell, of Collingham-road, South Kensington, Hollin-war-road, N., and Collingham, Kent, emery manufacturer, left nearly the

LATEST NEWS
Telephone: Central 8000

5

Different worlds

ON THE MORNING of Wednesday 9 August, at eight o'clock precisely, the sailors of 133 warships of the British Reserve Fleet began to dress ship. At five minutes to ten, having travelled overnight in the royal train from Scotland, King George arrived in Weymouth, on the English south coast, to inspect them. Like the ships, the streets of the town were gaily decorated with flags to greet His Majesty. In fourteen lines, each four miles long, the vessels stretched rank on rank across the wide bay, from Portland breakwater nearly to the cliffs at Redcliff Point.

As an inspection rather than a review, it was not just a show for the benefit of civilians; it was a fully naval occasion. Everywhere there were flag officers and commodores either accompanying the king or waiting in their ships for his arrival, and as a courtesy to the national ally, Amiral de la Flotte Jean Darlan, Chief of the French Naval Staff, was to be presented to His Majesty. For the journalists present, the serried grey shapes on the glittering water made 'a striking picture of grace and power in the brilliant early morning sunshine', but – unfortunately for the sailors lining the sides of the ships – when the time came for His Majesty to begin the inspection, a light rain was falling. The men had no option but to remain at attention and get wet.

The royal yacht *Victoria and Albert* was in attendance. From twenty-one designated naval guns a salute crashed out, reverberating across the bay. As all the other boat traffic ceased, the royal barge bearing the king sped among the warships. At the aircraft carrier *Courageous*, built in 1917 as a light battlecruiser and converted nine years ago, the barge stopped. Wearing the undress uniform of an Admiral of the Fleet, His Majesty transshipped to the carrier and remained on board for forty minutes, inspecting her 48 aircraft and 1500 crew. He would visit three more ships personally that morning, and in the afternoon would be taken in the royal barge past every other vessel in the fleet.

Watching from the shore, there was at least one journalist who did not grasp the fine distinction between an inspection and a review. Nevertheless his report was accurate enough: for the Reserve Fleet, this was the greatest occasion since 'the War'.

*

Ambassador Herbert von Dirksen was ready to go home on leave from London. Before departure he went to say goodbye to the Foreign Secretary, Lord Halifax, expecting a short interview. It developed otherwise.

Without preamble, Halifax asked him directly: 'Have you any explanation, Ambassador, for the present sharp tone of the press concerning Danzig? Sharp, I may say, on both sides.'

Von Dirksen was not surprised at the question – only a little at the Foreign Secretary's bluntness. He was ready with an answer: it was the fault of the Polish paper *Czas*, which had published a statement saying that if there was any attempt to incorporate Danzig into the Reich, Polish troops would open fire on the Free City.

'Moreover,' he added, 'the Polish Commissioner-General, Chodacki, has told Karl Burckhardt, the League of Nations Commissioner, that opening the customs frontier between Danzig and East Prussia would mean war. This further confirms our fear that, at any moment, the local Polish authorities might jeopardise peace.'

'You may be sure', replied Halifax, 'that I and the British Government will do all we can to incline the Poles to moderation. And I am certain that neither Foreign Minister Beck nor Marshal Smigly-Rydz desire a conflict with Germany.'

'Poland's great weakness has always been giving out many different political declarations,' von Dirksen retorted. 'Such is the case now.'

'Nevertheless,' said Halifax, 'it would be highly desirable for both sides to display moderation, as I am sure you will agree. Tranquillity might then be achieved, and then perhaps agreement by negotiation.'

But von Dirksen was not to be put off. '*We* have amply manifested calm and moderation. The danger is exactly that means of negotiations have been blocked on all sides. Not only the attitude of Poland, and the false information put out in the world's press; Mr Chamberlain's declarations too make the Danzig question practically unamenable to negotiations. We hear disquieting news of military commissions going from Britain to Poland or Moscow, news that Germany's potential adversaries are being strengthened financially by Britain. It goes without saying that we watch these things closely – and draw our own conclusions.'

In Bressay the Smith family's holiday was ending. Stella's dress had taken longer to finish than she expected: cutting out patterns from old newspapers, she always tended to get engrossed in the bits of news she had missed. But now it was done, four flared pieces with a short waist top, all of good quality cotton, green and blue on a white background. She put it on and twirled around, to the approval of the adults; while outside, Nanette, a tomboy at heart, who liked to ride the cows bareback in Foula, set off with their grandfather on the two-mile walk to the peat bank.

The diplomatic conversation in London continued. 'You must understand, Ambassador, how things have changed since Munich,' said Halifax, carefully keeping impatience from his voice. 'Then I thought we were embarking on fifty years of world peace. If I may, perhaps I could repeat my understanding as it was at that time.'

Von Dirksen inclined his head. 'Please.'

'Very well. Germany would have been the dominant power on the continent, with predominant rights in south-eastern Europe, especially in commercial policy, where Britain would engage only in moderate trade. Lines of fortifications on both sides would protect Britain and France from conflicts with Germany. We would have had friendship with America and Portugal – Spain, for several years at least, would have been an indefinite factor; Russia would have remained an out of the way, vast, scarcely surveyable territory; and we would have safeguarded our Mediterranean communications with the dominions.'

'Admirably put.'

Halifax lifted a hand. 'Ah – but then came the march into Prague. That changed everything. Above all, it destroyed the idea that world stability had been attained, and created doubt as to where Germany would stop, if at all.'

In the heart of France, the cycling pilgrims had an easy day's journey: sixty miles from Tours almost directly south to Poitiers, crossing the Loire and the Indre, along the right bank of the Vienne as far as Châtellerault. Although the whole thing had been Paddy Murray's idea – and he had organised it – Francis Vanek spoke the best French among the seventeen cyclists, and had been elected interpreter for the group. By now, the third full day in France, he was getting accustomed to a seemingly standard question, wherever they stopped: 'Monsieur, do you believe there will be a war?' The first time, he had been taken aback, and had simply answered truthfully that he did not. But that did not appear to be enough.

'Really, Paddy,' he said impatiently, 'they seem to think I know something they don't, just because I'm English.'

'So tell them what you think,' Paddy answered easily. 'A man like you can dream up something, that's for sure.'

When they stopped for lunch at Châtellerault, it came again; after orders for food and drink had been given, it seemed to be the only other question in anyone's mind. But this time Francis felt certain he had a better reply, and said with confidence: 'No, monsieur, absolutely not.' Pausing to add effect, he continued: 'And if you would like to know why, it is for two reasons – firstly, would we be here if we thought a war is coming? Of course not: we would be safe at home across the Channel. Secondly, it would be illogical for a war to begin; if France and Britain stand together, no one will dare attack us.'

The double appeal to logic and mutual patriotism was, he felt, clear and convincing; and so he was surprised when the waiter said pensively, '*Eh bien, monsieur*, let us hope you are right.'

It was not until they were leaving the town that Francis noticed a large building on the opposite side of the river, apparently with its own wharf. It was the national arms factory.

'Naturally,' von Dirksen answered Lord Halifax, 'these things look entirely different from the German aspect. I will not repeat how often our confidence has been deceived, nor what sad experiences have compelled us to rely on our own swift decisions, instead of negotiations. I understand your view of British policy; but you must put yourself in the mental position of a German statesman. Then you will understand that all we see is an ever bigger coalition being formed against Germany, and as far as we are concerned, the war potential constantly growing in our disfavour. At best, it is as if you had thrown a net over our heads – you tell us that if we keep quiet, nothing will happen to us, but if we move, we will suffer. So it is not surprising, surely, if Germany is rather sceptical when British statesmen say they are willing to consider German demands voluntarily, and by negotiation . . . On the English side, especially in view of the democratic system and the un-tutored behaviour of the press, the premises for a peaceful settlement do not exist.'

Nodding, Halifax said, 'I have to agree with you that, at present, public opinion in this country is', he paused, 'highly excited, and distrustful of negotiations with Germany; and indeed the difficulties you mention are, for the time being, insoluble.'

He must bring the interview to a close. It was not going as he had hoped; von Dirksen was being quite intransigent, and it was made no easier by the fact that he, Halifax, could understand at least part of the German's attitude. Odd how it was sometimes actually simpler to deal with diplomats one thoroughly disliked – von Dirksen's predecessor Ribbentrop, for example, who liked to use the noble prefix 'von' although he was almost certainly not entitled to it. Dreadful, pretentious man best summed up by that embarrass-ing episode three years ago, when, in presenting his credentials to the king, he had given His Majesty a Nazi salute. Ever since, he had been remembered as Brickendrop.

However, time for one last effort before letting von Dirksen depart. Rising to his feet, Halifax said firmly, 'Ambassador, I am *certain* that a period of calm will enable us here to pacify public opinion. Then, undoubtedly, it will be possible to discuss appeasement questions. I repeat, the British

Government keenly desire that this should come about, and would be prepared to go very far for the achievement of that aim.'

For the first time in the interview, von Dirksen was surprised. The Foreign
Secretary had actually used the word appeasement, virtually a dirty word
since the Reich had acquired Czechoslovakia. Perhaps it was only a slip of
the tongue; perhaps not. Politicians like Halifax were not prone to slips of
the tongue. Perhaps Chamberlain believed he could persuade the British
public that a return to his old contentious discredited policy was for the best,
after all. But, as impeccably discreet as ever, the Ambassador merely rose
to his feet as well, bowed and, shaking hands, said, 'Thank you, *Herr
Aussenminister.*'

'We may none of us be able to think of summer holidays for quite a while.'
Barkeley Goodrich had not heard Churchill's speech, and even if he had, it
would not have concerned him much. Coming out of the wooden two-holer
outhouse that served as a toilet, he had nothing whatever to think of except
summer holiday, and he loved it; he was in Vacationland. The car licence
plates said so, but he did not need to be told; he had lived all his fifteen and
a half years in the State of Maine, New England, and was certain there was
no better place in the world to be, at any time of year. A few weeks back his
father, a dentist, had closed up his office as he did every summer and taken
Mrs Goodrich and Barkeley, their only child, away from the city of Auburn,
40 miles north-east to the family cottage at East Pond. Now his parents had
returned to Auburn, their holiday over, but with an aunt and uncle, Barkeley
was still free at the cottage.

Deep, clear and unpolluted, East Pond was the smallest of the chain of
five that made up the Belgrade Lakes in central Maine. With lunchtime
approaching, Barkeley had already made his first trip of the day to the family
farm, half a mile away: the tenant farmer supplied them with milk, quarts of
heavy cream so thick it had to be spooned from the bottle, and water; although
they had electricity and electric lights, there was no running water in the
cottage.

It was a large, single-storey building set up on posts, the only private
dwelling on that cove. Its central room was big, thirty by forty feet, with a
brick fireplace. Off to one side were three bedrooms, with two more and the
kitchen on the other side; right across the front, facing the lake, was a broad
screened porch. That was where he preferred to sleep, snuggled deep in a
feather bed. Sometimes at night thunder would sweep across the lake; then
the adults would rush out and put down big wooden shutters, racing to beat
the storm, and he would snuggle deeper, loving the warmth of the bed, the

sudden freshness in the air, and the sound of the rain drumming on the tin roof.

Pausing on his way to the shore, he absently picked and ate some blueberries. 'Barkeley!' His aunt's voice came from the cottage, and he ran down. The kitchen was full of the smell of baking. 'Uh-huh?'

'Barkeley, are you busy?'

'I was thinking of going fishing again. Maybe catch some hornpout.'

'Mm-hmm, as long as you're the one to clean it. They're fine to eat, but I just cannot abide the sight of those ugly things until they're in the pan. But right now, I've got two cakes in, and I'm about to start the pastry. What kind of a pie do you want today?'

'Blackberries aren't quite ready yet. We had raspberries yesterday. The blueberries should be good.'

His aunt was a stern lady, even dictatorial at times. Straightening up, she looked at him: 'Should be? Barkeley Goodrich, I think you know that for a fact – unless that's a bruise all around your mouth.' He blushed and wiped the blue juice away. But then she smiled and relented. 'All right; blueberries it is. And pick a few peaches while you're out there – but just a few, mind – and then you can go fishing all you want.'

Colonel Josef Beck, Poland's Foreign Minister, was resting at a country retreat outside Warsaw when a report reached him from Prince Lubomirski, his Chargé d'Affaires in Berlin. What he read astonished and angered him. Lubomirski had been summoned to an interview with Ernst von Weizsäcker, the Reich Secretary of State, and there, to put it simply, he and Poland had been directly threatened. Evidently acting on instructions from Ribbentrop and refusing to let Lubomirski speak, von Weizsäcker had announced that any repetition of the Polish demands on Danzig, amounting to an ultimatum, would aggravate relations with Germany and lead to consequences which would be Poland's responsibility.

The semi-farcical customs dispute could have been contained and kept in its proper proportion, and would have been; but details of the affair had been officially released to the Polish press, picked up by French and British newspapers, and there made to appear as a victory for Beck over the Senate in Danzig. That in turn had led to the wave of mutual recriminations in German and Polish papers; von Dirksen's remark to Lord Halifax had been substantially correct. But what the ambassador had omitted to say was that Hitler, reacting furiously to the international publicity and the insufferable humiliation of the Nazi Senate, had ordered the German papers' anti-Polish campaign.

Colonel Beck was not the kind of man to spend time wishing away the past. If Herr Hitler did not care for demeaning publicity, that was his own business; relations between the Free City and the Polish government emphatically were not, and at once Beck sent a reply to Berlin saying just that. 'Now,' he observed grimly, 'it begins.'

At 6 p.m. the royal train left Weymouth. An hour later the fleet began to disperse, and at sunset, 7.36, the sailors began to undress ship. The inspection was complete; the British Reserve Fleet was now formally mobilised. Less than half an hour after that, at 11 p.m. Moscow time, the liner *City of Exeter* came cautiously into Leningrad harbour. André Beaufre, a member of the French delegation, reflected that it had really been an agreeable voyage. After three days of discussions in the liner's playroom a common policy had been settled, and its written text approved by every delegate, French or British. Essentially it proposed that France, Britain and Russia should agree to provide assistance to either Poland or Rumania, or both, as soon as requested; and as Admiral Drax had said, 'We've agreed; you've agreed; now all we need is for the Russians to agree as well.' It showed, thought Beaufre, that between *des hommes de bonne volonté*, men of good will, there need be no insoluble problems. All very satisfactory so far. Between working sessions there had been games of deck tennis, which the English admiral had always won. Beaufre's only personal regret now was that there would be no more of those excellent curries, heaped high by turbaned Indian stewards, which had made such pleasant interludes between the daily discussions. In business of any sort, he believed, one could tell a lot from the level of hospitality offered: a good meal and some good wine generated good humour; it made visitors affable and showed that hosts were serious. And of course the opposite was true too: if the only offering was a poor meal, poor wine, or even – he shivered – no wine at all, one might as well go home at once, for one could be sure that any agreement would be unsatisfactory, reached (if at all) only with reluctance. It would be interesting to see what the Russian table was like.

Despite the late hour, it was still light. Curious for an early look at Russia, Beaufre decided to leave his cabin and go up on deck. From there, what he could see of the port was not very prepossessing: merely a port, much like any other – quays, warehouses, office buildings – so he climbed higher, to the bridge, for a better view. And there, standing beside Admiral Drax, he was suddenly struck by the sight. No one appeared to be taking any great interest in the liner as it slowly drew in alongside the quay. The men busily warping the ship in were not dockyard workers, but *City of Exeter*'s own Indian crew; and apart from a small group of soldiers in green caps, with a vew few shabbily dressed bystanders, there was scarcely a Russian to be seen.

The bombers came in over England that night. With fighter support, there were 500 machines sweeping in from points east. People heard them first as a dull distant throbbing in the southern skies, growing steadily to a roar as they searched for targets across the country. Only five major cities were blacked out, Birmingham, Rochester, Bedford, Brighton and Derby, but around them all air bases were on maximum alert, and 800 aircraft were rapidly in the air, ready to challenge the attackers.

Only challenges were necessary. It was the largest air war exercise the RAF had ever mounted, and on the morning of 10 August the authorities declared it broadly successful: had it been real, Westland forces would have fought Eastland forces off, and bombers approaching London had had particular difficulty because of the balloon barrage above the capital.

Sir Kingsley Wood, Secretary of State for Air, visited Biggin Hill aerodrome in Kent to watch fighter exercises that day. As a member of the Air Defence Research Committee (and as a local resident, for the aerodrome was only five miles from Chartwell), Churchill accompanied him. There was a heavy drizzle, and at 800 feet the cloud base was low.

'Well, Winston, what do you think?' Wood asked. Pondering the final paper he would write for the committee, Churchill saw in his mind's eye the sky darkened with relays of enemy aircraft crossing the sea, hour after hour, and wondered aloud what toll could be extracted from them. 'One-fifth knocked out each go, will soon bring the raids to an end,' he remarked. It seemed a high target in the grey dismal light. However, he was confident it could be done; and afterwards, he predicted, the danger would alter. Heavy enemy casualties would force a change of tactic – with daylight raiding too expensive, random night-bombing of towns and cities would probably begin. These were gloomy thoughts; but staring across the rainy airfield, he added with grim reassurance: 'It is not child's play to come and attack England.'

With bags packed, Ginger the cat safely in a box and the budgerigar safely in its cage, the Smiths made their way from the Old Manse to the island's little pierhead and boarded the tiny ferry. By themselves they filled half of its single cabin. As their parents stowed the luggage under the narrow wooden benches, Jessamine ignored Stella's reprimand, ('Set dee *doon*, Jessamine, du'll fall o'er,') and knelt on the bench to wave to Uncle Lollie and their grandfather; Uncle Tommy was working on the roads, and had said his goodbye in the morning.

'Never leet, lass,' said their father. 'She'll no' fall very far, if she does.' Twelve-year-old Nanette stayed in the boat's open cockpit, glad she was old enough to do so. It gave her a chance for a last look at the island, a chance to set in her memory all the things she loved about the Old Manse: the spinning wheel and the upright chair her grandmother used to use; the big American clock on the wall; the green and red parakeet, from somewhere in South America – it could say 'Pretty Polly' but little else, and whenever it was in a bad temper (sometimes she would tease it on purpose) it would bend right over and squawk '*Waikeet!*' She had also learned from experience that, short as the trip was across the water to Lerwick, it was better done in the fresh air, even if it was raining: if the fumes from *Brenda*'s thudding diesel engine seeped into the cabin, she was sick at once. With a jerk, the ferry started from the pier. Caught in mid-wave, Jessamine fell over, and began to cry.

The Red Arrow express left Leningrad for Moscow at midnight on 9 August, too soon for the French and English delegations. They slept that night in the *City of Exeter*, and next day, since they had finished their joint preparation and had nothing better to do, they spent the whole day sight-seeing, escorted, naturally, by courteous Russians. It was a fascinating excursion, full of history and grandeur, visible culture and echoed brutality. Apart from containing upwards of 700 bridges crossing its many rivers and canals, Leningrad was the scene of the 1917 Revolution, and in a setting of squares, parks and wide avenues, neo-classical baroque buildings, pastel-painted with gilt spires and domes, the tourists saw Nevsky Prospekt, and the Peter and Paul Fortress; the home of the Kirov Ballet, founded in 1735; and not least, the Winter Palace of the tsars. It was a worthwhile tour by almost any standards – except, perhaps, those of immediate political need. For as Admiral Drax, the French General Doumenc and their colleagues admired their surroundings, 900 miles away in Berlin, Georgi Astakhov and Julius Schnurre were talking serious business.

Astakhov was Chargé d'Affaires at the Russian Embassy in Berlin; Schnurre was a member of the German Foreign Ministry's Economic Department. Just over two weeks previously, in a discreet and exclusive Berlin restaurant, their first discussion had begun on economics before slipping swiftly and permanently to politics. Schnurre was completely open, so much so that Astakhov, being both Russian and a diplomat, could hardly believe what he was hearing: a proposal that their two countries should abandon their ancient rivalry and dislike of each other, and instead work together as friends and partners to rechart the continent of Europe.

At first Astakhov demurred, pointing out that such a radical shift in German policy towards the Soviet Union would be scarcely credible in Moscow, and that moves were afoot to forge a link with Britain. 'What could Britain offer Russia?' Schnurre asked bluntly, and answered his own question: 'At best, participation in a European war, and the hostility of Germany – hardly a desirable end for Russia.' On the other hand, a link with Germany

69

could offer neutrality, no Russian involvement in a European war 'and, if Moscow wished, a German-Russian understanding which . . . would work out to the advantage of both sides.' He added specifically that German policy was now directed against Britain, and that from the Black Sea to the Baltic it should be possible to make a 'new arrangement' beneficial to Germany and Russia alike.

It was this extraordinary suggestion which had prompted the talk between Molotov and Ambassador von der Schulenburg on 3 August, one week ago. The Count came away from that 90-minute meeting with mixed feelings: Molotov had been less reserved than usual, but was plainly distrustful, insisting on proofs of honest German intentions. Two days later, however, Schnurre learned Molotov's own view of the session; positive, urgent and serious. So once again Schnurre and Astakhov met; and while the French and British delegations toured Leningrad, Schnurre spoke to Astakhov of the megalomaniac Poles; the likelihood that a serious conflict would break out any day; and the benefits to Russia of an early agreement with Germany. Astakhov promised to inform Moscow at once.

'Heat, and more heat every day from the blazing sun.' Niusia Zamecka was one of those millions, not important enough to be noticed individually, whose lives, slowly, almost invisibly, were drifting out of control. For diplomats and statesmen it was more abstract, lines on a map, changed or maintained by equations of military power and political agreement. But if a map is enlarged again and again, eventually it matches reality, inch for inch, and people fill it. In Julius Schnurre's scale of things Niusia was one of the megalomaniac Poles. In her own scale, she was a ten-year-old girl holidaying on her grandfather's smallholding outside Warsaw, sweltering in midsummer heat. 'The grass is brown,' she scribbled in her diary, 'the flowers are drooping, there's not much water in the well.' Thirty-eight Centigrade, 100 Fahrenheit was enough to make anyone do strange things. But Niusia followed the example of her pet dog Pempela, and took a long afternoon nap.

For Nanette Smith sleep would have been an unbelievable blessing. A hired car had carried the family across the mainland to the village of Walls. There they had clambered along a shingle and boulder dyke jutting out into the sea, and embarked in the Foula mailboat *Advance*. Although the 30-foot boat was completely open – only the engine was covered against the spray – Nanette's father Willie always enjoyed the three-hour crossing, especially when the weather was fine, as it was today: cool, overcast, refreshed by an occasional shower and a light southerly wind. But he was an experienced sailor. For the others it was simply an endurance test, and one which Nanette always failed. With an uninterrupted fetch of three thousand miles, the Atlantic swell was high even on the best of days. As the bow of the vessel began its rise and fall, nothing seemed to work; looking at the far horizon did not help; looking at something inside the boat was worse. She knew the sequence of signs all too well: first feeling hotter and hotter, then a dryness in her mouth, then the rising sourness. Within minutes she was leaning out, head down over the gunwale, watching with a glazed, distant fascination as the water changed from green to iron grey and the bubbles sped past, a foot below her face. 'Feedin' the fishes again, lass?' asked her father, as he always did. 'Wheesht, Willie,' said her mother's voice. 'Let the bairn be.' Someone's hand, she did not know whose, came protectively, affectionately on her shoulder, yet seemed so far away it could scarcely touch her.

At the same time in Wales, there was scandal and celebration. The conveners of the eisteddfod had expected a vintage year for poetry; now it was announced, to 'groans from the huge crowd', that neither the chair nor the crown could be awarded: the standard had been altogether too low. On the other hand eleven-year-old David Price from Pontardawe won the solo soprano for boys under sixteen: 'We have had a great deal of experience of competitions of this kind,' said one of the judges, 'but we do not remember having heard anything so satisfying, perfect and sweet as the performance given by this boy.' And in Germany, Hitler's interpreter Paul Schmidt was flying from one end of the Reich to the other. Recalled early from leave, as he had feared would happen, neither he nor the pilot knew where they were going until the time of take-off.

At midnight on 10 August Drax, Doumenc and their colleagues left Leningrad in the Red Arrow express for Moscow. That night in Britain the blackout was repeated and extended, covering half of England, and was generally a dismal failure. London in particular was as visible from the night sky as a blazing wreck at sea. In one sense it did not matter; finding weaknesses was part of the exercise. But on the following morning, 11 August, as the Anglo-French delegations finally arrived in Moscow, Lord Halifax in London learned that by the 15th Germany would be in a state of complete military readiness for anything.

'Wach' auf, so rufet uns die Stimme!' In the beautiful ancient university town of Tübingen, a thin man of late middle age was awakened by the sound of singing. It was an appropriate hymn for the morning, 'Wake up, a voice is calling us!' and he listened with pleasure. Outside his window, drenched in brilliant sunshine, was the market square with the old Rathaus, the Council Chambers, and the fountain around which, every year, people would gather

to celebrate May day. The sight gladdened his heart, softening his usual careworn, lined expression, and he decided to climb up to the castle which dominated the heights above the river Neckar.

He was Ulrich von Hassell, fifty-nine years old, a native of Hanover, ex-soldier, ex-diplomat and confirmed opponent of the Nazi regime. As a young man he had studied languages in England and Switzerland. Before the Great War he had been Vice-Consul in Genoa. In the army he had been badly wounded at the battle of the Marne. With the return of peace he rejoined the diplomatic service, finally becoming Germany's ambassador in Rome. He was sacked from the post in 1937 because he would not support the Anti-Comintern Pact, and since then, while lecturing on the economic situation in Europe, had become firmly anti-Nazi. It was a strange half-shadowed life, growing steadily more dangerous, with a constant uncertainty about whom one could trust. Nevertheless there were many like him, some he knew, most he did not; there was as yet no organised resistance to Hitler's rule. But one day he would join the conspiracy to kill Hitler, and would hang when the conspiracy failed.

That, however, was five years in the future. On 11 August 1939, Ulrich von Hassell gazed from the ramparts of the castle across the countryside. The Neckar was spread in its full splendour at his feet; the bells of the college chapel below seemed to him to ring out comfort and peace, and he could see people hurrying towards it. This picture, he thought with sad affection, represents the real German character.

Meanwhile Gauleiter Förster had returned to Danzig from his conference with the Führer. The message he relayed to his colleagues was simple: 'We know what is coming. We know we will return to the Reich, but we do not know when. The important thing is that we should prepare ourselves.' From Danzig, summoned to a private meeting at the Berghof, League Commissioner Karl Burckhardt flew south in Hitler's personal Condor plane. For Oscar Baker in Nottinghamshire it was a day much like any other, although it was his fifteenth birthday; his family did not mark birthdays particularly, but since it turned out to be warm and sunny he spent his time quite happily in his father's orchard, mowing the grass and trimming the hedges. Francis Vanek, Paddy Murray and the fifteen other cycling pilgrims were having another easy day's ride towards their goal, covering the fifty miles from Bergerac to Agen; and in Schloss Fuschl, close to Salzburg, the Italian Foreign Minister Count Ciano was listening with disgust and incredulity as von Ribbentrop (Ciano credited him with the noble prefix) said icily: 'The decision to fight is implacable.'

Ciano had come to Schloss Fuschl, a castle in theory rented, in practice commandeered, by Ribbentrop, with Mussolini's blessing: 'The Duce is more than ever convinced of the necessity of delaying the conflict.' Mussolini himself drafted a paper for the meeting, telling Ciano he absolutely must get the Germans to understand that a conflict with Poland should be avoided. 'It would be impossible to localise it, and a general war would be disastrous for everybody.' Ciano agreed wholeheartedly, but even before he left Italy he had been doubtful about the outcome; and now he was inside the Reich, his doubts grew every moment. The conversation was very tense; neither man trusted the other. Ciano, speaking with what he considered to be 'brutal frankness', found Ribbentrop completely unmoved, and began to realise that Italy counted for next to nothing in German opinion. For a long time Ribbentrop would not give a direct answer to any direct question of national policy towards Poland. He has lied too many times, Ciano thought contemptuously, not to feel uneasy now about what he must tell me. Eventually, in exasperation, he asked as plainly as possible: what precisely did Germany want of Poland – the Corridor or Danzig?

'Not that any more,' Ribbentrop replied. 'We want war.' From the way he said it and the way he looked, Ciano instantly realised that for once the German was probably telling the truth.

Tadeusz Orlicki was so tired he could not even curse any more. On Fridays he always went out to see his parents, and was very proud of his new Fiat: in it, the journey was only half an hour. His father thought little of the car – the family horse Samson was much better value in his view. 'He gives what he takes,' he had said when Tadeusz first showed off the car. 'At the end of each day there is enough manure to grow a sack of potatoes. And what do you hope to get from your Fiat?' Today the answer was, nothing but sore feet. The car had broken down irrevocably, leaving Tadeusz with an hour's walk. 'Well,' his father pointed out, 'it's silly to expect too much from a mere motor car.'

'Uncle Tadeusz revived at once,' Niusia wrote in her diary, 'and said something really naughty. I can't say what he said because I don't know how to spell it.' But to Tadeusz's annoyance, and his father's amusement, the only thing to do was to take Samson out and pull the car home.

At that moment, in his private tea-house far above the Berghof, Adolf Hitler was talking to Commissioner Burckhardt about just such people – or shouting, rather. He looks much older and whiter, Burckhardt considered, remembering the last time he had seen the Führer. Now there seemed a considerable change. An impression of fear, the Commissioner thought. Nervous, pathetic . . . almost shaken at times. Nevertheless Hitler's views came over loud and clear: 'If the slightest incident happens,' he bellowed furiously, 'I shall crush the Poles without warning in such a way that no trace of Poland can be found afterwards.' Ignoring the spectacular views across the mountains, he faced Burckhardt: '*Do you understand me?*'

73

'Very well, Chancellor,' Burckhardt answered, with extraordinary self-control. 'I quite realise that means a general war.'

Hitler glared at him. 'If I have to wage war, I would rather do it today than tomorrow.' Since his fiftieth birthday in April, he had said the same thing often, and would say it again: he did not know how long he would live, and Germany would never be better led than by him; therefore, if there was no alternative to war, the sooner it came the better it would be for the Reich.

Around the same time, Admiral Drax, General Doumenc and their respective colleagues paid a courtesy call on Commissar Molotov and Marshal Kliment Voroshilov, the Commissar for Defence. Their welcome was considerate: the visitors must be tired after such a long slow journey. Would it not be better to begin the talks tomorrow? All could have a pleasant evening beforehand. The western delegates accepted and were entertained with a banquet and a concert in a thoroughly cordial atmosphere. Only Drax felt uneasy – *iron hand in a velvet glove*, he thought to himself.

As the French, British and Russians wooed each other towards an alliance, dinner in Schloss Fuschl was an altogether more frigid affair. Ciano and Ribbentrop were, of course, allies already, yet during their meal the two Foreign Ministers did not speak a single word to each other. Though he was host Ribbentrop made no attempt to break the icy silence. As for Ciano, he had made up his mind. Later that evening he wrote down what he thought about Ribbentrop in particular and Germany in general: 'He rejects any solution which might give satisfaction to Germany and avoid the struggle. I am certain that even if the Germans were given more than they ask for they would attack just the same, because they are possessed by the demon of destruction.'

6

Can the Red Army march across Poland?

FOR FIVE HUNDRED YEARS the city of Bradford had grown on the backs of sheep from the West Riding of Yorkshire into a centre for woollen and worsted manufacturing. It was a place composed of mills and factories where, like a Muslim priest calling the faithful to prayer, sirens would blare out twice daily to call the men and women to work, while smoke poured constantly from the tall chimneys. Wool was the very fibre of Bradford's muscle, smoke its breath, thunderous noise its heartbeat; but on Saturday 12 August, the whole city lay silent, and Elsie Harmes rejoiced. It was the first day of Bradford's annual holiday week, the one day in the year when the mills were quiet and the chimneys ceased. Then the wind blew the smoke away, and for that day alone, high above the city, the moors were visible, wild, empty and beguiling, visible as they had been to her only fifteen times in her short life. But it was not only the peace that made the girl rejoice: the following day would be her sixteenth birthday. Then, her parents had agreed, she could officially change her name from Elsie to Elspeth; and for the first time she would go away from Bradford on holiday, travelling with two girls from work. Even though Hilda and Margaret had been to posh grammar schools, and she had not, all three were close friends. Together they would travel 80 miles by train to Silverdale on the coast of Lancashire where they would see the sea, strange and mysterious, a thing only dreamed of, read of, in Elsie's many books of poetry. Jumping from the tram a stop early, she walked through Ivegate, a narrow street leading to Westgate, short and steep (Bradford was full of hills) and started the climb towards her work in the ribbon and lace department of Lingard's clothing and hosiery store. It was a tiring walk, guaranteed to leave you breathless; but with her head full of the sea Elsie was happy, for she had saved another penny towards the journey.

Far away across the invisible water the USS *Tuscaloosa* was being prepared for a distinguished passenger. One of the perks – and there often seemed to be few – of being President of the United States was the chance of vacationing on board an American warship. It was perhaps not everyone's idea of the perfect cruise ship but it offered virtually complete security, and like his distant cousin Teddy, President before the Great War, Franklin Delano Roosevelt was particularly fond of the sea and the US Navy. Both Roosevelts had been assistant Secretary of the Navy before reaching the presidency, and both knew well the US Navy League's formula for world peace. Only two things needed to be done – 'Abolish: Kings, Oligarchs, Race Antipathies, Unfair Competition, Land Grabbing, Injustice and Sin. Establish: The Rule of the People, A Satisfactory World Tribunal, Justice, Charity, and A Changed Human Nature.' And in case of difficulty in achieving those goals: 'Ad Interim: MAINTAIN A STRONG NAVY.' Teddy had seen the transition from an antiquated navy of sail and wood to a completely modern one of steam and steel, and had dreamed up the world cruise of the Great White Fleet; Franklin (who one day would be asked by a general to stop referring to the navy as 'we' and the army as 'they') would oversee the American navy's transformation into the largest maritime fighting force in history. But today he was simply weary, very weary. 'I think', he wrote to his wife Eleanor, 'I shall spend most of the first few days sleeping.'

'I look at the papers anxiously,' she wrote back, 'but hope you get the whole of your cruise, not just for your sake but for the sake of the poor people in Europe.'

Curiously enough, her sympathetic thoughts would have seemed kind but unnecessary to some of those poor people. In Northern Ireland David Howarth felt just then that he was living in a pretty good approximation to paradise; and certainly his situation was one which Elsie Harmes or even President Roosevelt might well have envied. His weekly work as director of talks for the BBC was more stimulating than Elsie's job on the shop floor at Lingard's, and infinitely simpler than Roosevelt's in the White House. Sometimes it was helpful in a practical way to the ordinary folk: the series given by a housewife and a doctor on feeding a family with a healthy diet on one shilling per person per week had been a splendid example. There was a certain *frisson* in the private knowledge that the doctor was reputed to be a chief in the IRA. Once Howarth had lunch with the IRA doctor, followed by dinner with Lord Craigavon, the British Governor of the province – an odd but interesting contrast. Never once, though, did he feel any fear or threat from such strange combinations: though he suspected it was only because they all wanted to get their points across, it seemed as though he was accepted by both sides as a friendly neutral. And with the week's work done he turned again, as he always did, to the peace and solitude of Strangford Lough, half a mile from his rented cottage, the Porter's Lodge outside Killinchy. There was nothing left of the big house. That, when he thought about it, was somewhat spooky: next to the Lodge was a pair of large gates leading to a long drive, leading to nothing; the IRA had burnt the house down. On the sea-lough, however, there were no politics. One of the first things he had done after moving to Ireland from London was to rent a boat 22 feet long, with a small cabin and two berths. After a few sails he was glad he had not actually bought her – she was dead rotten, falling apart. Nevertheless within the lough, almost land-locked, she was safe enough, even for someone whose sailing experience was confined to the Norfolk Broads.

David Howarth had come to the conclusion that he was not cut out to be a city dweller. The whole of the Irish north coast, especially Antrim and Donegal, was his idea of a good coast – in the north-west the extraordinary Giant's Causeway and the mountains of Antrim reaching almost to the sea; in the north-east the Derryveagh and Blue Stack mountains, the rocky bays and inlets with their evocative names, Sheep Haven, Bloody Foreland, Inishfree Bay. He could, and would, walk or drive for miles without seeing a living soul, hearing nothing but wind, larks, sea and gulls; or, as he was doing this weekend, he would range where he chose across the 75 square miles of Strangford Lough, learning by trial and error how best to work the boat with wind and water. Some time, sooner or later, he would find a suitable anchorage for the night; and then, with a hurricane lamp, some simple food, a book and a flask of gin, there was a depth of peace he would not have exchanged for worlds.

Yet one important link with the city remained: Richard Dimbleby, his closest friend in broadcasting. Both young men were prone to wild enthusiasms, and when Richard was around life was always exciting; he bubbled with new ideas, and David, a physics graduate, worked out how to put them into practice, even if the BBC hierarchy disapproved. Together, three years ago, they had covered the burning of the Crystal Palace in a live outside broadcast – something no one had done before. They had reported from the tarmac when Chamberlain returned from Munich; they had gone to Germany together when the Sudetenland was annexed. Around the time David left for Ireland, Richard was informed that should war come, he could be the world's first radio war correspondent, an offer he accepted eagerly, with the request that David should be allowed to go with him. The BBC agreed. On the quiet waters of Strangford Lough, David Howarth knew at the back of his mind that one day a call would come from London, and that he would respond.

In the grandeur of the Spiridonyevka Palace, Admiral Drax was deeply embarrassed. On the other side of the large round table Marshal Voroshilov waited. Beside him was an impressive array of senior officers: the Chief of the General Staff of the Red Army, the Commissar for the Navy, the Chief of the Air Force and the Deputy Chief of the General Staff. All were full of expectation. Close by, General Doumenc let a flicker of uneasiness cross his face: surely the British admiral was not so ill-prepared? This first session had begun with an amiable talk on procedures, after which Voroshilov, rising from his seat, had ceremoniously produced a paper giving him authority to conduct and conclude military negotiations. General Doumenc in turn provided his credentials, which were examined and pronounced satisfactory; yet now, though some such authorisation to negotiate was obviously essential, it seemed that Admiral Drax had none.

In fact he did have a document giving him the appropriate power, but by an absurd oversight in London, it formed part of his instructions; and they were secret. He could not show one without revealing the other. Caught off guard at the outset, angry with himself for not having noticed the flaw and mentally cursing whoever was responsible, Drax did the best he could, and explained that full plenipotentiary powers had never been granted to a British military delegation. Knowing it was hardly a sufficient explanation, he could sense the surprise and exasperation of all those around the table. Everything else and everyone else was ready, but the negotiations could not proceed. The only thing to do, and he did it at once, was to send a telegram to London requesting written credentials, and wait. It was not a good start.

Count Ciano was not enjoying himself very much either. He was in the Berghof with Adolf Hitler. Very cordial, Ciano noted mentally, but he too is impassive and implacable in his decision. Stretching from side to side of the large drawing-room, there was an enormous picture window with a terrace beyond. Visitors usually gasped at the view outside, and gasped again when the Führer demonstrated how a concealed mechanism could lower the entire window silently into the floor. It was an enviable gadget; today, however, Hitler was not showing off his house, but his war plans. A wide table was covered with maps. With them he explained to Ciano just how powerful Germany had become under his rule, impressing the Count with his profound military knowledge. Ciano was not sure if it was a pretence or if Hitler was saying what he believed to be the truth. Interpreting between them, Paul Schmidt decided that Ciano had considerable debating power: he was decisive, he was cool, he was statesmanlike. Nevertheless he could not dent Hitler. Several times Ciano tried to persuade him that a war with Poland could not be localised, but though he listened the German leader shook his head. 'I personally', he declared, 'am absolutely convinced that in the last resort the Western democracies will recoil from unleashing a general war', and added that the war must be fought while he and the Duce were still young. Privately considering this an exceedingly selfish reason for such a course, Ciano took the opportunity of pointing out how badly it would affect the Italian people. Hitler's reaction was, if anything, even more disconcerting than before: he paid attention, but a faraway look came into his eyes. Clearly he was not interested.

'Hitler has decreed *Spannung* for the 15th,' wrote Sir Alexander Cadogan. By that date, only three days away, Germany would be fully ready for war. *Spannung* means 'tension' or 'suspense'; in his diary Cadogan translated the word as 'the opening of the "battle of nerves"', adding, 'Hope mine will be all right!'

In Poland ten-year-old Niusia Zamecka was quick enough to have grasped that Germany posed a real threat to her country – her parents spoke often of it, and at school she had learned how to wear a gas mask – and trusting enough to believe her teachers: 'I don't think the Germans have a chance. One can buy a lot of bullets for one zloty, and if everybody saves, then we can give Hitler a proper thrashing.' But that afternoon she had forgotten such things; she was sitting on a blanket in the shade of a cedar tree, learning to crochet. Her mother had a wind-up gramophone, and as they crocheted they listened to all their favourite records: the tango *Jealousy*; songs by Jan Kiepura; and the Charleston, which her mother adored. Niusia had to choose a good sharp needle for that, and clapped with glee as her mother danced. 'I've never seen you do it so well!' she cried, and then asked what it was her mother was making – a tiny white lacy garment.

'Well –' Her mother paused, clearing her throat, and Niusia guessed at once. Their maid Irka was 'with child'. Niusia had heard it from her brothers, and told her mother so. 'Mama's eyes nearly popped out of their sockets . . . I thought it best', she concluded innocently, 'not to ask Mama whether Irka was getting her baby from a stork or from under the gooseberry bush.'

Cycling through France the pilgrims were making excellent progress; from Agen that morning, they had passed through Auch and were on their way to Tarbes, capital of the Hautes-Pyrénées. Eleven hundred years earlier it had been occupied by the Saracens, and for the past hundred years English and Arab bloodstock had given it an international reputation in the horse-breeding world. But more importantly for the pilgrims, it was barely 15 miles from Lourdes, their target. They would get there easily next day, with a full forty-eight hours in hand before the Feast of the Assumption of the Blessed Virgin Mary.

They were a happy group, young, fit and full of faith. A glance ahead showed the Pyrenees, a high blue and brown line in the distance. But while they were pedalling cheerfully south along the rising N21, Count Ciano, with deep unease, was watching one of the most sinister sights he had seen: Adolf Hitler in a state of joy.

Moments before, a message from Julius Schnurre had been delivered to the Führer. It contained galvanising news. As he had promised, Georgi Astakhov had reported to Moscow, and his new instructions were that Russia was ready to talk. All issues outstanding between Germany and the Soviet Union could be discussed, in particular the Polish problem. His piercing blue eyes glittering with delight, Hitler told Ciano that Danzig must be settled: 'one way or another,' he said, 'before the end of August'. After that the weather would be too bad: the autumn rains always turned Poland into a colossal quagmire. And he revealed one further reason for his confidence that his move could be made soon. Would Russia, Ciano inquired, intervene on behalf of Poland? Hitler's reply was triumphant: 'Probably never.'

Ciano realised that there was nothing more he could do. 'He has decided to strike, and strike he will,' he wrote that evening. 'As far as the Germans are concerned, an alliance with us means only that the enemy will be obliged to keep a certain number of divisions facing us . . . They care for nothing else. The fate that might befall us does not interest them in the least.'

'Everything,' wrote Neville Chamberlain on Sunday 13 August, 'is going wrong here from the fishing point of view . . . I am sending you a salmon (not caught by me) and will be glad if you will distribute such of it as you don't want yourself to any of the staff who are on duty.' Cecil Syers, the Prime Minister's Principal Private Secretary, could not avoid a wry smile at the last part of the patrician letter: 'The cook or the kitchen maid at No 10 will cut up the fish.' Whatever his faults, the PM was a considerate, kindly man and meant well.

It was, of course, an appropriate day to arrive in Lourdes. After early Mass before breakfast in Tarbes, Francis Vanek, Paddy Murray and their fifteen friends rode the last few miles of their pilgrimage at a leisurely pace, but with a sense of mounting excitement. Bernadette Soubirous, the girl whose visions of the Virgin Mary in 1858 had focused world-wide Catholic attention on the town, had been declared a saint only six years ago, and for most of the cyclists, including Francis, this was their first visit to the holy place.

They were not disappointed. Lourdes is set in a fine Pyrenean landscape on both sides of the river Gave de Pau. Passing through the old town, on the east bank they could see the ramparts of Château Fort, the medieval fortress which once – for more than forty years at the end of the fourteenth century – had been held by the English; but it hardly interested them. Parallel to the Rue Bernadette Soubirous ran the Boulevard of the Grotto, and along that they rode, directly to the river bridge. With the year's main religious festival only two days off, the streets were packed with other pilgrims, but in spite of the crowds they decided it would be quite safe, and more suitable, if they dismounted and left their bicycles. The last half-mile to the grotto with its sacred spring should be done on foot, with reverence.

Simultaneously, after a second, briefer talk with Hitler, Galeazzo Ciano was returning by plane to Rome. During the talk the interpreter Paul Schmidt had been astonished to see how Ciano had transformed overnight – *folded up like a jack-knife*, Schmidt thought. He had not seemed to care any more what happened, telling Hitler wearily that for all he knew he, Hitler, was the one who saw things most clearly: 'You have been proved right so often before, when we others held the opposite view.' But in his diary the Count confided his true feelings: 'Completely disgusted with the Germans, with their leader, with their way of doing things,' he wrote. 'They have betrayed us and lied to us. Now they are dragging us into an adventure which we do not want . . .' And he decided the advice he would give to Mussolini: 'I think that our hands are free, and I propose that we act accordingly, declaring that we have no intention of participating in a war which we have neither wanted nor provoked.' For Italy's safety and survival, he was determined to break the Pact of Steel.

The following day was a busy one for Ulrich von Hassell. Back in Berlin from his visit to Tübingen, from ten in the morning until late at night he had meetings with other Germans who felt as he did. First, Karl Goerdeler in his lodgings on Askanischer Platz. In the two years before Hitler came to power Goerdeler had been Reich Price Control Commissioner, a hard and thankless task as depression took root after the nightmare inflation of the 1920s. Subsequently he had been mayor of Leipzig, but resigned, sickened by the Nazi government's measures against the Jews. Von Hassell found him 'fresh, clear-headed, active . . . One hears generally that he is imprudent and is being closely watched.' No doubt; any form of protest, even simple resignation, could well be called imprudent. *It is a relief, though, to speak with a man who wants to act rather than grumble.* Von Hassell found his company a tonic: Goerdeler was sure that resistance, albeit scattered and disorganised, was growing again in Germany, and that world war would be no solution. Heartened by their shared confidences and agreeing to use whatever influence they could for peace, they parted warmly.

Goerdeler too would be arrested in 1944, after the plot on Hitler's life failed, and after protracted torture would die in Plötzensee Prison.

He and von Hassell met again on 14 August 1939, unexpectedly, in the Hotel Adlon. Goerdeler was accompanied by Hans Gisevius. *No doubt intelligent, informed and active*, von Hassell thought with faint suspicion, *but I don't quite make him out.* It was only sensible to be cautious: Gisevius had joined the Gestapo in 1933, then the army, and was now attached to the Legation in Switzerland. They decided to go for lunch together to the Esplanade, and there encountered what von Hassell called 'a veritable stock exchange', including the President of the Deutsche Bank and Herbert von Dirksen, who had arrived from London that morning. From one of the 'stock exchange' came the sombre affirmation that at best Germany had only six weeks' supply of the raw materials of war. Greeting von Dirksen as an old colleague from diplomatic days, von Hassell inquired whether he was on holiday or had been summoned back. Von Dirksen snorted derisively, 'Ha! Of course I was summoned!' before explaining that try as he might, he, the Ambassador to Great Britain, could get no appointment with either Hitler or von Ribbentrop.

Von Ribbentrop's name came up again later that afternoon, when von Hassell had tea with Baron Ernst von Weizsäcker and his wife. Their house, 'next to the verdant garden of the Krupp building', was new and beautiful, but the baron, Under-Secretary in the Foreign Office, was too worn out to enjoy it. Von Ribbentrop's behaviour was worrying him greatly: the Foreign Minister would tell him hardly anything about what had happened with Count Ciano. 'What do you suppose the Italians will do,' he asked von Hassell, 'now that they have been turned down?'

'As a matter of fact,' came the dry response, 'they are no longer free to choose.'

For Ulrich von Hassell, that Monday ended with a private dinner with Ludwig Beck, 'a most cultured, attractive and intelligent man'. Not only that: he was a colonel-general and until 1938 had been Chief of the General Staff of the Army. Like Goerdeler, he had resigned his post, but in his case, because of Hitler's policies during the Sudeten crisis. 'Unfortunately,' von Hassell noted in his diary, 'he has a very low opinion of the leading people in the Army. For that reason he could see no place where we could gain a foothold.' Nevertheless the ex-diplomat and ex-soldier were in absolute agreement on one matter: both were 'firmly convinced of the vicious character of the policies of the Third Reich'.

That was the reason why in 1944, when Hitler survived the plot against his life, Colonel-General Ludwig Beck committed suicide.

Monday, 14 August 1939 was also the third day of the military discussions in the Spiridonyevka Palace. Marshal Voroshilov came to the meeting knowing that that day he would find out exactly how influential, how prepared and how committed the French and British delegates, and by extension their governments, really were. To do so, he had to ask only three questions. Yesterday he had indicated what they would be, when he pointed out an elementary fact of geography: the Soviet Union did not have a common border either with Britain or with France. How, then, he had enquired, did the British and French missions imagine there could be joint action against an aggressor? Today, chairing the session, he wanted to know the answer.

If Russia were to fight in Europe on behalf of Britain and France, Russian troops would have to cross over either Poland or Rumania – merely by looking at an atlas, even a schoolchild could see that. It was no trap or trick on Voroshilov's part; the question was obvious and legitimate, the reply critical. Yet on that very question, both the French and British governments had just crossed their fingers and hoped it would not arise. The ideal offer, from their point of view, would have been a promise of a steady supply of military hardware manufactured in the Soviet Union. There was very little likelihood, indeed virtually no chance at all, that the Polish or Rumanian authorities would allow tens of thousands of Russian soldiers to cross over their territory. So, seeing no easy solution to the problem, neither London nor Paris had made any preparation for it; and neither Drax nor Doumenc knew what to say.

Voroshilov put his questions clearly. First: if Poland was attacked would Russian land forces be allowed in to help with its defence? Second: would the Red Army be allowed passage over Poland in order to make contact with the enemy and fight him in the south? Third: if Rumania was attacked, was it proposed to allow Soviet troops across Rumanian territory? 'These,' he finished simply, 'are the three questions which interest us most.'

For a long time Doumenc and Drax whispered together. Being military men themselves made the situation even more embarrassing and difficult for them – they understood Voroshilov's point and privately agreed with it: hardware was all very well, but it would not be enough. Yet they were not authorised to say that kind of thing. Doumenc, doing his best to avoid the question, gave the first reply. Agreeing that Voroshilov had indicated the right areas of Soviet troop concentration, he remarked that their distribution would be at the Marshal's discretion. 'I think the weak points of the Polish–Rumanian front are their flanks and point of junction,' he concluded. 'We shall speak of the left flank when we deal with the question of communications.'

Voroshilov was not to be diverted. 'I want you to reply to my direct question. I said nothing about Soviet troop concentrations. I asked whether the British and French General Staffs envisage passage of our troops towards East Prussia or other points to fight the common enemy.'

Doumenc's next words sounded disarming and candid: 'I think Poland and Rumania will implore you, Marshal, to come to their assistance.'

'And perhaps they will not,' Voroshilov snorted. 'It is not evident so far.'

Drax and General Heywood conferred at length. Eventually the Admiral spoke: 'If Poland and Rumania do not ask for Soviet help, they will soon become German provinces . . .' The listeners around the table stiffened; everyone knew he was speaking the military truth. 'Then,' he continued, 'the USSR will decide how to act. If, on the other hand, the USSR, France and Britain are in alliance, then the question of whether or not Rumania and Poland ask for help becomes quite clear.'

As far as Voroshilov was concerned, it was not at all so. Once again he pressed for a plain response, and this time Drax gave the pathetic political truth. In his own view, Poland and Rumania were almost certain to ask for help; but, he acknowledged, that was only his personal opinion. 'To obtain a precise and satisfactory answer, it is necessary to approach Poland.'

So there it was, just as Voroshilov suspected and feared. The Soviet Marshal stared heavily across the table; his voice was stern. 'I regret that the Military Missions of Great Britain and France have not considered this question and have not brought an exact answer.' How, he wondered silently, could they have been sent to the conference table so ill-prepared, at such a critical time? The only conclusion seemed to be that their governments were not trying seriously to negotiate. 'Without an exact and unequivocal answer to these questions,' he declared, 'further conversations will not have any real meaning.'

There was no getting round it – he was right in every way. Shortly afterwards the meeting adjourned, and the French and British delegates walked despondently through the palace gardens. 'At least he's agreed to carry on until we get replies,' said Admiral Drax. 'But quite frankly, I think our mission is finished.' As André Beaufre noted, everyone felt the same; and had they known the instructions Count Werner von der Schulenburg had just received, their suspicions would have become certainty. Schulenburg was to tell Commissar Molotov that Hitler's Foreign Minister, Joachim von Ribbentrop, wished to come in person to Moscow, at the earliest opportunity.

The authorities had been quick enough to provide a plane to bring Paul Schmidt down to the discussions with Ciano, but to his disgust he was not given one to take him back. After a long slow journey, he had just arrived back in his beloved Norderney, 'only too thankful that Ribbentrop let me continue my leave'.

In Italy hymns were being sung. Walking on the sea-shore with the Polish Ambassador, Count Ciano could hear them, and noticed that the churches were full. Word had come from the Italian counsellor in Warsaw that the Poles would fight to the last man, and Ciano, speaking in roundabout terms, was trying to advise moderation. The words of one of the hymns drifted out to him: 'Oh God, help us save our country . . .' *These people will be massacred by German steel tomorrow,* he thought with anger and compassion. *They are innocent. My heart is with them.*

7

This is no time for half-measures

WITH NOTHING BETTER TO DO, Herbert von Dirksen decided to pay a call on Bernardo Attolico, Italy's Ambassador in Berlin. Both had served their respective countries years before in Moscow, and had become close friends, so von Dirksen did not feel any appointment would be necessary; and sure enough, Attolico was delighted by the visit. With profuse and exuberant apologies, he explained that he did have another visitor at the moment, but that he was about to leave, after which there would be plenty of time for the two old friends to chat. Attolico had not altered, and in amusement, von Dirksen settled himself down to wait.

While he was waiting the telephone rang and he could see Attolico becoming highly excited and disturbed at the conversation. Then, shoving the receiver down, the Italian rushed through.

'My dear friend, I am so sorry, I have to go to Rome – at once! Oh, I am so sorry! Now: listen to me – I must talk to you immediately, man to man, friend to friend. There are times, I think, when this must be done. It is Ciano. You know of his discussions with Herr von Ribbentrop? Yes, of course, of course. Well, it seems there have been decisions made which might easily result in war, namely with Poland. And what is more, much more, those decisions are based on the notion that England will not join in!'

'Wait, wait.' Von Dirksen raised a calming hand. 'I have just returned from England. What are you saying? That we are going to war with Poland? And that the Foreign Minister believes England will not fight?'

'Precisely. But they will. And so I must go to Rome this instant and present my report.'

'No, this cannot be right. I too am on the brink of presenting my reports and I assure you, my friend, I know the English mind well now, and I know that full account will have been taken of the possibility that they will fight.'

Attolico refused to accept it, saying that von Dirksen must do his duty and change the opinion of the leading German authorities. Their whole conversation lasted less than five minutes, and with Attolico as hurried as he was excited, von Dirksen was only able to throw in a few brief remarks before, in a shower of hasty apologies, the Italian Ambassador ushered him to the door.

Left alone, von Dirksen frowned thoughtfully. It was difficult to conduct diplomacy, even between friends, at such speed. But at least he had conveyed his own view. He had felt instinctively that it was important to challenge Attolico's double assertion, that war with Poland was inevitable, and that Germany had not taken the British factor into account. If only von Ribbentrop would consent to see him! Hoping, not very optimistically, that Attolico had registered his comments, he decided it might be as well if he returned home and put it on record.

For their part, Taddeus and Zofya Olscholwski had decided it might be as well if their two small boys, Stefan and Andrew, were taken from Gdynia to the family estate of Moniaki, three hundred miles away. Deep in Poland, it was the safest place they knew, and in the large, bustling household the children would be surrounded by relatives, Zofya's father and two of her aunts; her sister Ann, Ann's husband, who ran the 8000-acre estate, and their three children, as well as the cook, the maids and the housekeeper. Their silver, and the carpets from the villa Sadyba in Gdynia, could go for safe keeping to Taddeus's parents in Warsaw. These were not easy decisions; Taddeus and Zofya knew they would miss the children, but also that it was a sensible precaution. As for the precious objects, 'There doesn't seem to be much point in owning such things', said Zofya, 'if we can't use them; and the villa will look very dull and empty.'

'Better to lose the use for a while than perhaps lose them all for good,' Taddeus reminded her. And then, to her delight, he told her he had a little surprise for her. With the demands of his work, he felt they had not been seeing enough of each other. 'So I thought we'd take two or three days together, just by ourselves, and go to Copenhagen. What d'you say?'

Putting her arms round his neck, she smiled. 'I say: I love you, Taddeus. You're such a kind and thoughtful man. The boys are very lucky to have you for a father – and I'm very lucky to have you for a husband.' Kissing him, she added, 'But I do hope we can all be back together, very soon.'

'*Entschuldigen Sie, bitte, Herr Kapitan – ein Ferngespräch aus Berlin für Sie.*'

Captain Karl Dönitz, head of the U-boat arm of the Reich Navy, nodded his acknowledgment and followed the receptionist through to the hotel's front desk. The deferential Austrian handed him the telephone receiver, and busied himself with some papers. If he hoped to overhear any news, he was disappointed: punctuated with short pauses, the conversation was brief and one-sided.

'*Hier Dönitz. Ja, guten Morgen. Ja . . . also, wann? Heute? Ja, natürlich; ich bin jederzeit bereit – und auch seeklar. Sie auch, nicht? Gut. Also, danke schön; auf Wiederhören. Heil Hitler!*'

Handing the telephone back to the receptionist, Dönitz informed him that, regrettably, he would have to cut short his holiday and leave the hotel today. Could his bill please be made up at once?

Climbing the stairs to his bedroom, Dönitz's regret was genuine: for the past few years since he had learned to ski he had usually taken his holidays in the south Tyrol and liked it as much in summer as in winter. Bad Gastein, his chosen resort this year, was particularly attractive. The hot springs which gave it its name ran at a constant temperature of nearly 120 degrees Fahrenheit, blissfully comfortable. The town was small, with a population of about five thousand. Lying on the northern slopes of the Austrian Alps, it was tucked between the Hohe Tauern and Niedere Tauern mountain ranges. Against a backdrop of steep evergreen forests, its pretty colour-washed buildings were divided by a river. Dönitz could see it from his window, and could hear the roar of the great waterfall which cascaded under the stone bridge in the very heart of the town. Yes, he would be sorry to leave.

As it happened, Bad Gastein was only 40 miles south of Hitler's fortified mansion, the Berghof. Not that Dönitz needed to be close to the Führer to have him constantly in the back of his mind at least. They had met once so far, nearly five years ago, but on that occasion Hitler had seemed to Dönitz 'brave and worthy', and nothing had happened since to make him change his opinion. True, the recall to duty in Kiel was sudden, prematurely ending his scheduled six weeks' leave, but not entirely unexpected; and as he had said, he was always ready.

That was virtually all the receptionist had been able to overhear, that and the words 'and ready for sea too'. It was tantalisingly little, but while adding up the neat columns of figures in Dönitz's account he reflected that it was more than anyone else in the hotel knew. When the captain had gone it would be interesting to gossip about it, and speculate on what it might mean.

Neither the humble receptionist nor even Karl Dönitz could guess, but his early recall was intimately connected with events taking place that day in Moscow. In one part of the Russian capital the Anglo-French delegates faced Marshal Voroshilov again; in another part Commissar Molotov and Ambassador von der Schulenburg were deep in discussion, unknown to the Frenchmen and Britons. The timing of Hitler's next move depended on the outcome of these separate, rival talks, and whatever happened he would have his forces ready in all respects.

The previous evening, under Voroshilov's threat of suspending the military talks, the chief foreign delegates and their respective ambassadors had held an emergency meeting and sent urgent telegrams to London and Paris. Sir William Seeds, the British Ambassador, had sent his already: 'All indications so far show that Soviet military negotiators are really out for business,' he had said, stressing that unless Admiral Drax was given much greater freedom of action the Russians would conclude that there was no serious British intent to reach agreement. But that telegram had gone on the 12th, three days ago, and there was still no reply. Today, in a state of nervous tension, the delegates could only wait, hoping for a rapid and suitable response, and listen to Voroshilov expounding at length on Soviet military power and plans.

Molotov's session with von der Schulenburg was of an altogether different character. Where there had been suspicion, there was now a growing candour. Before nightfall the German Ambassador was able to send to Berlin a telegram with staggering implications. Though hesitant about the idea of von Ribbentrop coming in person to Moscow and supervening the normal channels of diplomacy, Commissar Molotov stated he was now confident of Germany's good faith, and wondered what the German government might say to three proposals. First, would a non-aggression pact be of interest? Second, could Germany offer assistance in Russo-Japanese relations? Third, might it be possible for Germany and Russia jointly to guarantee the frontiers of the Baltic states? As he drafted the telegram, von der Schulenburg shook his head in pleased surprise: Molotov had gone further than he would have imagined possible, actually explaining the benefits that Russia would gain if agreement on those three points could be reached. All came down to one word: security. When, not if, Poland was attacked, a Russo-German non-aggression pact would leave Russia in peace. Russia's long-running dispute with Japan concerning the border with Manchuria could, with German influence, be solved; and the safety of Russia's Baltic borders could be ensured by Germany to a degree that was simply impossible for either France or Britain.

Signing his name with a flourish, von der Schulenburg half-wished he could be with von Ribbentrop and the Führer when they received the message. Perhaps it was not quite so swift as they might like – Molotov's seeming unwillingness to receive von Ribbentrop was coupled with a desire to conclude economic agreements before political ones – but it was promising progress. The Ambassador felt a professional satisfaction.

Five years later, he too would be one of those involved in the conspiracy against Hitler's life; he too would be executed when it failed.

*

Never in his life had Francis Vanek seen such a huge crowd of people – tens, scores of thousands, maybe more; he could not begin to estimate the numbers. The day before, feeling the need of another long ride, he had cycled out thirty-five miles from his lodgings in Lourdes to Gavarnie, nearly 4500 feet up the Pyrenees and five miles from the border with Spain. It had proved one of the most tiring stretches he had done so far, but worth it if only for the exhilarating return trip down the mountains. He had slept soundly that night, and quite early on the morning of 15 August, the Feast of the Assumption of the Blessed Virgin Mary, had gone with his friends towards the Esplanade des Processions, the wide avenue leading arrow-straight to the Church of the Rosary and the grotto where St Bernadette's visions had taken place. There was a spring there, which had arisen miraculously when, on the directions of the Holy Mother, Bernadette had scratched the dry ground. This was literally the fount of holiness, the place where all the pilgrims most wanted to be, for its waters could cure. Not everyone who drank them was so blessed, but in the eighty-one years since it first began to flow more than 200 people whom doctors declared incurable had been restored to full health. Francis himself was exceedingly fit and healthy, for which he thanked God; and as he approached the bridge across the Gave de Pau, he thanked God too for giving him the sense to have visited the grotto already. There would be precious little chance of doing so today.

Even before they reached the bridge they could hear the people. More and more were coming from each direction, from the Quai St Jean, the Rue Bernadette Soubirous and the Boulevard itself, all congregating on the bottleneck of the Pont St Michel. As they made their way slowly over, they could see ahead the sombre Breton Calvary, a 40-foot granite crucifix from Brittany, towering over the heads of those in front. The 500-yard Esplanade was filling steadily. Many of the people were blind or crippled, hobbling on crutches, trundling in wheelchairs, even being pushed in wheeled beds, their faces shaded from the climbing sun; and all were praying. Some were silent: an old lady moving only her lips as fingers distorted by arthritis struggled to move the beads of her rosary; a young man crossing himself with his left hand as his right hand dangled limp and withered beside him. Others were crying out loud in English, French and languages Francis did not understand, *Dear Lord, restore my sight – Oh God, let me walk again.* Instinctively crossing himself, overwhelmed by the enormous demonstration of faith, Francis closed his eyes in prayer, and felt tears on his cheeks.

Elsewhere in France a pilgrimage of entirely secular purpose was beginning: Winston Churchill had come as a guest of General Joseph Georges, Commander-in-Chief of the armies in France, to see for himself the Rhine sector of the Maginot Line, the main French land defensive barrier against

Germany. Begun ten years previously and named after the then War Minister, André Maginot, it had been fabulously expensive, and was very well equipped indeed. Telephone exchanges, power stations, ammunition dumps, miniature railways, underground barracks, cookhouses and hospitals, ammunition hoists and drainage systems, a garrison of 300,000 men, and gun emplacements elaborately planned to cover every square foot of ground ahead; everything was there. Their tour lasted three days. Starting from Lauterbourg, the north-easternmost corner of France, where the border with Germany made an acute angle, they continued south for a hundred miles up the Rhine to the Swiss border. The first thing that struck Churchill was the harsh contrast in atmosphere with England. He wrote of it later, in his lucid, dramatic fashion. At home, he knew, there were families holidaying on the sands, contented and carefree. But here any temporary bridges crossing the river had been moved to one bank or the other; all permanent bridges were under heavy guard on both sides and, at least on the French side, mined as well; they could be blown up at the touch of a button. French riflemen crouched in pits; Germans shovelled earthworks. Any person or vehicle crossing, and there were very few, was subjected to close scrutiny on both sides, though the border posts might be only a hundred yards apart. Between such posts there was absolutely no contact, and for long stretches of the river no civilians were allowed to walk. *Yet*, he thought, *Europe is at peace. There is no dispute between Germany and France.*

Perturbing though it was, he admired what he saw; but it had flaws, and he saw them too. 'The French Front cannot be surprised. . .' he reported to the British Secretary of State for War. 'The flanks of this front, however, rest upon two small neutral States.' To the north, Belgium; to the south, Switzerland. Since 1815 no nation had threatened Switzerland's neutrality, and (although Hitler once remarked that after conquering Europe, he would take Switzerland with the Berlin fire brigade) in Churchill's judgment the French were safe from that side. Nevertheless their defences there were as strong as on any part of the Rhine, whereas along the Belgian frontier, from Montmédy to the sea 170 miles away, there were only occasional pillboxes; and it was through Belgium, neutral in 1914 as in 1939, that Germany had invaded France.

For the Englishman inspecting the defences of France, however, the single most remarkable effect of the Maginot Line was its psychological influence on the French: 'the complete acceptance of the defensive which dominated my most responsible French hosts, and imposed itself irresistibly on me . . . France had no longer the life-thrust to mount a great offensive. She would fight for her existence – *Voilà tout!*'

In Lourdes a prayer went up from every French-speaking mouth: '*Dieu nous donne la paix!*' Many of the French there had come especially to offer that prayer, and Francis Vanek echoed it, although he still believed it unnecessary. At his side, Paddy Murray nudged him.

'What was that they said, Francis?'

'They said, "God give us peace." They really are frightened.'

Paddy crossed himself. 'Amen to that. God give us peace.'

At 5 p.m. on 15 August, the Foreign Secretary Lord Halifax and the Minister for the Coordination of Defence, Admiral of the Fleet Lord Chatfield, approved for dispatch a draft telegram written by the Deputy Chiefs of Staff in reply to Sir William Seeds. The chance of an alliance with Russia, which for so long had seemed undesirable and awkward, began to seem more and more attractive as the possibility of losing it increased. Released from their previous political constraints, the Deputy Chiefs wrote their response eagerly. Accepting in full Seeds' urgent recommendation that Admiral Drax should be given a looser rein, it authorised him to bring the military discussions to a satisfactory conclusion as quickly as possible.

As soon as the telegram was sent, the second plea arrived from Moscow. Its tone was emphatic: Voroshilov appeared sincere, but the question of Russian passage rights over Poland must be resolved, or all might fall through. Around the same time, the French version of the same telegram arrived in Paris; and for once in both capitals, a condition of extreme urgency was immediately recognised. For their own good, the Poles and Rumanians had to be brought with the utmost speed to the same point of recognition: they must be persuaded to allow the Russians through.

Tuesday 15 August, the Feast of the Assumption, ended in Lourdes as it always did. From the Basilica, a nineteenth-century building in the style of the thirteenth century, came a torchlight procession of pilgrims of many nations. Above them in the darkening sky rose the Basilica's 230-foot bell tower. Turning right, they commenced the winding march past the Stations of the Cross, climbing half a mile to the top of Mount Calvary.

Such processions, lit by flickering brands in gathering darkness, always have an instinctive and powerful effect on those who see them or those who take part. Adolf Hitler, an instinctive man in many ways, understood this; which was why he preferred such processions, above all others, as a conclusion to any Nazi rally. There too the cheers would ring out: *Heil Hitler! Sieg heil!* Hail Hitler! Hail victory! *Ein Volk, ein Reich, ein Führer!* One people, one empire, one leader! and the daunting, rousing anthem, *Deutschland, Deutschland, über alles.*

In torch-lit Lourdes, the pilgrims sang hymns of Christian faith. They sang with hope, and with fearful defiance; and their power was greater than they knew.

*

By noon on 16 August Marshal Voroshilov was thoroughly annoyed. The talks had been in progress for four days, and he still had not seen or heard anything which could be called proof of firm intention from either the French or British delegates. He was also losing interest. After his own account of Russia's plans and forces the previous day, General Doumenc had followed with an outline of western naval plans, and this morning was continuing with an account of western air strength. The general was making some play of the idea that this was all very secret information, trying thereby to convince the marshal of good intentions. Instead Voroshilov merely felt insulted. Secret? What rubbish! He wondered if the general thought him a simpleton or a schoolboy. There was no intelligence service which did not know all this supposedly secret information already. Moreover the British and French kept on asking for agreed principles, when all he was interested in were physical realities, the totals of men, ships, guns, planes and tanks that all three nations together would put into action, and when, where and how it would be done. And central to it all remained the unanswered question of passage rights across Poland and Rumania.

At last he had had enough. Abruptly, saying it was a waste of time, he called the session to a halt and repeated his warning of the previous night: firm answers must come, and soon, or the entire idea would have to be abandoned.

In the British Foreign Office, Cadogan was very worried about how much of this to let out to the press. Publicising the progress, or lack of it, and all the difficulties surrounding the talks could easily make everything even worse; yet there was no escaping the fact that people were eager, desperately and naturally eager, for news, and if nothing was said they would go by guesswork, which could be equally bad. Among the many millions around the world who found the skimpy newspaper reports of the Moscow talks a subject of consuming interest were John Neville Scott, a rebellious English teenager, and Charles King, an idealistic Australian. Their roots and circumstances had little in common, yet they shared one basic attitude. Nineteen-year-old Scott was a brewing research chemist; forty-one-year-old King was an unemployed teacher, the father of three daughters. King's own father, long dead, had been a womaniser and a heavy drinker, while Scott's father, recently retired from work as a supply manager, was a man of stately appearance and strict moral rectitude. The young Englishman and the middle-aged Australian had never met, and never would meet, but in direct reaction to their very different backgrounds, both were firm, paid-up supporters of the Communist Party.

Within a year neither would belong to the party. King, the unpaid editor of its monthly publication *World Peace*, was expelled in 1940 for writing a leading article which savagely criticised Russia's invasion of Finland. Scott had Communism knocked out of him by his wartime service. His parents had learned not to ask where he had been when he came home late in the evenings; if they did a bitter political argument usually followed. But real working-class people, in destroyers and the Fleet Air Arm, saw through him. They did not mind that he had been given his middle name in honour of the Prime Minister; and he, helping illiterate seamen to write their love-letters, was honest enough to realise that distributing the *Daily Worker* and going to smoky, conspiratorial meetings was little more than an intellectual game.

Nevertheless in August 1939, both John Scott and Charles King were certain that peace in Europe could only be maintained by an alliance between France, Britain and Russia, united against Fascism. As Communists it was much easier for them than for many others, mistrustful of Bolsheviks, to accept the idea; and since nothing definite was published to the contrary they assumed that progress was satisfactory. Actually, though they would never have admitted to panic, the professional diplomats of Britain and France were frantically trying to stave off a complete collapse.

The first pressure on the Poles came from Paris. The Polish Ambassador to France was urged to recommend co-operation with the Russians; the Polish Foreign Ministry was given the same strong advice from its French counterpart; and a French delegate from Moscow was sent to Warsaw with the same message for the Polish General Staff. Meanwhile in Britain the Deputy Chiefs of Staff were writing a passionate second report to Whitehall:

> This is no time for half-measures . . . every effort should be made to persuade Poland and Rumania to agree to the use of their territory by Russian forces . . . It is perfectly clear that without early and effective Russian assistance, the Poles cannot hope to stand up to a German attack on land or in the air for more than a limited time . . . We suggest it is now necessary to present this unpalatable truth with absolute frankness both to the Poles and to the Rumanians.

This was plain speaking from men who had until now been held back from expressing their full opinion – the same men who, in the event of war, would be responsible for Britain's strategy. 'To the Poles especially,' the Deputy Chiefs continued, 'it ought to be pointed out that they have obligations to us as well as we to them; and that it is unreasonable for them to expect us blindly to implement our guarantee to them if, at the same time, they will not co-operate in measures designed for a common purpose.'

A Polish soldier was shot dead by a Danzig frontier guard that day. During the course of the afternoon Francis Vanek relaxed in the unaccustomed luxury of a train ride from Lourdes to Paris. Winston Churchill gazed in amazement at German and French propaganda posters facing each other across the Rhine. Galeazzo Ciano, trying to avert disaster for Italy, attempted to persuade Mussolini to renege on the Pact of Steel; and Captain Dönitz arrived in Kiel. Taking over from his Chief of Staff, he began to implement Hitler's instructions for *Fall Weiss*, Case White, preparations for an assault on Poland; and Joachim von Ribbentrop sent an urgent telegram to Ambassador Count von der Schulenburg in Moscow, telling him that Commissar Molotov's three proposals were acceptable and could all be met at once.

8

In order to escape

AT 4.47 A.M. on Thursday 17 August, the sun rose over the North Sea. Looking out from his cabin under the trawler's bridge, Lionel Tomlinson again had that feeling of confidence he could never quite explain, even to himself. The forecast was good, and as the stars dimmed he could see, as he had sensed all night, that the sea was smooth and the wind almost non-existent. Under his feet the 115-foot *Evelina* vibrated rhythmically with the regular thump of her triple-expansion steam engine. He had had her command for only a month – his first job as a skipper, although he had got his master's ticket more than a year ago, when he was twenty-two. He knew that everything about her was in perfect condition: with the different members of the crew he had checked it all himself the previous morning, before leaving Tynemouth. But since then they had been steaming for twenty hours, including two sessions of shooting the nets, with no result. Weather, ship and men could all be perfect, but sometimes the fish just would not come. Today, however, he was sure they would. He could not say why; he simply felt it.

A bowler hat bobbed past his window, and a moment later the third deckhand stuck his head in the door. 'Mornin', skipper – just checking you're up. Chuck's about to mash a brew.'

'Morning, Darky; looks like a good one. I'll be with you in a moment.'

The half-caste nodded. 'See you in the wheelhouse.'

As the door closed Tomlinson smiled. Darky Coates was a rum one, all right, what with that bowler he always wore, never wanted a sou'wester, even if it was pouring with rain – and was it his pa or his grandpa who was a black man? Tomlinson could never remember, but whichever it was, it did not matter a jot. No one ever thought of calling him anything other than Darky, and no offence was meant or taken. Born and bred in Sunderland, Darky Coates was pretty well as much a Tynesider as Tomlinson himself, and a good deckhand; those were the important things.

When he came into the wheelhouse, Chuck the cook was already there, handing out big mugs of tea. He was a little man, thin but wiry, always lively. 'Here's yours, skipper,' he said chirpily. 'Strong and sweet, just like me.'

Tomlinson took it gratefully. 'Good and hot, too. That's grand.' Even on the best mornings, and this was definitely one of them, it was always cold on the water first thing. 'Hot?' said the cook. 'In India we'd've called that cold. That's the thing about tea, if you're cold it warms you, if you're hot it cools you down. Now, in India it was hot enough to –'

'To cook a canary?'

India and canaries were almost Chuck's sole topics of conversation. He had been with the army in India ('How long did you say, Chuck? Two years?' 'Huh! I was under chloroform for longer than that!') and he was mad about canaries, with a whole room of his house set aside for their breeding. Now he looked pained.

'Not a nice thing to say, with all the work I do for you. Anyway,' he added with comic dignity, 'you'd only get a mouthful from a whole canary.'

The chief engineer came in, his flannel shirt damp with sweat. 'Mornin', skipper. Mornin', all. Got a cuppa there, Chuck? Ta.' He drank thirstily: whatever the weather the engine room was always hot, and with only one assistant and the need to keep steam up constantly, his job was five hours on and five hours off. 'No problems below, skipper; everything sweet as a bell. I'm off to get my head down now.'

'Right, Chief. See you later. I think we'll be busy.'

As Tomlinson checked their course on the pelorus, flicked on the Marconi echosounder and turned to the chart, the man on the wheel glanced briefly at him. 'Reckon we'll lucky today then, skipper?'

'I do. Don't ask me why. I just feel we're going to get a big haul.'

'Certainly could do with it – just as long as it's not one of them bloody German mines again.'

Although the war had been over for twenty years, fishing boats still netted ancient mines from time to time. It had happened twice to Lionel Tomlinson. The first time, just to begin with, he had been excited. Born in 1915, he had never seen a real mine before. But he had learnt quickly that it was no laughing matter. The thing could not be cut free to drift, and it was too dangerous to try and blow it up at sea, so it had to be towed very gingerly all the way back to the coast, until some official boat with trained people could come out, take it over and explode it safely. Then, briefly, the fishermen were local heroes and would have their picture in the paper, with one of the explosion alongside. But that was all; there was no reward or anything, so at best, netting a mine was a bad waste of time and money for the skipper and crew concerned. And at worst they could all be killed. It had happened before, and no doubt would happen again.

1. With an elegance to rival that of any royal court, senior Nazis and their guests gather for a concert in the Berlin house of Reich Foreign Minister, Joachim von Ribbentrop. In his Field Marshal's dress uniform, Hermann Goering sits at the left of the picture, next to Frau von Ribbentrop; the Führer is in the place of honour; to his left, the actress Olga Tschechowa, and beyond her, on the far right, Frau Emmy Goering. Also visible in the second row are the Japanese Ambassador, General Hiroshi Oshima; Frau Gertrud Scholtz-Klink, leader of the Reich Women's Movement, and Major-General Wilhelm Keitel, Chief of the High Command of the Armed Forces.

2. Behind the facade of cultural appreciation, however, is the reality of a nation where even children and teenagers are already semi-militarised. In the middle of August 1939, the subjection of Czechoslovakia is symbolised by a contingent of Hitler Youths marching with banners flying through the Invalidenplatz in Prague...

3. … while in Germany, where the growth of the armed forces leads to a civilian labour shortage, the harvest is gathered in by numerous members of the *Bund Deutsche Mädel*, the League of German Maidens.

4. Across the border, by the third week of August, the Polish Army is also ready – not merely the famous, archaic cavalry, which rode vainly against German tanks, but also fully equipped soldiers sufficient to make Poland the world's fifth military power, with an army larger than that of France.

5. Wednesday 9 August: breaking his holiday at Balmoral Castle in Scotland, His Majesty King George VI has travelled overnight in the Royal Train to Weymouth Bay on England's south coast. There, 133 warships – the British Reserve Fleet – await his inspection, the ceremony marking their mobilisation. Wearing the uniform of an Admiral of the Fleet, he boards HMS *Effingham*, the Fleet's flagship.

6. Tuesday 15 August: at Salzburg airport in Austria, Count Galeazzo Ciano, the Italian Foreign Minister, shakes hands with Joachim von Ribbentrop, Reich Foreign Minister, after two days of discussion with him and the Führer. A German spokesman states that complete unity had been achieved on all questions concerning the Axis; yet over the next two weeks, Ciano will successfully do his utmost to save Italy from fulfilling the obligations of its Pact with Germany.

THE ILLUSTRATED LONDON NEWS

The World Copyright of all the Editorial Matter, both Illustrations and Letterpress, is Strictly Reserved in Great Britain, the British Dominions and Colonies, Europe, and the United States of America.

SATURDAY, AUGUST 12, 1939.

"UNDER THE SPREADING CHESTNUT-TREE," SUNG BY THE ROYAL FAMILY DURING THEIR VISIT TO THE KING'S
ANNUAL CAMP FOR BOYS AT ABERGELDIE, ON THE BALMORAL ESTATE.

By invitation of its royal founder, the King's Camp for boys from Public Schools and Industrial Areas took place this year at Abergeldie Castle, on the Balmoral estate. Some 200 boys from 17 to 19, were the guests of the Royal Family for tea at Balmoral on August 6. On August 7 the King and Queen, with Princess Elizabeth and Princess Margaret motored the two miles from Balmoral in perfect weather to visit the Camp, and above they are seen with Captain J. G. Paterson, the camp commandant (seated next to the King), and boys joining in the action-song, "Under the Spreading Chestnut-Tree," conducted by the song-master, Mr. Robert Hyde, director of the Industrial Welfare Society, from among whose member-firms the boys are selected. The little Princesses joined in with appropriate gestures. *(G.P.U.)*

7. [*Opposite*] 'Back at Balmoral'.

8. [*Right*] Sir Reginald Plunkett-Ernle-Erle-Drax (left) and Joseph Doumenc (right): on Saturday 5 August, on board *City of Exeter*, the British Admiral and French General, heads of their respective military missions, look cheerful enough at the start of their long journey to Moscow in search of an alliance with Russia. Knowing their task will be difficult, they do not realise that centuries of antipathy between Russia and Poland will make it virtually impossible.

9. Biggin Hill RAF Station, Kent: on Tuesday 8 August, pilots sprint to their machines. Not only fifteen groups of the Civilian Observer Corps, but also 500 barrage balloons, 1,300 aircraft and 1,400 anti-aircraft guns are engaged in a test of British air defences and counter-offensive strikes. This is the beginning of the most comprehensive air exercises ever planned in Britain.

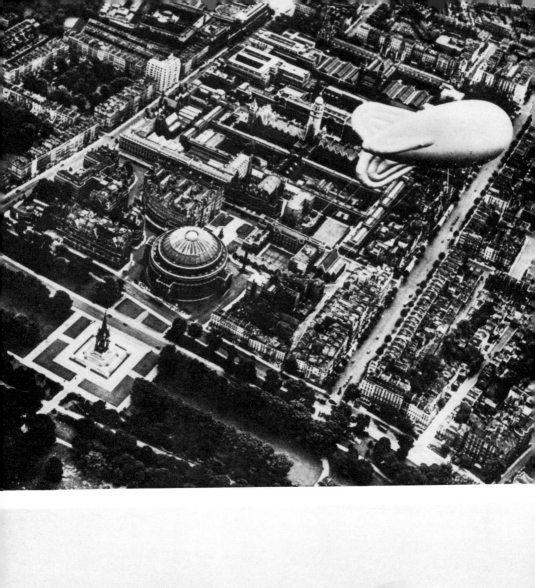

10. [*Opposite above*] Tests of barrage balloons have already begun: the first five hundred are ready by 28 July, moored in a circle 14 miles across and centred on Tower Bridge. From 2,000 feet up – their maximum daytime flying height – the Albert Hall's dome is dwarfed, and the Albert Memorial becomes a tiny spike. In war conditions the balloons will fly at altitudes between 20,000 and 30,000 feet, forcing attackers above the zone where accurate bombing is possible.

11. [*Opposite below*] Gradually the strange and abnormal becomes a familiar, comforting sight. On 3 September, the day war is declared, hundreds more balloons are in position, and at ground level their huge size is apparent: even when partially inflated, they dominate the busy thoroughfares of London.

12. Conscription in Britain: compulsory military training began at the end of April 1939. By the beginning of June, 234,000 20-year-old men were registered; in July, 34,000 of them were called up. By mid-August, when this photograph was taken, enrolment centres were inundated...

13. ... and even statesmen put on uniform. Anthony Eden, Member of Parliament and ex-Foreign Secretary, was also a major in the Territorial Army. On Sunday 13 August, at the head of his TA unit – the 2nd Battalion The Rangers (King's Royal Rifle Corps) – he marches from their Bloomsbury headquarters to Waterloo Station, *en route* for their training camp in Beaulieu, Hampshire.

Inside the photograph (railway notices):

SPECIAL NOTICE OF TRAIN ALTERATIONS
On Friday, Saturday & Sunday, Sept 1ˢᵗ, 2ⁿᵈ & 3ʳᵈ

Charing Cross Station

Time	To	Remarks

SOUTHERN RAILWAY

SPECIAL ANNOUNCEMENTS

EVACUATION OF LONDON CHILDREN

Friday, Saturday & Sunday, Sept. 1ˢᵗ, 2ⁿᵈ & 3ʳᵈ

The following steam trains are required for the evacuation of children, and will not be available for ordinary passengers

9.15 A.M. Margate.   2.25. Hastings.
9.25 A.M. Hastings.   3.30. Tun'Wells.
11.15 A.M. Margate.   4.15. Ramsgate.
12.10 P.M. Ashford.   4.20. Hastings.
                        Gillingham.

The Enquiry Office staff will gladly give further information of alternative services.

14. Beaming with optimism at the apparent strength of French defences, Winston Churchill arrives at the Gare de l'Est in Paris on Thursday 17 August. Although, like Eden, he is out of office and acting as an ordinary backbench MP, he has just returned from an inspection of the Maginot Line – while, as many people note despondently, the only line the Prime Minister is inspecting is his fishing line: Chamberlain is on holiday in Scotland.

15. The eve of evacuation: on 31 August posters in every railway station in Britain herald the greatest migration of British people ever known. In four days, more than 1.4 million children and crippled, blind or elderly men and women will be moved from the urban centres to places of comparative safety. Already well rehearsed, the whole vast operation is outstandingly successful, without a single accident or casualty taking place...

LCC

0 3 4 1

ENGLISH MARTYRS

16. ...except, of course, the traumatic, inevitable separation of children from parents. After a last brushing of the hair and straightening of the socks, and wearing the knapsacks made by their father, 11-year-old John Brown of Clerkenwell Green, London, leads his brother and two sisters, aged 10, 9 and 4, away from home. There is no promise they will see their parents again...

17. ...and yet for some it is all a great adventure. Leaving for the West Country, pupils from a Roman Catholic school in the south-east London suburb of Walworth are exhilarated by the prospect of a long train journey, and with unintended irony, wave the banner showing their school's name.

18. For those left in the cities, other posters indicate what they may have to endure. In Covent Garden, London's great fruit and vegetable market, porters read of air-raid warnings and the possibility of poison gas attacks...

19. [*Opposite left*] ...and even away from the city centres, it is sensible to take precautions against air-raids. Wielding unfamiliar tools, a mother and daughter make wooden shutters, after covering their windows with sticky tape to minimise the danger of flying glass...

20. [*Opposite right*] ...while some fathers come to terms with the outrageous new realities by reducing them all to a more manageable scale.

21. [*Opposite above*] But as the nervous strain increases, practical activity is the best means of coping. Everywhere, busy groups of soldiers and civilians are filling sandbags: outside the Royal Eye Hospital at St Geroge's Circus in London, women volunteers help nurses fill the bags.

22. [*Opposite*] For months, the Government's repeated advice has been 'Take your gas mask with you'. By the end of August, slung in a box over the shoulder, they have become a part of nurses' uniform, and by Christmas even toy dolls will have them too.

23. Friday 1 September: war may be only hours away. The Bank Rate has been doubled; the price of gold has leapt, and Britain's reserves have been massively depleted, with up to thirty million pounds' worth leaving the country in a single day. Now even the Stock Exchange is closed...

24. ...and although heavy-handed, whether posed or not, a bit of humour helps to keep things in perspective. *'What – again?'*: these men from the Royal Artillery are too young to have fought in the Great War, but the memory of victory bolsters morale.

25. Wednesday 23 August is Soviet Air Day, and, accompanied by Foreign Commissar Vyacheslav Molotov, Defence Commissar Marshal Kliment Voroshilov and other high-ranking Soviet officials, Stalin watches an air-war exercise over Moscow's Tuchino Aerodrome. This marks the humiliation of Drax and Doumenc: their mission has failed entirely, and Communist Russia's impending pact with Nazi Germany has just been announced.

26. Both the King and the Prime Minister returned from their Scottish holidays well before the end of August, and on Friday 1 September were together at Downing Street. In bowing to his Sovereign, Chamberlain observes the ritual formalities, yet looks exactly as he feels – old, sad and terribly worn.

27. On Wednesday 30 August, steel-helmeted men of the SS crouch beside a grenade thrower near the Polish border ...

28. ... while in Danzig harbour, crowds assemble under a welcoming banner to stare at the German cruiser *Schleswig-Holstein*. Within 24 hours, the grenades will be launched and the cruiser will bombard the city.

29. Sunday 3 September: Great Britain declares war on Germany. For once the paper's name is entirely appropriate. On a London street-corner, by a tree striped white for the blackout, a newsvendor's face shows the unutterable bleakness of the future...

30. ...while the artist Henry Moore sees people swimming below the cliffs of Dover. With pencil, wax crayon and watercolour, he gives them hideous, mechanical, mask-like faces; the world has changed for ever, and no one will ever be the same again.

'That'd make things go with a bang, that would,' said Chuck, gathering up the empty mugs. For a moment Tomlinson went cold inside: he could imagine it all too clearly. 'Mind you,' the cook continued, 'in India, if we wanted things to go with a real bang, we'd have a good hot curry. That'd clear you out, and no mistake. That's the thing about curry –'

'Chuck!' He was glad to hear the cook chattering on, but there was business to be prepared. 'Get out of it, will you, and cook us all some breakfast. It's fish we're after, and I think there's going to be a lot of them.'

'Aye, aye, captain.' With mock formality, Chuck saluted. At that, Tomlinson smiled: he was a member of the Royal Naval Reserve, and Chuck's salute was an army one, as incongruous at sea as Darky's bowler hat.

Commanded by Heinrich Himmler, the *Schutzstaffel*, the Nazi police force, was best known by its insignia, a pair of twin bolts of lightning which depicted its initials: SS. One branch of the SS was the SD, the *Sicherheitsdienst* or Security Service.

Something Adolf Hitler liked about General Reinhard Heydrich was his appearance, tall, blond, blue-eyed, muscular, handsome: the perfect Aryan, emblem of the perfect German. Another agreeable attribute was his character, devious, unscrupulous and utterly ruthless: the perfect chief of the SD. On 17 August he had a proposal for the Führer which Hitler could only admire as typical of the man.

It was a solution, simple but effective, to the problem of how to justify, at least in German eyes, an assault on Poland. The old-fashioned phrase was *agent provocateur*: if the enemy would not oblige with a timely offence, an offence would be provided and made to look like enemy action. In this case, Heydrich suggested, it would be very suitable if Polish soldiers launched an attack on German soldiers near the border. Even better if they targeted, say, a radio station such as the one at Gleiwitz, took it over, and broadcast insults against Germany. No doubt some of the attackers would die in the process. So if Admiral Canaris, the head of the *Abwehr*, the Intelligence Service, could obtain 250 Polish army uniforms, a corresponding number of Polish weapons with appropriate ammunition, and suitably identifying Polish military pay-books, he, Heydrich, would arrange the rest. Just call it a 'special SS operation', there was no need for Canaris to know any more than that. Soldiers from the SS, trained to obey Polish commands, would play the active part. But there was a passive part as well. It could not be merely a set of reported episodes. 'Physical evidence,' said Heydrich, 'is essential for the foreign press and for German propaganda purposes.' That evidence would be provided by the corpses of some of the 'attackers', bodies taken from a concentration camp (there were more than enough) and kitted out in Polish uniform.

There was one little thing which worried Hitler in what was otherwise an excellent plan. One could not refer in orders to the use of dead bodies; presumably General Heydrich had thought of that? Indeed he had; in any written orders, the corpses would be described as 'canned goods'. Cynical but suitable; and without further hesitation, the Führer approved the plan in every detail.

Less than three years later, on 4 June 1942, when he was Reich Protector of Czechoslovakia, General Heydrich ('a man with an iron heart,' said Himmler) was blown up and killed by Czech resistance fighters. Admiral Wilhelm Canaris lived a little longer: as another of those who plotted against Hitler's life, he was arrested by the Gestapo in 1944, and executed in 1945 in Flossenburg concentration camp.

From the Foreign Office in London, the report of the Deputy Chiefs of Staff was telegrammed almost word for word to Sir Howard Kennard, Britain's Ambassador in Warsaw. He should ignore the government of Rumania, at least for the time being; the Polish authorities posed the critical problem. In order to persuade them, he should support his French colleague Léon Noël and do everything he could to convince the Polish Foreign Minister, Colonel Josef Beck, that Soviet troops must be allowed free passage across Poland. Kennard was empowered to point out to Colonel Beck that if he did not agree, responsibility for any breakdown of talks in Moscow would be on his shoulders.

A dramatic sideshow took place at the same time in Harland and Wolff's shipyard in Belfast. At noon a brand-new aircraft carrier, HMS *Formidable*, launched herself:

> Sir Kingsley Wood, the Air Minister, and Lady Wood had just arrived on the launching platform [newspapers reported] when pieces of timber were seen to be breaking away from the cradle supporting the vessel on the slips, and, to the consternation of everybody, the vessel began to move. Shipwrights, hundreds of whom were below the vessel ready to play their parts in the launch, ran for their lives, while pieces of timber from the broken cradle crashed around them . . . Iron nuts and bolts were flung into the air, and some of them fell among the thousands of spectators . . . Tugs had been standing by to take charge of the *Formidable* after the launch, and when they saw the ship entering the water they had to proceed at full speed ahead in order to escape.

As the tugs sounded their warning sirens in a scene of great excitement, Lady Wood showed astonishing presence of mind, and despite everything, managed not only to call out the name of the new ship, but also to crack a bottle of champagne across *Formidable*'s bow. But in the drama, nineteen people were injured, and a woman called Mrs Isobel Kirk was killed.

In Moscow the annual Soviet air exhibition was taking place. Not far away the foreign delegates in the Spiridonyevka Palace were aware that they were only spinning things out: nothing had been heard yet from London, Paris or Warsaw. Even so, at the end of the morning session, they were not expecting Marshal Voroshilov to say what he did.

'The Soviet Mission,' he announced, 'considers that we shall have to end the work of our conference until we get a reply to our questions.' Pausing, he added smoothly, 'Until receipt of this reply, I recommend our dear guests to rest, see the sights of Moscow, visit the Exhibition, and make themselves at home.'

In the circumstances a dispassionate observer might well have said this was a sensible and reasonable thing to do. Certainly Voroshilov considered it so: as things stood the conference was getting nowhere, and until there was a chance of progress it was a waste of time to talk for the sake of talking. But the decision hit Admiral Drax and General Doumenc like a hammer-blow. True, they had not yet been able to offer the confirmation wanted by the Russians, but neither had Voroshilov accepted in principle their desire for agreements. Unless they could keep the Soviet delegation at the conference table, or at least leave with a firm commitment to meet again on a definite date, both the Frenchman and Englishman felt they would lose even the limited control they had on events. Joining in a strong protest, they could not change Voroshilov's mind; until something was received from abroad he saw no point in carrying on. At length, though, and with reluctance, he agreed that there should be a specific date for the end of the adjournment. The conference could begin again in four days, on 21 August.

Otherwise he was adamant, and eventually Drax and Doumenc accepted that they could move him no further. Doumenc was angry and concerned, but Drax was furious. The episode inflamed his latent distrust of Russians. 'Something devilish is going on behind the scenes, I'm sure of it,' he fumed in private to his colleagues. 'Some kind of intrigue of which we know nothing. Just what the hell d'you think they're up to?'

Of course no one could give any definite answer, and the admiral took everyone aback with his next remark: 'Be blowed to diplomacy. I'll tell you what I'm going to do, next time we see them – I'm going to ask them straight to explain exactly what they're playing at. Then we'll see what happens.'

That precipitated a welter of argument. Finally, acknowledging that he might feel calmer by the 21st, Drax was persuaded to await developments. He still grumbled in dissatisfaction. But he would have been even more disturbed if, instead of Moscow, he had been in Washington DC; for then he might have learned how well-founded his suspicions were.

By that time Lionel Tomlinson was six feet of pure concentration. The routine for shooting the nets was long-established and familiar to all on board, but the skipper could not afford to miss a beat: ship and men were, in the end, his responsibility – his own life, theirs, the livelihoods of all. Accidents were rare, but if they happened they were bad. Poisoned fingers pierced by wire or fishbones were commonplace, taken as a risk of the job, and a man – especially a family man – would continue to work in spite of the pain; but there could be clumsiness, and sheer bad luck could never be ruled out. Recently, in another vessel belonging to the Tomlinsons, one man had been standing in the wrong place when a huge bag of fish was being lifted. The masthead block swivel had broken under the strain, and, though the fish were inboard, the block caught the man on his wrist and broke it. He would be off work for months, possibly never to work at sea again. Tomlinson wanted to do all he could to prevent such an accident while he was skipper of *Evelina*.

The men were good. Even so, from his decision to shoot, it always took half an hour to get the lashings off the nets. Then warps were run out from the heavy-duty steam winch on deck. They were connected to the trawl doors, two weighty metal contraptions designed to move one to each side as the water flowed through them, opening the mouth of the net. Normally they were stowed between the gallows and the rail, but once over the rail they were hung on a preventer hook until the time came to let them go. Then came the bobbins, each fourteen inches high, fixed on the ground range at every two feet, to keep the line rolling sweetly over the seabed.

From amidships the net was streamed to windward, with the ship going to leeward. Over went the bobbins. Now all was hanging by two 50-fathom ground cables. In rapid response to his orders, the ship turned to bring the net off her quarter, then stopped before the wind. Now the net was pulling heavy astern, taking out the rest of the 50-fathom line. Over the tops of the gallows the patent clips to the trawl doors were unclipped – lower away the fore door – amidships – lower away the aft door – slow ahead. Everyone knew what to do, but the orders were essential: only one man was in charge; the others moved at his bidding. Full ahead: the warps leading off the sides began to pay out. Their final length would be three and a half times the depth of water. Judging that was the mate's job, and his alone. Every 25 fathoms the steel warps, 2½ inches thick, had rope markers spliced into them. When there was sufficient out, the mate gathered the two warps and locked them together with a block of heavy steel. From there they spread out in a V, and *Evelina* began to trawl. If the V closed and the warps drew together astern, it could mean a good bag of fish or that they had netted a rock. It could also mean – and there was that shadow again – that they had netted a mine.

Since the spring the Roosevelt administration had known far more than anyone in Britain about the political relationship between Nazi Germany and Communist Russia. For fear of compromising their source the Americans hitherto had passed on hints, but nothing more, to the British. However the hints had not been enough, and today in the State Department it was decided the time had come to sound a clear alarm. The British Ambassador, Sir Ronald Lindsay, heard it in the elegant setting of the office of Sumner Welles, the Under-Secretary of State.

Welles's message was unequivocal. He gave Lindsay a complete run-down of the conversation, only two days earlier, between Molotov and von der Schulenburg: the German suggestion that Ribbentrop should come to Moscow very soon; the Russian proposals of a non-aggression pact, help with Soviet–Japanese relations, and guarantees for the Baltic frontiers; everything. In the assessment of the US State Department, Welles explained, a Russo-German pact was imminent, which, freeing Hitler from any fear of attack from the East, would immediately bring about war.

At the end of his tour of the Maginot Line, Winston Churchill gratefully checked into the Ritz Hotel in Paris. About the same time Francis Vanek and his friends, spiritually fulfilled by their visit to the shrine of Lourdes, were going shopping in the French capital. Francis needed new cycle clips for his trousers, and to his delight the others bought a bottle of champagne. The group shared it, all seventeen of them, in honour of their achievement. As they did so Count Ciano, in Rome, was struggling through another day of Mussolini's changing moods. After his experiences in the Reich, Ciano was positive that come what may, Italy must avoid the commitments implied by the Pact of Steel; but the Duce dithered, caught between his own sense of military honour and Ciano's blunt practicality. Since Ciano's return from the visits to Ribbentrop and Hitler, Mussolini had (as Ciano noted in his diary) 'refused to act independently of the Germans', then became 'convinced we must not march blindly with Germany', then thought it might be 'a good idea to reaffirm his determination of going along with the Germans'. That, Count Ciano thought, would be 'a mad venture, carried out against the unanimous will of the Italian people'. They might not yet know quite how things stood, but 'having had a sniff of the truth', said the Count, they reacted with 'a sudden fit of rage against the Germans'. By 17 August, in spite of everything, old scruples of loyalty were returning to Mussolini: now he felt after all that if the democracies threw themselves into the furnace of war, Italy should join with Germany. All day long Ciano fought against the idea. Believing in the end that he had prevailed, he conducted individual interviews with other ambassadors, ending with Sir Percy Loraine from Britain:

> I tell him that Europe needs a great deal of common sense if it is to avoid the crisis. He answers that the common sense is there, but that Europe will not tolerate the periodical diktat of Hitler. If the crisis comes, England will fight. Personally, he would like to participate in such a fight. He regrets only one thing: that for the first time in our history, our two countries may be at war with each other.

Ciano did not reply to that; yet he felt sure that Loraine understood he did not wish for such a thing to happen.

That evening in Moscow, Commissar Molotov and Count von der Schulenburg met once again. A strange meeting, thought von der Schulenburg. The Commissar, comparing the status of Germany's proffered visitor adversely to the British, was positively jaunty; yet still he seemed to have misunderstood the speed at which Germany was willing to proceed, and spoke of the need for trade agreements and credit agreements. But he did mention also the desirability of each government drafting a non-aggression pact, and in that context brought up the idea of a secret protocol, 'defining the interests of the contracting parties in this or that question of foreign policy'. Ambassador von der Schulenburg reported it all dutifully; von Ribbentrop could make of it what he would.

Evelina's decks were covered with blood and silver. Somehow they had found the shoal, a dream shoal, net after net. Shooting and hauling were continuous as Lionel Tomlinson, with the master's prerogative, stood at the wheel and gently coaxed the vessel in the direction he thought the fish were going. It was not all magic – the echosounder, bouncing back from apparently unnaturally shallow depths, revealed them – but there was an essential element of feel in it, the touch that came only with experience. And as Tomlinson would have been the first to admit, there was an element of luck too. Once they seemed to have lost the shoal: he searched for half an hour before the tell-tale trace showed on the echosounder again, and during that time he had had no real idea where to go, not that he said so to anyone. By then their haul was already big enough to have justified the journey; but still he was glad when the fish were relocated. This time he knew the only limit to their catch would be *Evelina*'s capacity or their own physical exhaustion.

Each time the fishermen hauled in the net it took fifteen minutes; with everything prepared, the shortest shoot and haul took between twenty-five minutes and half an hour, with a good haul being fifty baskets of fish at six stone each. As soon as the fish were inboard, still flapping and flipping, the men began gutting them, sorting them by size and type, passing the clammy corpses below, where they were stacked on shelves between layers of ice. From time to time someone would sluice water across the quivering deck, washing livers and stomachs and small tubular joining bits through the scuppers and over the sides for the gulls and the other fish still swimming below. Silver and blood, blood and silver; and every fresh-iced fish a payment towards the coal, the ice, the oil, the carbide, the food and the welfare of the men and their families. But what precise payment no one could tell, until after the catch was landed and auctioned next day.

There had been public signs of a possible Russo-German reconciliation since April, when a defector known as Krivitsky announced to American newspapers that in 1934 Stalin had tried to negotiate with Hitler along such lines. It was also in April that Hitler's speeches lost their powerful anti-Soviet tone. But though Krivitsky's information was later found to be correct, in the summer of 1939 British intelligence, having nothing to corroborate it treated it with caution and some scepticism. The Americans, with good reason, did not: from members of the German Embassy in Moscow, their Ambassador there was receiving a steady supply of completely reliable material, and had been doing so since before the Munich agreement.

In Washington, summarising the whole, Welles pointed out to the shocked and excited British Ambassador that when he reported to London there must be no mention in any telegram of the source. Lindsay gave his promise on that, agreeing that no cipher could be guaranteed completely secure; he would put the identity of the source in the diplomatic bag only. On 17 August, at nine o'clock in the evening Washington time, he sent his ciphered telegram, containing the most reliable and accurate information on Russo-German negotiations ever yet seen by British eyes, to London. Hoping that it might enable his colleagues to pre-empt any deal between Molotov and Ribbentrop, Lindsay remarked: 'It should be there first thing tomorrow morning, their time.' It was; but it sat there, undeciphered, for four crucial days.

The third week

18–25 August 1939

9

The present unusual situation

IT MAY HAVE BEEN ACCIDENTAL. In these weeks of crisis, abnormally large quantities of telegrams were flowing in to the Foreign Office. Extra staff had been taken on to try and cope with them, but the volume of traffic and inexperience of many of the clerks meant that serious delays were occurring all the time. Moreover first attention was being given to messages from Europe, and Lindsay had not attached any special priority marking to his. But its deciphering and final delivery may have been held up, at that critical time, on purpose. For some years past the Foreign Office suspected that at least one of its members had been leaking classified information. Early in September, on new evidence, Sir Alexander Cadogan noted in his diary a positive 'fear that someone in the office is compromised'. Soon after, an investigation produced an 'awful' discovery: Captain John King, one of those who handled the Communication Department's cipher traffic, was actively spying for Russia. On 27 September he was arrested; three weeks later he was sentenced to ten years in gaol.

It was not revealed whether King was personally responsible for that particular delay, or whether, as one of the Foreign Office's senior officials said regretfully, it was simply 'a bad oversight'. It would be interesting to know. But by the time King was convicted, it was, of course, an academic question – by design or default, the damage had been done, and Europe was at war.

When that telegram arrived in the Foreign Office, and by active or passive neglect became buried in someone's in-tray, Cadogan received something which also required early attention – a salmon from the Prime Minister. Chamberlain seemed to be sending them to everyone. *Hope he's having good sport*, Cadogan thought, a trifle enviously. With the PM in the north of Scotland and Lord Halifax in Yorkshire, he was having what he called 'a rather complicated time' in London. However, one item of news that day caused him to reflect that if it was complicated trying to stave off a war, it seemed to be just as complicated, in unexpected ways, for someone trying to start one. The head of the Secret Intelligence Service, Admiral Quex Sinclair (whom Cadogan always discreetly referred to as 'C'), told him from a very good source that two days previously, Hitler had had an interview with a worried man, the chief of the Reich railways. Orders were out already for the mobilisation of 25,000 men. Hearing rumours of further mobilisation and knowing that a Nazi rally was scheduled for 2 September, the railway boss wanted to find out which he should prepare for. 'He could arrange transport for Party Rally or for mobilisation,' Cadogan learned with amusement, 'but not for both!'

Nevertheless, good as the source was, it seemed that even though arranging for the physical transport of troops was a basic requirement of mobilisation, no one yet knew for certain what Hitler's reply to the railway chief had been. It was reported he had chosen the rally; but Cadogan noted soberly that this was 'unconfirmed'.

The Reich navy's U-boat arm contained at that time a total of 56 boats. In Kiel Captain Dönitz found that, much as he had expected, 21 were undergoing various repairs and periodical maintenance work, while 35 were fully *seeklar*, ready for sea in all respects. At once he began dispatching them to their positions, planned long before. Eighteen would go to the eastern Atlantic, scattered from the Straits of Gibraltar (where three boats, U-39, U-40 and U-41, patrolled up to 1000 miles out into the ocean) all the way to the north-west of Ireland, where U-53, U-27 and U-30 were stationed. Between them the 18 boats could work an enormous area: approximately 1.5 million square miles of sea. The other 17 were all destined for the Baltic, ready for operations against Poland, and, in accordance with existing plans, against Russia too.

'Got you!' As the boys hurtled out of her orchard, Betty Haigh collared the youngest and smallest. Kicking and punching in his efforts to escape, he screamed up at her: 'You let me go! My dad'll come, an' 'e's a boxer!'

'Listen to me,' she answered, breathless but calm. 'You don't frighten me with that kind of talk, so don't try. I'm going to let you go, don't worry. But if you want apples, come and ask for them, all right? There are plenty of them, and I'll give you some. But what you're doing is stealing – d'you understand?'

Still holding the urchin tight with one hand, she reached up and picked an apple. 'There you are. That's much better than the ones on the ground.' He snatched it from her, baffled and suspicious. 'It's all right,' she said. 'That's for you. And when you want more, just come and ask.' With a sudden twist the boy broke free and ran off. As he ran, he turned, throwing the apple hard at her, and yelled again: 'My dad'll come! 'E's a boxer!'

Over lunch in the lighthouse, their nickname for the three-storey detached house which was both home and workplace, Betty told her husband of the episode. 'It's so depressing, Michael,' she finished. 'I don't think he understood anything I said.'

He nodded. 'The same sort of thing happened to me in a different way the other day,' he replied. 'I haven't mentioned it before – it's not really important – but a little lad came into the surgery. He knocked on the door before he came in, very respectfully; shut the door behind him; and then he knocked again, on the closed door. Then when I asked him what his name was, you'd never guess what he answered, "Dunno, Jimmy or summat." He wasn't just being shy. The kid honestly didn't know his own name.'

One day Michael Haigh would retire as an Emeritus Professor of Social Medicine. In the summer of 1939 that was many years away, but he was put on the road to academic distinction by much of what he saw with Betty in the suburbs of Birmingham. At that time Britain's second city seemed to contain all that was worst and unhappiest in the nation: severe economic depression, high unemployment, grime, poverty and all the illnesses that went with them. The redbrick 'lighthouse' was an intensely ugly building, uncomfortable and inconvenient in many ways. The fire in the living-room smoked badly; the wooden floor tiles were loose, clattering underfoot, always threatening to trip you up; apart from the smoky fire there was no main heating; fungi grew on the cellar walls, and for lack of other space the dispensary had had to be set up in the garage. However, the house had two acres of land including the prolific apple orchard, and the Haighs knew how fortunate they were compared to most of their patients. Close by, living on the banks of the canal, were the vagrants and gypsy types, the publican who beat his wife and once, when she called the doctor for help, turned on him too. Behind the house, on Balsall Heights, were long straight rows of council houses; inside them you could smell the wallbugs. Delivering babies there, which happened about once a week, Dr Haigh could feel the fleas as they jumped on his wrists and ankles, and even as the mother gave birth could see the flat, blood-sucking bedbugs writhing around her and the new-born infant.

After such sessions he always needed to scrub down from head to foot, standing naked on a large white bath-towel: it was the only way to be certain all the parasites had gone. But he did not resent it. The respect shown by almost everyone to him as a doctor, an educated man who could cure their ills, embarrassed him. They trusted him to do his best and did not blame him when he failed. Yet he knew how little he could really do, and, with babies and children dying from measles, whooping cough and diphtheria, how narrow were his resources. Chalk and opium for diarrhoea; bismuth and chloradine for stomach complaints; bromide with strychnine as a tonic;

quinine, insulin and arsenic: until 1936, when anti-bacterial sulphonamides were introduced, that was virtually the complete range of his effective drugs. Often, seeing in his surgery the large glass Winchester jars filled with different coloured solutions, patients would know exactly which they needed, pink, white or yellow, because it had worked before. What they did not know was that all the different solutions were simply aspirin. Convinced that the pink would fix them up and the yellow would do no good, they were given the pink, and more often than not it worked. Haigh was not tricking the patients: it was simply the best that could be done within the system he and they had inherited. It was that which he resented; and he wondered sometimes about the council estates. Certainly they were better than the city slums they had replaced, but people had been moved there willy-nilly, to strange new areas they did not know, without shops or pubs or any of the neighbourly things of the past.

'You know I'm not being romantic about slum life,' he remarked to his wife. 'God knows they were dreadful, but people don't seem to be healthier outside them, and every day I see how unhappy they are in these council houses. I think it's possible a lot of their illnesses come from plain old-fashioned unhappiness.'

'A conversation with the Duce in the morning,' Ciano wrote dully in his diary. 'His usual shifting feelings.' Mussolini still thought the democracies would not go to war, and his latest worry was that 'Germany might do good business cheaply, from which business he does not wish to be excluded.' With the candour of privacy, Ciano noted that the Duce was also chicken. 'He fears Hitler's rage . . .' Gnawing at the Italian leader's mind was the fear that if he denounced the Pact of Steel, or even did something like it, Hitler might abandon the Polish question altogether and turn his full wrath on Italy. 'All this makes him nervous and disturbed.' As well it might; but dictators should not dither. The only thing on which Mussolini's mind appeared to be made up was a refusal to accept any further advice on foreign affairs from his Foreign Minister, and so Count Ciano turned his mind to a more congenial subject, and made ready for an official visit to Albania.

About the same time Sir Percy Loraine, Britain's Ambassador in Rome, was sending another report home to London. The first part of it might have reassured Mussolini, or at least helped him make up his mind, had he cared to listen: one of Ciano's senior officials, who had accompanied the Count to Berchtesgaden, was convinced that unless Danzig was surrendered, Hitler had definitely decided to take it and then march on Warsaw. But the second part would, no doubt, have thrown Mussolini off beam again, for the same official judged also that 'Herr Hitler's language and behaviour showed clear signs of mental abnormality.'

Count Ciano should have taken some little consolation from the fact that even if Mussolini ignored what he said, he would at least listen to him. Herbert von Dirksen was itching to present Ribbentrop with his assessment of the likelihood of British involvement in a war. On that subject, which had, after all, an undeniable bearing on Germany's best move, von Dirksen was probably the best informed person in the Reich; yet try as he would, he could not get an interview with Ribbentrop. In exasperation he decided to go on holiday to Silesia, as he had intended all along. From there he would write to Ribbentrop, but not direct. He would send his letter through Ernst von Weizsäcker, Secretary of State at the Foreign Office. That way the Foreign Minister might be forced to take a look at it.

Meanwhile in Warsaw Ambassador Kennard was having no success at all either with Colonel Beck or with the Polish Commander-in-Chief, Marshal Edward Smigly-Rydz. Both were as immovable as Marshal Voroshilov, 'absolutely obdurate', Kennard reported to London. In no circumstances would the Poles consider allowing Soviet troops to pass over their country. They had two central reasons: first, Beck judged that if he were to agree, Hitler would go over the edge: 'Given his anti-Bolshevik complex, he would see red, and not hesitate to precipitate a war.' There was something in that: undoubtedly the Führer would regard such an agreement as provocative. Smigly-Rydz gave the other reason, one which encapsulated centuries of battered Polish pride. 'With the Germans we risk losing our lives,' he explained. 'But with the Soviets, our souls.' Apparently he did not consider the possibility that persistent refusal might result in Poland losing not only its life, but its soul as well.

This was the essence of *Spannung*, the war of nerves. For the politicians and diplomats most closely involved, these weeks constituted the toughest many had ever known or would know; and for the ordinary people too. A decision, any decision, could offer release from increasingly awful uncertainty. But in the meantime life carried on as best it could, with all its enormously differing degrees of innocence and experience. Returned safely to the isle of Foula and back with the few friends the island offered, Nanette Smith cavorted again, riding the backs of cows, while her uncles in Bressay gloomily foretold disaster to each other. In eastern Australia, following the politics of Europe and communism as closely as possible, Charles King prepared the next edition of *World Peace*. In rural Devon Kit Dennis and her farming family followed the season, with harvesting and hunt balls and meetings of the Young Conservatives. In the state of Maine, Vacationland USA, perhaps the farthest removed from Europe's desperate situation, Barkeley Goodrich prepared for a visit to the New York World Fair, to get a look at the 'World of Tomorrow'. In the English towns of Bradford and Newcastle, firmly planted in their world of today, Elspeth Harmes and Molly McAndrew sold ribbons and lingerie, Elspeth happy with her fleeting visit to the sea and her silver bracelet, an unexpected birthday present from a friend in the shop; and Molly happy with thoughts of Ernie, her fiancé. In Northern Ireland David Howarth pondered the BBC's radio talks for the coming week, while in London, on his last day of holiday, Francis Vanek could not resist going straight to his cycling club; and in East Sussex Bob Leaney, a parish priest, was walking through the tranquil village of Mountfield.

In time, like Dr Haigh in Birmingham, he too would become a professor, the Revd Professor Robert Leaney; but in August 1939, just thirty years old, he was still a humble Anglican vicar ministering to the six hundred or so souls in his parish. It was a job he enjoyed enormously. He and his wife Liz had been there only a short time, and found nothing humdrum about the quiet little village nor anything unpleasant about their lives in it. Indeed before coming to Mountfield they would hardly have believed that such a place still existed. Both were born and bred in Birmingham, and after studying and being ordained in Oxford, Bob had returned to the Birmingham suburb of Oldbury to take up his first post as a curate. It had been ghastly in almost every way. Facing the same social conditions as Dr Haigh, he felt even less able to deal with them effectively: anyone could see the need for a doctor and would go to him if they were physically unhealthy, but the need for a curate was not so obvious. For Bob Leaney, life in Birmingham and the depressed industrial Midlands had been a deep well of unhappiness and frustration.

He would have agreed with Dr Haigh's suggestion that unhappiness caused illness; in Birmingham he too had spent much time with the poor and unemployed. Mountfield was like another world – as if, in a flash, one had been taken back forty or fifty years to a more stable England. Because of a prosperous gypsum mine outside the village there was hardly any unemployment. Being a small place it was easy for him to get to know his parishioners; each afternoon, after studying, preparing sermons and gardening in the morning, he would visit several households; and best of all he was welcomed by all. Even those who did not go to church (and he knew they were the majority) felt the village needed a vicar.

There was no deception in Mountfield's traditional atmosphere and appearance. In its centre the level crossing of the railway line from Hastings to London was one of the few signs of intrusion by the nineteenth century, let alone the twentieth. In the graveyard surrounding the small, sturdy church generations of Mountfield villagers were buried. Its registers went back to

1517, and in one of the earliest Bob Leaney had been delighted to discover a record of the burial of one Mercie Leny, no relation, he was sure, but it made him feel at home. The vicarage, originally an Elizabethan farmhouse, was an enormous rambling building, all tile-hung walls and tall heavy chimney stacks. Opposite was the entrance to the drive of Mountfield Court, residence of Commander Sydney Egerton; and he, the vicar reflected, was one main cause of the village's character, for he virtually ran it, filling to a T the role of squire.

In this idyllic, archaic setting the Revd Leaney sensed himself blossoming into his task and position. Yet no one and nowhere was immune that August. *Spannung* touched everyone, a sense of imminent probing evil, even in Mountfield's rural obscurity. It felt as if, creeping through the hedgerows and across the sunlit fields, there was a poisonous mist which you could not see or smell but knew was there, and which might at any instant rise and choke you.

But he did have one defence. For him the more serious crisis was not one of politics but of conscience, and with the help of his bishop, George Bell of Chichester, he had faced and overcome it. It was the classic dilemma of a Christian: if war came, what would he do? One by one Bishop George had asked all his ministers the same question. In his modulated voice he had spoken of General Montgomery. The memory still amused Bob: 'Favourable to our work – helps chaplains,' the bishop had said. 'But he's queer, you know; he's Irish, you know . . .' However, it was something else which had helped him to his solution. Bishop George knew Dietrich Bonhoeffer well – indeed he was probably the closest English friend Bonhoeffer had. For six years the German theologian, a Lutheran pastor, had opposed the Nazi regime in every way he could; in 1943 he would be arrested, and in 1945 (when still only thirty-nine years old) he would be executed. Talks with Bonhoeffer gave a special insight into the nature of the potential enemy. In other circumstances Bob would probably have been a pacifist; but not against the Nazis. A war against such a creed would be, he decided, the nearest possible thing to a morally justified war. He had discussed it with Liz and she agreed; so it was arranged that if necessary he would become chaplain to a battalion of the Royal Sussex Regiment, a part of the Territorial Army.

There was nothing further he could do; whatever happened next was out of his hands. Once the decision was taken the weight lifted; his crisis was over. With confidence in God, he gave himself back to his family and his ministry. *Spannung*, the time of tension, ceased to affect him. But for others that day, less fortunate in faith, it was reaching its highest pitch.

'I don't usually take tickets in the "dates" lottery,' wrote Sir Nevile Henderson from the British Embassy in Berlin. 'But I did venture to write to the Secretary of State [Lord Halifax] early in July to the effect that I foresaw the big crisis around about 27 August. I am afraid that I may not be far out.'

Cadogan was dining at home that evening with his wife Theo. They were just finishing the meal when the government's chief diplomatic adviser, Sir Robert Vansittart, telephoned 'in a high state of excitement'. Vansittart had just been talking on the phone to Halifax, and now was so worked up that Cadogan could barely grasp what he was saying: Halifax must come back at once, and the Prime Minister too. Realising there was little point in trying to make sense of this over the phone, Cadogan insisted he should come round at once and talk; and when Vansittart arrived, Cadogan noted later, 'I have never seen a man nearer nervous collapse.' Providing his distraught guest with a cold supper, he heard the reason: '*His* source has told him Hitler has chosen war, to begin between 25th and 28th.' Cadogan did not entirely credit the report. *Still*, he thought, *one can't ignore it*, and telephoned Halifax himself. Before long it was agreed that the Foreign Secretary would come to London next day, but that the Prime Minister need not be summoned yet.

'Eventually calmed Van down a bit,' the phlegmatic Under-Secretary wrote, 'and packed him off about 11. This is the beginning of the "War of Nerves". And I have seen the first casualty!'

It was just about then that a telegram was sent from Joachim von Ribbentrop to Ambassador von der Schulenburg. Its priority coding was 'Most Urgent'. Von Ribbentrop understood Commissar Molotov's caution at his proposal to bypass the usual system of diplomacy by coming in person to Moscow. 'We too, under normal circumstances, would naturally be ready to pursue a realignment of German–Russian relations through diplomatic channels, and to carry it out in the customary way.' But that would take time, and 'the present unusual situation makes it necessary, in the opinion of the Führer, to employ a different method which would lead to quick results'. To be more precise, that meant von Ribbentrop's 'imminent departure for Moscow.' Von der Schulenburg should make this possible. 'Please', von Ribbentrop concluded, 'emphasise that German foreign policy has today reached an historic turning-point.'

On that Friday *The Times* published a letter signed by no less than 375 notable academics. It was an appeal to the Prime Minister to drop his prejudice against Winston Churchill and include him again in the Cabinet. On Saturday 19 August, 'at this grave hour' and 'on behalf of some of my friends here informally assembled', Captain Alfred Henderson-Livesey of the Army Educational Corps sent Churchill a private letter:

We pray that God will give you health and strength to discharge the great task which awaits you. We feel that the continued exclusion of yourself from the ranks of the Government is a monstrous scandal which cannot long continue. We note that you have been spending your vacation inspecting the defences of France, while the First Minister of the Crown has been absorbed in the mysteries of rod and line in remote Highland streams. At this juncture your name alone can do for the people of this country what that of Kitchener did in 1914.

It was ponderously worded, but honestly meant; throughout the country there was a powerful feeling that putting Churchill back in government would be the clearest possible sign to Germany, specifically to Hitler, that if it came to it Britain meant business. At that moment Churchill was in Dreux, 50 miles west of Paris, resting after his tour of the Maginot Line in a château belonging to his cousin Consuelo Balsan: 'some sunshine days,' he wrote later, 'with a pleasant but deeply anxious company'. One of his fellow guests was the wife of the British Minister of Transport: 'She was expecting him to join her. Presently he telegraphed he could not come, and would explain why later . . . I found painting hard work in this uncertainty.'

On the same morning – a brilliantly sunny morning in every part of Great Britain – Andrew Hole, a young schoolmaster in Plymouth, received a letter from his Uncle James, who had lived in Germany since 1910. 'Can't quite believe Hitler will go to war,' said Uncle James. He should know, shouldn't he? He'd been there for twenty-nine years, since before the Great War. He'd seen that through; and after Germany's defeat and humiliation, he'd seen the Weimar Republic, the depression, the rule of President von Hindenburg, and since 1933 the renaissance of national spirit and confidence. It wouldn't be thrown away on a whim, on the throw of a dice, would it? He should know. But Andrew Hole was, he put in his diary, 'very depressed.' He was twenty-nine years old and had grown used to his pupils' jokes about his name, 'A. Hole', and that was not the cause of his mood. Uncle James might well be right, 'but there's little sign of tension slackening or of weakening in the German policy over Danzig'.

In Warsaw that day Colonel Beck had a session with Léon Noël, the French Ambassador to Poland. Like his British counterpart Sir Howard Kennard, Noël did his utmost to gain permission from the Polish Foreign Minister for the passage of Russians across Poland; and like Kennard, Noël failed. Beck's response was *un "non" catégorique*.

At twelve noon, as arranged, Lord Halifax, Sir Robert Vansittart and Sir Alexander Cadogan met in 'the Office'. Cadogan had already written down his proposals for an approach to Mussolini. By lunchtime they had agreed to send a telegram to Rome, to draft a letter for the Prime Minister to send to Hitler, and to let the Prime Minister stay a little longer in Scotland. Since he was due to return early on Monday morning there seemed no point in bringing him back two days early: they could handle all that needed to be done in the meantime.

Chamberlain's holiday had two main purposes: to relax and strengthen him in preparation for whatever might come next, and to maintain as far as possible an air of normality in the country and in Britain's dealings abroad. Nations might be panicked into war, but no one had ever been panicked into peace. Merely being on holiday did not mean, however, that he was unreachable or out of touch with developments; daily telephone calls to and from London kept him up to date, while key telegrams and digests of the situation were continuously forwarded to him. One such, sent this day, was a thousand-word letter drafted by Cadogan and signed by Halifax, summarising recent events, action taken and action proposed. Government and diplomacy did not go to sleep, but as usual in any parliamentary recess, their continuing work was more or less invisible to ordinary folk. The system functioned as well in this recess as in any other, and Chamberlain would have been going against his nature to have altered it. But whether it was publicly or politically appropriate in the August of 1939 was another matter. The intended signal of confident stability could easily be misread at home, as Henderson-Livesey's letter to Churchill made plain: 'We note that you have been spending your vacation inspecting the defences of France, while the First Minister of the Crown has been absorbed in the mysteries of rod and line.' This was less than fair to the Prime Minister: for better or worse, Churchill was not a member of the government, and he toured the Maginot Line as a private citizen. Since 1933 he had advocated increased defensive and offensive preparations for Britain; his tour was as natural a reaction for his pugnacious character as fishing was for the Prime Minister. In their different ways both were striving for peace. What if they had changed places? What if Churchill had travelled in an official governmental capacity? The questions are unanswerable today, except theoretically; and they were unanswerable then, when it was all real and urgent.

Chamberlain was as fully informed and aware as any individual could possibly be. He knew that the military talks in Moscow were temporarily halted until a reply came from Poland. He knew the Poles had not yet given in to diplomatic pressure. He knew that Hitler might respond to a visit from a German-speaking Englishman of high military rank, or to a personal letter from himself. He knew of the predicted possibility that war might begin in eight or nine days. 'All this,' Lord Halifax had written to him, 'may have its place in the general nerve storm which we have been told was designed to rage during these weeks . . . If the appreciation is in fact a true one, it is also a black one, and there is no time to lose.' Chamberlain knew too that the Italians were frightened, and were being encouraged in every way to restrain Hitler; in short, he knew that the diplomatic system was at full stretch in every country, but was still functioning and might yet succeed.

But in Moscow that Saturday afternoon, 19 August, Ambassador von der Schulenburg was trying hard to persuade Commissar Molotov to short-cut the system. Naturally Chamberlain did not and could not know this; and at first it seemed to von der Schulenburg that his efforts had failed. The Commissar could not be persuaded to act with speed, but kept on putting up problems, arguing details, and apparently doing all he could to avoid making any commitment. Von der Schulenburg left disheartened; then only half an hour later he was asked to return.

He had no idea what had happened in the interim, but as soon as he got back to the Kremlin it was obvious that some transformation had occurred. Welcoming him in, Molotov apologised for the inconvenience of a second meeting in one day, and without more ado presented him with a draft pact of non-aggression, and an invitation for Reichsminister von Ribbentrop to come to Moscow next week.

10

I have them!

FOR A MOMENT the Ambassador's heart leapt. At once, and correctly, he assumed that Stalin must have intervened personally. Never mind why, the important thing was that Molotov had done an about-face. But then, as the Commissar continued to speak, the Ambassador realised that there were, as there were bound to be, conditions attached. First the trade agreement being negotiated by Julius Schnurre and Georgi Astakhov must be concluded and signed as a preliminary; secondly, because the reception for a guest as important as Reichsminister von Ribbentrop would take time to prepare, a week must be allowed before his visit.

As conditions went, they scarcely seemed onerous. With a handshake, a bow and a murmur of thanks, von der Schulenburg took his leave and went directly back to his Embassy's communications room. At ten minutes past seven that evening, Saturday 19 August, his message was received in the Foreign Ministry in Berlin; and there it caused mixed delight and consternation – delight because it was an enormous advance, something firm to build on, and consternation because of the two seemingly light conditions. Those conditions were critical to the timing of Germany's – and Europe's – immediate future. Negotiations on the trade treaty had been concluded the night before with complete agreement: Germany would extend to Russia a merchandise credit of 200 million Reichsmarks at 5 per cent annual interest, to finance industrial plant, machine tools, armour plating and optical instruments; Russia would repay the loan with raw materials. Signature of the treaty had been expected today, but Julius Schnurre had just reported a delay: his Russian counterparts were awaiting instructions from Moscow.

This could hardly be coincidence. The Russians had manoeuvred themselves into a position of complete control. Worse yet, from Ribbentrop's and Hitler's point of view, they had put a timetable on the possibility of continued peace in the East. A minimum of seven days must elapse, they said, between the signing of the trade agreement and the signing of the non-aggression pact. Therefore, if the treaty was signed tomorrow, the 20th, the pact could be signed on the 27th. But all German plans in motion were targeted on an assault on Poland taking place at dawn on the 26th. Captain Dönitz's U-boats were in position. The pocket battleship *Graf Spee* was alert in the Atlantic. General Heydrich's 'Operation Himmler', the pseudo-Polish attack on the German radio station at Gleiwitz, was ready. German troops in sealed trucks were being moved to points on the Polish border. Yet if the attack should be launched with Russia unallied, what then? Before 26 August, Russia must become a German ally or else remain an imponderable, perhaps an unacceptable, risk.

Some people might have seen a certain irony in this. Hitler had inaugurated *Spannung*, the time of tension, and now he was falling prey to it himself.

Locked in the Rosau barracks in Vienna, Hilda Richter was all alone. There were other female prisoners there but none of her family. She was not certain how much her gaolers knew. Nor was she certain where her husband was, only that he had left Vienna for Britain. So had the Revd Grimes. Her twenty-three-year-old son Richard was there already, and had been for the past three years, since he had left the Hitler Youth. Now he was living just outside Kenilworth, close to her brother Edward. Indeed Richard was well settled, with a clerical job at A. C. Wickman's machine tool company in Coventry. Thinking of her family made her feel less alone; they would get her out of this place. But until they or someone else did so, all she could do was wait, hope, keep quiet, and try to avoid giving anything incriminating away.

She had not been badly treated – yet; but it was a strange thing, to say the least, for a girl from Tipperary to be a prisoner of the Gestapo. *It's been a long way from Tipperary indeed*, she thought unhappily. Her husband was Austrian-born but had become a naturalised Briton nearly forty years ago. After the Great War he had joined British Intelligence, and when their son Richard was six the family had moved back to Vienna, ostensibly so that Mr Richter could take up a job with the British Council in the Wöhlnerstrasse. Actually he was continuing his work for British Intelligence – the Vienna operation used a cardigan factory as its cover. It had been a pleasant life, spending Saturday nights at the English Club in the centre of Vienna; working for the church, Christ Church, opposite the British Legation in Lustigprienstrasse; watching Richard grow up – he had all his schooling in Vienna, and learned to speak German like a native. Smiling sadly, she remembered how even when he spoke English, he had a pronounced German accent. *I wonder if he's lost it yet? Probably not, probably never will.* He had joined the Hitler Youth simply because everyone else at school did; his parents, treating the organisation like a suspicious form of the Boy Scouts, knew that he was sufficiently level-headed not to fall for the propaganda side of it, and when he decided he would like to try and join the British army, his father had instigated his return 'home' to a country he had not seen for fourteen years.

That had been in 1936; then after the Anschluss last year, the forcible union of Hitler's homeland, Austria, with Germany, life in Vienna had begun to change radically. In the first two or three weeks it had not been as bad as they had all feared, but then the Gestapo had arrived. Their threat to all Jewish people was self-evident: she had seen for herself old Jewish men being forced, on hands and knees, to clean streets with sacred scrolls, degraded, humiliated. If they refused, the sneering Gestapo laughter stopped, and they were kicked and beaten mercilessly; she had no doubt that some died.

It was then that the Revd Grimes, a tall, lean, reserved man already in his sixties, began secretly baptising as many Jews as possible into the Christian faith. Hilda Richter helped him. Both understood they were placing themselves at some risk; but neither realised that they were doing so unnecessarily, and to no effect. Under Nazi race laws, simple baptism did not purge the crime of being Jewish.

Eventually the Richters sold their house and moved into a hotel, the Malek. It seemed a sensible precaution; in emergency they would be able to leave the country swiftly. Then unexpectedly the Gestapo had come – it was pure coincidence that Mr Richter was away. They had taken Hilda from the hotel garden one afternoon. Wearing her housecoat, she was not even allowed to change, but peremptorily invited to step into a waiting car. Such invitations were not open to refusal.

At the barracks her passport was confiscated and she was interviewed by an English-speaking officer. Where was her husband? Where was the Revd Grimes? Since she was not an accomplished liar, she was relieved to be able to answer truthfully that she did not know; but then with a surge of apprehension she remembered that in the pocket of her housecoat was a completed baptismal certificate, waiting for a ceremony that had not yet taken place. In sudden fear she asked if she might go to the lavatory. To her astonishment she was allowed to go unescorted, and she was able to flush the incriminating paper away.

They released her then. At once she went to Captain Thomas Kendrick, passport control officer at the British Legation. Without hesitation he gave her a new passport, and advised her to get out as soon as possible. Perhaps, if she had gone direct to the airport she might have got away, but she returned to the hotel. She should not have done that: she was promptly re-arrested.

An Austrian clerk in the Legation, himself under threat from the Gestapo, had overheard her worried discussion with Kendrick and reported it all.

Since then only four or five days had passed but it seemed an eternity. What day was today? Counting up, she realised it must be a Sunday – Sunday 20 August. What could she do? Nothing but go over in her mind again and again the things she had said, the answers she had given; wait and pray that she would be released before a war began. *Hold on, hold on.*

'Hold on, Zofya – here, take my hand.' At the quayside in Gdynia, Taddeus Olscholwski helped his wife down the ship's gangway to the shore. Their trip to Copenhagen, anticipated so happily, had been an ordeal which Zofya never wanted to repeat. The outward voyage, 300 miles across the sheltered southern waters of the Baltic, should have been pleasant, and was, until suddenly she understood who the majority of their fellow passengers were, and why they were there. At first she had thought only that the ship was unusually crowded; but gradually she overheard snatches of conversation. Some was in Polish, some in a German-sounding language she did not recognise at once. All sounded tense and nervous, and in a sickening instant of comprehension the whole scene made sense: the complete families huddling together as if for protection, the mothers with confused large-eyed children, the old women, the long-bearded men dressed entirely in black, pebble glasses under wide-brimmed hats.

'Taddeus,' she whispered urgently, 'are all these people Jewish?'

He looked at her in mild surprise, and nodded.

'But where are they going? I mean, so many of them. What are they doing?'

He answered in one word: 'Escaping.'

'But what from? Surely they're Polish? I heard some speaking Polish.'

'And Yiddish. I expect they're all Polish, or most of them. I suppose some might come from the Corridor. But that's what they're doing, anyway, getting out while they can. I don't suppose they really need to, but I don't blame them; I expect we'd do the same in their position.'

Dizzy with the intensity of her realisation, she leaned against him, clinging to his arm. With concern in his voice, he asked, 'Zofya – are you all right?' For a moment she could not answer. Taking the carpets and the silver from the villa to safety in Warsaw seemed all of a sudden like some kind of a game. Taking the children to Moniaki had felt, more than anything, like part of a family holiday. She was not stupid; she read the papers, listened to the wireless, but it was not until she saw for herself all these poor people in this horrible ship that she truly grasped, deep inside, what kind of a reality might be coming. I expect they're all Polish . . . and yet they were fleeing from Poland. She knew then what she must do. From its coldness, she was aware that her face was still white with shock, but she straightened up, opened her eyes, and spoke as firmly as she could.

'Taddeus, I want to go back as quickly as we can. I must go to the children.'

He looked at her steadily, silently, sadly before replying: 'Yes, you must go to the children.'

That had been two days and nights ago. Until they reached Copenhagen, Zofya had only felt the distance between them and the children increasing. In the beautiful Danish capital, she and Taddeus had walked hand in hand together, both trying to be cheerful. They took coffee in Tivoli park, admired the intricate spire of the Börsen, the Stock Exchange – it was formed by the spiralling tails of four dragons – and strolled out along the Langelinie promenade to see the Little Mermaid. Perhaps it was a mistake: the statue's delicate, chaste innocence spoke to Zofya only of their own small children.

'Of course they're not all like that,' remarked Taddeus. 'Mermaids, I mean. Lorelei, and the Greek ones, the Sirens, looked beautiful and sang delightfully, just in order to lure sailors on to the rocks, to their doom.' He grunted and smiled. 'But then Lorelei was a German mermaid, so what could you expect?'

'Dear God, Taddeus, I don't know what to expect at all.'

His attempt at a joke did not work; and at night in bed, he could only hold her until, tired of crying, she fell asleep at last.

Now, on Sunday, hastening from the ship, they found their car, went quickly to the villa, and set off on the drive south-eastwards to Lublin. There, they had agreed, Taddeus would leave Zofya to stay overnight with one of her aunts before proceeding in the morning to Moniaki; he would have to return at once to Gdynia, to be ready for work the next day.

As they travelled, Zofya could feel her spirits rising again. It was a long drive, 300 miles or so; and while they were on the road, two crucial developments took place in Germany. The first, at 2 p.m., was the signature of Germany's commercial treaty with Russia, delayed since the day before by lack of instruction from Moscow. With that signature achieved, Commissar Molotov's timetable came into effect: Reichsminister von Ribbentrop could visit him in seven days. But for Adolf Hitler that would be too late – by then he intended to have commenced his attack on Poland. The possibility, remote as it might be, of Russian aid then coming into Poland was an unacceptable risk: he could devastate Poland, no doubt, but at what cost, and for what result? At the cost of an eventual German defeat, and without gaining either the minerals or the land, the *Lebensraum* he so avidly sought; without even gaining the humiliation of Poland, a nation he had learned to loathe. No; it could not be done so. And yet to retreat from his plan was equally unbearable.

For hours he struggled with it, conscious that he was for once in the hands of another, that Josef Stalin, the Communist, had outmanoeuvred him, the Nazi, just as surely as he himself had in the past outmanoeuvred the democracies, and bloodlessly gained for the Reich the Saarland, the Rhineland, Austria, the Sudetenland. At length he decided.

If the message that followed at 4.35 p.m. had not been of such importance, its address would have appeared ridiculous: 'Herr J. V. Stalin, Moscow.' A personal appeal from the leader of the Nazi world to the leader of the Communist world – diametrically opposed ideologies, the opposite extremes of politics. But extremes can meet and touch. The Führer sincerely welcomed the new commercial agreement: it was the first step in a proper adjustment of relations. With a few small reservations which no doubt could be swiftly clarified, he accepted the Russian draft of a non-aggression pact. But speed was vital. Herr von Ribbentrop would have plenipotentiary authority: let him come at the earliest opportunity, the 22nd or the 23rd.

It was impossible to tell what the unconventional move cost in pride for Hitler; though couched in the language of a dictator, it was a begging letter. Nerves on stretch, he could only wait in the Berghof, pacing to and fro in agitated silence. No one dared to speak to him. *Geduld – halt' aus*. Patience – hold on.

Galeazzo Ciano's patience was also close to breaking point. The previous day he had left Italy to visit Albania, going first to Tiranë, or as he called it, Tirana. He had been much encouraged by the country's spiritual and material progress, and especially gratified to receive news that the Collar of the Annunziata had been conferred upon him, making him an honorary cousin of the King of Italy. He felt confident that in a few years Albania could be the richest region of Italy, 'if we can work in peace'. But still he was distracted by thoughts of what was going on in Europe, events 'serious and sad'. He proceeded by the steamer *Duke of Abruzzi* sixty miles down the coast to an enthusiastic welcome in Vlórë (which he called Valona). His first thought on seeing it was, *What misery*! Tirana, a humble enough place, was a metropolis in comparison. Nevertheless there was an excellent bay, the sea was rich and the locality was beautiful; all that was needed was a few years' work.

But then a telegram reached him: he should be in Rome that evening. Cancelling the rest of his tour, he returned at once to the Italian capital. 'This is what had happened,' he wrote later. Though the British had sent Mussolini an appeal to try to settle the dispute peacefully, he had finally made up his mind 'to support Germany at any cost'. Ambassador Attolico, who was present, was to return to Berlin with a communication stating that intention. Pressing Mussolini for his reasons, Ciano was exasperated to find they were feeble in the extreme: if the Pact of Steel was broken 'the whole world would say that Italy is cowardly, that she is not ready, and that she has drawn back in the face of the spectre of war'. The fact that Italy's genuine military unreadiness made withdrawing from the pact common sense, not cowardice, cut no ice with the Duce; he was not going to have people saying he was a coward. *Holds very stubbornly to his idea*, Ciano noted. By pushing hard and using the British appeal as an excuse, he managed to get the final decision deferred until the morning, and left the conference with some hope remaining; but he saw that Attolico departed in tears.

It was about then that Ambassador Kennard in Warsaw was making up his own mind about a telegram from Lord Halifax. The Anglo–French–Russian military talks must not be allowed to fail because of Polish non-cooperation. 'I am convinced,' wrote Halifax, 'that such failure must encourage Herr Hitler to resort to war, in which Poland would bear the brunt of the first attack. On the other hand, I fully believe that the conclusion of a politico-military agreement with the Soviet Union would be calculated to deter him from war.'

From his conversations with Colonel Beck two days before, Kennard knew at first hand that Beck's assessment was exactly contrary. He had told Halifax so, of course, but realised that the first-hand emphasis had not come across; things looked different in London, as somehow they always did. For his own part, he sympathised with the colonel's point of view, and, feeling there would be no point in trying any new arguments on him, told London so. By then, however, as the Prime Minister was settling into his sleeping cabin in the overnight train from Scotland, Lord Halifax was pondering a cryptic message from Berlin. It proposed that Hermann Goering, Commander-in-Chief of the Luftwaffe, should secretly fly to London, meet the Prime Minister and explore any remaining avenues of peace.

Adolf Hitler could not sleep that night. Prowling through the rooms of the Berghof, he seemed near to nervous collapse. Close by, his doctors kept a discreet but watchful eye on him.

'The very confident attitude of the crews deserves special mention,' Captain Dönitz recorded on 21 August. 'In my opinion it is a sign that the broad masses of people have great faith in the government.' He certainly seems to have had such faith: that day he moved his command ship 170 miles eastwards to Swinemünde. Since he had already decided to move 120 miles west to Wilhelmshaven 'if *Fall Weiss* should develop into a major war', it appears that he was still not expecting any serious conflict in the West. Ironically, Swinemünde today is called Swinoujcsie, and is part of Poland.

Meanwhile, deep in Poland, Zofya Olscholwska was travelling with an almost light heart from Lublin towards Moniaki. This last three-hour stage of the journey was always her favourite. In winter it would be done by horsedrawn sleigh, with people's ears protected from the brisk cold by foxtail muffs; in summer, as now, the conveyance was a horse and trap. As they bowled along, the clop of the hooves, the rumble of the wheels and the merry musical jingling of the harness combined into a lively harmony. Quietly she hummed, and sometimes sang to herself, little songs of love and Poland. Her emotions were mixed: she was nearly with the children, but Taddeus was already back in Gdynia. When they had parted last night it had been with a prayer that very soon they would all be reunited, yet now as the kilometres passed her fear began to slip slowly away, to be replaced by a growing confidence that all would be well. In fact Taddeus and Zofya did not see each other again for more than five years.

As Chamberlain's train drew into London that Monday morning, Sir Alexander Cadogan picked up Lord Halifax early and at 11.30 took him to No 10 Downing Street. 'Discussed letter to Hitler, and all phases of the crisis,' Cadogan noted two days later. 'Frightful day, but don't remember all details.'

Among other things, they agreed to accept the suggestion that Goering should come to London, and accordingly made secret arrangements for 23 August. From William Strang, head of the Foreign Office's Central Department, they also learned of a drastic French initiative in the Moscow talks, communicated by Charles Corbin, French Ambassador to London. Acting on the advice of his colleague in Moscow, and of General Doumenc, the French government had decided to override Colonel Beck's refusal to allow Russian troops across Poland. The talks, Corbin pointed out, were due to resume, indeed should be under way even now, and as soon as he was authorised Doumenc was going to give consent in principle to the Soviet demand. Corbin requested that Great Britain should cooperate with this, and when asked on what basis such consent could be given, explained that Colonel Beck had insisted his refusal should not be made known to the Russians. It might be a pretty loose interpretation of the truth, but giving consent in principle would certainly keep knowledge of Beck's refusal secret. 'In short,' said Strang to Cadogan, 'the French Government have gone ahead without consulting and now ask for our support.' And he gave his own view, 'It may well be that their judgement of the Polish attitude is the right one.'

But it was already too late. That very morning, to his great excitement, Admiral Drax had at long last received the written credentials authorising him to negotiate. Marshal Voroshilov, however, had decided that pending a definite answer on the Polish question the talks should be postponed indefinitely. The foreign delegations agreed reluctantly; but before they parted company both sides spoke their minds frankly. Voroshilov had it put on record that he and his colleagues could not grasp how the negotiators had been sent without exact instructions on the passage of Soviet troops across Poland, 'such an elementary matter'. Drax and Doumenc responded in kind: the Soviet insistence on 'difficult political questions' was beyond their understanding. Complete mutual incomprehension was all the two sides shared.

Shortly after twelve noon a message was sent from the German Embassy in Moscow to the Berghof. Seizing and scanning the paper, Hitler cursed in frustration: Count von der Schulenburg would not be permitted to see Commissar Molotov until 3 p.m. In Germany, that would be the early evening.

Mussolini and Ciano argued all day. As soon as Ciano arrived at the Palazzo Venezia, the Duce confirmed his decision to go along with the Germans. Vehemently opposing this, some inspiration gave Ciano a new line: 'I went to Salzburg in order to adopt a common line of action. I found myself face to face with a diktat. The Germans, not ourselves, have betrayed the alliance . . . We were to have been partners, not servants.' Sensing that Mussolini had not thought of that angle before, he followed it up dramatically: 'Tear up the Pact. Throw it in Hitler's face, and Europe will recognise in you the natural leader of the anti-German crusade.'

He knew that to be thought a coward was the one thing which would make Mussolini act. Hitherto it had seemed to the Duce that reneging on the pact would be seen as cowardice. On the contrary, declared Ciano, it would be cowardly to follow in Hitler's footsteps. Proud defiance, not humble servitude, was the proper reaction for Italy. 'Do you want me to go to Salzburg? Very well, I shall go and speak to the Germans as they should be spoken to.'

Finally, by needling, cajoling and thundering, Ciano got the reaction he was after: Mussolini approved his proposal to invite Ribbentrop to a meeting at the Brenner Pass 'to reaffirm our rights as Axis partners.' The Duce made it clear he did not want the Axis to collapse. *If it should*, Ciano thought, *I would not be the one to weep over it.* They tried to telephone Ribbentrop, but could not get through to him until half past five. The German Foreign Minister stalled, explaining that he could not answer at once: he was waiting for 'an important message from Moscow' and would telephone Ciano later that evening. *Strange* . . . For the time being, however, Ciano put that to the back of his mind and conferred again with the Duce. Between them they drew up a list of four points covering what seemed to be all the possible eventualities. Privately Ciano felt that three of the four were irrelevant, 'but one is fundamental: we shall not intervene if the conflict is provoked by an attack on Poland'.

Harold Nicolson, author and Member of Parliament, dined on shore that evening. During the adjournment debate of 2 August, in spite of his own deep doubts about its wisdom, he would have accepted the government line. In the end, though, he gave his support again to Churchill – 'I cannot let the old lion enter the lobby alone' – and commiserated when the majority of members decided they should all go on holiday. Since he could do nothing further personally, Nicolson did go on holiday, and had been enjoying himself enormously. The previous year he had borrowed £2000 from his wife, the writer Vita Sackville-West, and bought a yawl, a small two-masted yacht. 'Really this is just the boat I wanted,' he told her in the spring of 1939. 'I didn't really want a swank boat, even as I never wanted a Pekinese.' But it was not until the summer that, accompanied by his son Nigel and close friend, John Sparrow, he was able to get some decent sailing in. In the course of later events he would never sail his yawl again.

Unlike David Howarth in Northern Ireland, learning by trial and error how to sail single-handed, Nicolson employed a professional crew of two, sometimes three, under a skipper named Captain De'Ath. Confronted with his employer's lightheartedness, De'Ath turned out as humourless as his name. 'We tried all yesterday to cheer him up,' Nicolson wrote to Vita in the middle of August:

> We threw a mattress into the sea (not a smile): we shot at jellyfish with the air-gun (not a flicker of interest): we fished for jellyfish with the canvas bucket (not the slightest attention paid to us, until we dropped the bucket overboard and it sank: he then said, 'There's the bucket gone, and one can't get buckets in France.' 'But you can, Captain; truly you can.')

It was not until they ran into heavy seas and fog off the dangerous rocky coast of Ushant that De'Ath was able to show his skills. 'The Captain, when tiresome things occur, is perfectly charming,' Nicolson wrote. 'I am getting to like him.'

They had hoped to sail to Brest, but judging it too risky, they headed back across the Channel 'feeling cheated, frustrated but wise', and ended up in the Cornish port of Fowey. After seventeen days on board, the idea of dinner in the Fowey Hotel was irresistible; but when the meal was over and they were walking back down the hotel corridor, reality came in. From the wireless in the hotel office they could hear the news. 'It looks as if the Germans have arranged with the Italians . . . to stage their coup at once. The Germans are half-mobilising and the French are doing the same.' With a sense of 'terrific imminence', the small party rowed out across a satin-smooth harbour to their boat; and on board Nicolson jotted in his diary: 'How strange it is that this war which I have dreaded for six years and which I have so repeatedly forecast now seems close upon us.' Three months ago he thought there had been some chance of a negotiated settlement over Danzig, but 'we have missed that chance as usual. It looks like war. I am glad that fate has given me these weeks of happiness before the great ordeal begins.'

In the Berghof, Hitler dined late. The meal was tense and silent, his own mood dominating the others'. Among them were Albert Speer, his favourite architect, and the photographer Heinrich Hoffmann, trying to diminish the clink of their knives and forks, when a messenger came and handed a telegram to Hitler. Everyone paused. Appetites already dwindling because of the strained atmosphere vanished altogether. Covertly they watched him read the telegram. His face turned scarlet with passion. He put the paper down and gazed unseeingly out of the window, then abruptly turned back towards his guests, clenched both hands into fists and crashed them so hard on the table that the plates jumped. '*I have them!*' Speer recalled that Hitler's emotion was so powerful he could scarcely speak, and he said it again in pure ecstasy: 'I have them!'

That was all: he did not explain but, evidently worn out, lolled back in his chair and signalled to the others to continue eating. They did so in unbroken silence. It was not until after they had finished that, calling for champagne, he revealed that the telegram came from Stalin. Ribbentrop could go to Moscow on the 23rd; the non-aggression pact would be signed in time for *Fall Weiss*. Instantly the mood in the dining room changed to huge excitement. Amid the hubbub of toasts and congratulations, everyone present knew that they had just heard the first news of one of the century's most important strokes of diplomacy.

By an odd coincidence, the day before, Hitler's cry of delight was pre-echoed six hundred miles away by Winston Churchill, in grim, sombre tone. At his cousin's château in Dreux, accompanied by the French artist Paul Maze, he was painting the Moulin. He and Maze had been friends for over twenty years; the Frenchman was one of the first to encourage him in art. As they sat side by side at their easels, Churchill suddenly turned to Maze and said: 'This is the last picture we shall paint in peace for a very long time.' It was hardly a sentence calculated to help Maze's concentration, and Churchill's ability to think hard and simultaneously about painting and war astonished him. From time to time as they worked the Englishman threw out further remarks about the French and German armies: '"They are strong, I tell you, they are strong," he would say. Then his jaw would clench his large cigar, and I felt the determination of his will.' *I have them!* It is almost as if Churchill anticipated the Führer's distant shout of joy, for in his diary Maze noted Churchill's own resolute remark: "'Ah," he would say, "with it all, we shall have him.'"

The day is charged . . . and full of threats

BY MIDNIGHT on 21 August it was known in every press agency and government office in Europe. In Britain, on the morning of Tuesday the 22nd, *The Times* summarised it in four headlines:

FULL CABINET TODAY

GROWING TENSION

GERMAN TROOPS MASSING

NAZI PACT WITH RUSSIA

'The sinister news burst upon the world like an explosion,' Churchill wrote later. 'A complete bombshell,' said Leslie Hore-Belisha, British Secretary of State for War. 'A sensation,' wrote Paul Schmidt, 'to Germany and the world.' In Westphalia a young German soldier called Bernt Engelmann heard his 'Uncle Franz', an old friend of the family, say pensively, 'This can't possibly turn out well.' In Australia Daphne King saw her father turn pale as he listened to the announcement. He opened his mouth, stood up straight, closed his mouth again and left the room without a word. Charles King, the Communist editor, was experiencing his first terrible doubt about the party. 'A tactical master stroke,' said Ulrich von Hassell, 'and at the same time . . . proof of absolute unscrupulousness and lack of principle.' Harold Nicolson, sailing from Fowey to Plymouth Sound, did not hear the news until the evening. 'This smashes our peace front . . . How Ribbentrop must chuckle,' he wrote. 'I feel rather stunned by this news and sit on deck in bewilderment with the fishing smacks around me.' In Sheffield the teacher Andrew Hole was no less bewildered: 'What on earth can it mean?' In unheard answer, Harold Nicolson added: 'I fear it means we are humbled to the dust.'

Galeazzo Ciano's reaction was unusually muted: 'A new act opened . . . There is no doubt that the Germans have struck a master blow.' But it did not take a politician to see the implications, which Andrew Hole expressed as well as anyone: 'It has given Germany a big fillip towards confidence and action.'

Just how big a fillip would be known in London by the end of the week. Not a minute was being wasted in Germany. Early in the morning, armed with the Führer's final instructions 'to make every offer and accept every demand', Reichsminister von Ribbentrop left the Berghof for Berlin. Shortly afterwards a line of staff cars with fluttering swastika pennants raced up the winding road to the Mountain Court. Senior military commanders followed by their Chiefs of Staff strode over the crunching gravel, up the famous flight of stairs and into the spacious reception hall. There, facing an enormous desk, a semi-circle of chairs were ready. Greeting each other, the officers settled themselves; and then Hitler came in. As one, his audience stood up, their right arms rigidly outstretched in salute – 'Heil Hitler!' The hall echoed.

His excitement was obvious. As he spoke, some of the officers took notes, and one general passed his to a member of his staff. Later he in turn gave them to a journalist in Berlin, who passed them on again to the British Embassy. They were immediately forwarded to London. From newsreels and wireless broadcasts, Hitler's rasping, metallic voice was almost as familiar there as it was in Germany, and reading the notes was a peculiar experience, almost as if one was standing outside a window at the Berghof eavesdropping:

There are only three great statesmen in the world, Stalin, myself and Mussolini. Mussolini is the weakest, for he has been able to break the power neither of the Crown nor of the Church. Stalin and I are the only ones who visualise the future. So in a few weeks I shall stretch out my hand to Stalin at the common German–Russian frontier, and with him undertake to redistribute the world. Our strength lies in our quickness and our brutality . . . I have given the command and I shall shoot everyone who utters one word of criticism, for the goal to be obtained in the war is not that of reaching certain lines but of physically destroying the opponent.

He spoke like a man possessed, in an atmosphere filled with the vibrant, dominating intensity of his will and confidence. 'I have put my Death-Head formation in place with the command relentlessly and without compassion to send into death many women and children of Polish origin and language. Only thus can we gain the living space we need . . . Poland will be depopulated and settled with Germans.' Prime Minister Chamberlain and Premier Daladier of France, 'those poor worms', might institute a blockade but would be too cowardly to attack. 'As for the rest, gentlemen, the fate of Russia will be exactly the same . . . After Stalin's death – he is a very sick man – we will break the Soviet Union. Then there will begin the dawn of the German rule of the earth.'

As he continued, his language became coarse and crude. He admitted he had one worry: 'namely that Chamberlain or some other such *Saukerl* [filthy wretch], will come at the last minute with proposals . . . He will fly down the stairs, even if I personally have to trample on his belly in front of the photographers. No, it is too late for this. The attack upon and the destruction of Poland begins on Saturday, early.' Explaining that German soldiers disguised as Poles would open the attack, thus giving a reason for Germany's assault, he added: 'Whether the world believes it is *Scheissegal* [lit. shit-equal]. The world believes only in success.'

He had begun by speaking of the greatness of Genghis Khan; he ended in the same way, telling his commanders that for them an era of fame and honour was opening, such as had not been seen for centuries. 'Be hard,' he exhorted them, 'be without mercy, act more quickly and brutally than the others. The citizens of western Europe must tremble with horror. This is the most humane way of conducting a war – it scares the others off.'

At that point, according to the notes, 'Goering jumped on a table, thanked bloodthirstily and made bloodthirsty promises. He danced like a wild man.' Perhaps he did, but different perceptions can give quite different accounts of one event. Years later, on trial for his life at Nuremburg, Goering indignantly denied this particular episode. 'I want you to know', he told his judges, 'that the speech was made in the great hall of Hitler's private house. I do not have the habit of jumping on tables in private houses. That would have been an attitude completely inconsistent with that of a German officer.' Nevertheless, as Hitler's speech in the Berghof ended on the morning of 22 August 1939, his audience responded with enthusiastic applause – some because they believed it all, others because, if nothing else, they believed the threat that any opponents would be shot.

As the Nazi officers applauded their Führer, Winston Churchill was being driven from Dreux to Paris. There had been enough in the news bulletins to be profoundly unsettling, but too few details. He felt he must go home, and explained apologetically to his hostess: 'At least there I can find out what is going on.' During the drive his secretary Mary Shearburn took notes from his dictation. When he finished, they sat in silence as the car proceeded, and watched the passing countryside – a beautiful pastoral scene of wide corn-fields, the crop heavy with ripeness and waving gently like an undulating sea. Churchill gazed at it for some time, deep in thought, looking more and more grave, until at last, slowly and sorrowfully, he voiced his thoughts: 'Before the harvest is gathered in – we shall be at war.'

His return through Paris gave him the opportunity of inviting to lunch his military host, General Joseph Georges. Over the meal they discussed the relative strengths of the French and German armies. General Georges had all the figures to hand, and was able to classify the divisions by quality as well as quantity. Churchill was deeply impressed by the results. Digesting the balance sheet of potential war, he said something he had never said before to the French: 'But you are the masters.' General Georges hesitated. War, they both knew, was not a simple matter of accountancy. After a moment he replied. 'The Germans have a very strong army, and we shall never be allowed to strike first. If they attack, both our countries will rally to their duty.' For the British people, Churchill believed it; he had faith in them. Looking closely across the table at Joseph Georges, he sensed that the French general had the same faith in the French people. Churchill was willing to accept it; he wanted to accept it, not as an Oriental placing of spirit over matter but a sum which began with a blunt comparison of material strength and which then added the immeasurable spirit of the nation. 'Yes,' he answered. 'They will both rally, as you say. And now, if I may say it, *bon appétit!*'

The formula for the sudden recall of Parliament was fairly well known in Westminster; as Chamberlain had pointed out, it had been used at least six times in the past four years. Whatever feelings it hid or provoked, its style was calm and authoritative:

I, Edward Algernon Fitzroy, Speaker of the House of Commons, do hereby give notice that I am satisfied, after consulting with His Majesty's Government, that the public interest requires that the House should meet at an earlier time than the 3rd day of October.

By virtue, therefore, of the Resolution of the House of Commons of the 2nd day of this instant August, I now give notice that the House shall meet on Thursday the 24th day of August.

Given under my hand this the 22nd day of August, 1939.

[signed] E. A. Fitzroy, Speaker.

The recall was only one result of a three-hour meeting of the Cabinet that afternoon, its first session since the adjournment twenty days earlier. The mood in the Cabinet room was of concentrated high anxiety, the imminence of peril emphasised by a ghastly announcement made that morning by the Town Clerk of Westminster. Parents and guardians residing in the area were asked to 'bring their infants up to two years of age to one of the below-mentioned centres during the week commencing Thursday 24 August . . . to be fitted with gas helmets'.

That was the reality of late August 1939. If anyone beforehand had failed to grasp the full seriousness of the threat they faced, the dreadful idea of having to fit infants with gas helmets brought it savagely home.

The Cabinet meeting was hectic but productive. Lord Halifax briefed his colleagues on developments in Moscow, both of the Anglo-French mission and the astounding new initiative from Germany, and pointed out that the critical problem was still Danzig. Solving that was still the only way to preserve peace, whatever might transpire between Ribbentrop and Stalin. By 6 p.m. ministers had agreed to make preparations for evacuation; to activate Civil Defence, including blackout; and to call up a further 5000 naval reservists and all squadrons of the Auxiliary Air Force including balloon squadrons, along with key groups of all coastal defence and anti-aircraft units. The remainder could be called up without reference to the Cabinet at the discretion of Leslie Hore-Belisha, the War Secretary. They also agreed to prepare measures to stem an alarmingly large outflow of gold from the Bank of England – in one single day 30 million pounds' worth – for as the Chancellor of the Exchequer, Sir John Simon, pointed out, what was left was 'the minimum required for our War Chest'. After prolonged discussion they agreed too that Chamberlain's letter to Hitler should be sent; but perhaps their most important agreement was to declare publicly that whatever arrangement Germany and Russia came to, it would make no difference to Britain's obligations towards Poland.

The question of the letter had been difficult. Some ministers felt a public announcement would be just as effective; others did not want to drop the idea of a personal emissary. Chamberlain's own view was that a firmly worded letter with practical proposals for a solution would be the best. Hitler would have to pay attention to this, but could ignore a public announcement. A trained diplomat would handle the delicate situation best; and, since Parliament's duty on the 24th would be to pass the Emergency Powers (Defence) Bill, that would be the best time for the letter to be sent. As they were debating the matter, they were interrupted by the arrival of a telegram from the British Consul-General in Danzig. Ernst von Weizsäcker of the German Foreign Ministry had sent a colonel there, pleading for an emissary to come while Ribbentrop was away. Whether an emissary or a letter was sent, it would have to be by the next day. Faced with such immediacy, the Cabinet chose the letter. Just after 6 p.m. Sir Alexander Cadogan was called over from the Foreign Office 'to give effect to their decisions'. At ten minutes to ten ('awful rush,' he noted) it was sent. Sir Nevile Henderson, British Ambassador in Berlin, would take it personally to Hitler the following afternoon.

By the time the letter was dispatched, Ribbentrop and his team of thirty were past Danzig and in the East Prussian port of Königsberg. Two large Focke-Wulf Condor aircraft, their tails emblazoned with giant swastikas, had been provided for their transport, and the Park Hotel taken over for their accommodation. Among the delegation, to his own astonishment, was Paul Schmidt, Hitler's interpreter. Hauled unwillingly yet again from leave, he had known no more than anyone else about the impending pact until he arrived in Berlin. Even then he did not see what use he could be, because he did not speak Russian; nevertheless he was to report on and record negotiations and agreements. Once over the initial surprise he rather liked the idea, and friends envied him his journey to 'the distant planet'. But it was not exactly a holiday. At Königsberg Ribbentrop kept the team frantically busy, preparing material for the forthcoming discussions, constantly telephoning Berlin and Berchtesgaden ('asking for the most un-get-at-able papers,' Schmidt remarked), and filling sheet after sheet of paper 'with notes in handwriting which grew larger and larger as the night wore on'. At one point Schmidt and some of the other younger delegates were able to get away 'from this statesmanlike activity' to the Park bar. Back in Berlin, people had generally been pleased at the possibility of a pact with Russia, feeling it would obviate war. Schmidt disagreed. In his judgment Hitler would become still rasher and more irresponsible if a pact were concluded; so in the bar with his colleagues he drank 'a farewell toast to peace'.

In Moscow the Anglo-French missions had spent the day in a fever of frustration. At last, with their governments' authority to override the Polish refusal, they were able to present Marshal Voroshilov with the answer he wanted; but mysteriously he had been unavailable all day. They did not track him down until the evening, and when they found him, he made it absolutely plain that they were too late.

> The question of military collaboration with France [he told Doumenc] has been in the air for several years, but has never been settled. Last year, when Czechoslovakia was perishing, we waited for a signal from France, but none was given . . . The French and English Governments have now dragged out the political and military discussions too long. For that reason the possibility is not to be excluded that certain political events may take place . . .

That same evening the British Ambassador, Sir William Seeds, gained an interview with Molotov. It was little less than a confrontation. Infuriated at the Russian's secretive system, Seeds accused him face to face of having acted throughout the military discussions in bad faith. It was hardly diplomatic language, Seeds knew, but he was sure now that it could do no harm; and

135

'after months of patience and self-control' he was glad to have the chance to say what he really felt.

The port of Königsberg was nearly seven hundred years old. It had been founded by the Teutonic Knights in 1255, and in the Middle Ages had been capital of East Prussia; it was German through and through. As Joachim von Ribbentrop worked there in nervous excitement through the night of 22 August 1939, the last thing he could have imagined was that by the end of 1945, as a more or less direct consequence of his efforts, little would remain of the original town, and Königsberg rebuilt would become Kaliningrad, a major naval base and the third largest port in the Soviet Union.

'Of course, with the naval base more or less just down the road,' Frank Harding said thoughtfully, 'I suppose that if the worst comes to the worst we might be rather a good target.'

'Really, dear,' his wife protested, 'I do wish you wouldn't say such things. Or if you must, then not in front of the baby.' Richard, thirteen months old that morning, gave no sign of being interested in anything apart from breakfast.

'Sorry . . . Just thinking aloud. I see Parliament's going back tomorrow. About time too, lazy so-and-sos. Not much they can do about this extraordinary Russian business, I imagine. Perhaps I ought to stand as a member – must be easier than selling furniture.'

His wife, engaged with the baby, had not been paying full attention, but now she looked at him in surprise. 'And leave Harding's? Surely not!'

Smiling, he shook his head. 'Of course not. Harding's without a Harding – Grandfather would turn in his grave. Anyway, I'd better be off now. Don't forget, I'll be late back; ARP tonight.'

'Yes, of course, darling. I'll keep something hot for you.' Following him to the front door, she added, 'I wonder how many people they'd have for ARP if the instruction took place somewhere else – a church hall, say, instead of a pub.'

'Oh, just as many, I'm sure; they all take it pretty seriously. The Tamar's very suitable in many ways – good-sized room. It's not as if we actually practise in the bar, after all. Lucky little fellow,' he said, fondly stroking his small son. 'Lying in a pram on silken pillows while Daddy's hard at work. Well . . . off we go.'

At the roadside, turning back for a moment, he saw his wife holding up Richard's tiny hand in a farewell wave. It was only a short bus ride from Hartley to the family store in the centre of Plymouth. Proud, happy and apprehensive, he looked out at the city. It would certainly be a target. Curious to think that his brother Denis, for all that he was a soldier, would probably be in less immediate danger in the barracks in Rangoon than they would at home. If, if. Air Raid Precautions, there was a sinister ring to the phrase. ARP sounded so much less ominous. Yet 'precautions' had a sensible sound as well. Be prepared.

As the bus trundled along, on the other side of the city Harold Nicolson was walking grimly towards North Road railway station. Waking to a warm, cloudy, almost windless morning, he had hoped at first for a pleasant little potter around in the yawl; but then he too had read in the papers the announcement that the House of Commons was to be summoned next day. Leaving his son Nigel and his friend John Sparrow on board, he said goodbye with a sad heart.

Eight thirty in Britain was 10.30 a.m. in Moscow. By then the two Condors had been in the air for two and a half hours, droning over the apparently endless Russian plains. Peering through the windows Paul Schmidt saw vast forests unrolling below, with widely scattered villages and isolated farms with dark thatched roofs. He was particularly struck by that: German farms had red tiled roofs, which looked bright and cheerful from the air. These in contrast looked very dour, very sombre; very Russian.

In Paris citizens were being advised to leave the capital if possible. Trains and aircraft were already filling steadily with Britons and neutral nationals making a hasty return to their own countries. In London the American Ambassador Joseph Kennedy came to express his concern to Lord Halifax. Referring to the latest development between Russia and Germany, he said, 'I believe there's a real danger that the Poles just don't appreciate their true position,' and added that in his view, pressure must be brought to bear upon them. Halifax's reply, that it was impossible, jolted him badly. He sought and gained an interview with the Prime Minister. What, he wondered, could now be done? There must be something. Chamberlain, seeming deeply depressed, did not think so. 'I have done everything I can think of,' he said unhappily, 'and it seems as if all my work has come to naught.' Then in a sudden access of angry energy he told Kennedy what was upsetting him most. 'The futility of it all,' he burst out. 'That is the thing that's frightful. After all, we cannot save the Poles – all we can do is carry on a war of revenge. And that will mean the destruction of the whole of Europe.'

Yet that had always been a possible outcome of the Prime Minister's method of coping with Nazi Germany.

The Condors landed punctually at noon. During their final approach the entire German delegation, including Ribbentrop, had been staring fascinated from the aircraft windows. Schmidt's first thought on sighting Moscow was that from the air it looked exactly like London or Berlin, a sea of houses; but once on the ground, taxiing to a halt, a sense of pervading unreality took hold of him. It was all so completely improbable, yet it was happening. There was a shield with 'Moscou' written on it in French, and the red and gold hammer and sickle flag leaned across the black, white and red swastika flag in a most friendly manner. There was the Italian Ambassador Rosso, whom he had known in Geneva, in the welcoming committee and their own Ambassador, Count von der Schulenburg, stood alongside a group of high Soviet officials, including Molotov's deputy Potemkin. *Couldn't have had a more appropriate name*, thought Schmidt.

With his colleagues he allowed himself to be ushered into one of a fleet of Russian cars, large and comfortable, looking like American Buicks. The motorcade sped off towards the capital, down a dead straight, very broad road. It reminded him of the autobahns at home. *Dictators seem to delight in the magnificence of broad roads*, he reflected, deciding at the same time that the immediate surroundings were unutterably bleak and dreary. First stop was the German Embassy, where the delegation had a hurried meal; and at that point, to his consternation, Schmidt discovered his suitcase had been mislaid somewhere between there and the airport. It contained his only dark suit, which 'even in Moscow' was essential for formal occasions. Without it he could not go any further, and Ribbentrop, who was in a great hurry, was definitely not going to wait around. The Reichsminister was taken to see Commissar Molotov, and Schmidt, to his chagrin, had to remain at the Embassy. Rather than waste his time, his host's wife (who spoke perfect Russian) suggested they might go for a tour of Moscow. Schmidt accepted, and they walked for several hours; but apart from the incongruous luxury of the underground railway system, with its chandeliers and marble walls, he found the Soviet capital unexpectedly dull. To begin with he thought it was merely that it all looked like any other great European city, until suddenly he realised 'the essential difference' – no one looked at all cheerful. The people were clean and neat but colourless in faces and clothing, and 'a melancholy grey pall seemed to hang over everyone and everything'. He wished again he was with the delegation: it was frustrating not to know how they were getting on.

In other towns and capitals, other people were equally on tenterhooks. 'The day is charged with electricity,' wrote Ciano, 'and full of threats.' Mussolini had authorised him to give the British Ambassador, Sir Percy Loraine, a plan for a solution. First Danzig should be returned to the Reich, then negotiations and 'a great peace conference' would follow. Rome was intensely hot, and either through emotion or the heat Loraine fainted, or nearly fainted, in Ciano's arms. In Warsaw, in one final joint effort, Ambassadors Kennard and Noël were trying again to make Colonel Beck change his mind. In Washington President Roosevelt was writing an appeal for peace to Hitler; and in the Berghof Hitler, highly agitated, was reading in Chamberlain's letter to him that Britain's guarantee to Poland still stood.

Late in the Moscow afternoon Ribbentrop hurtled back from the Kremlin to the German Embassy, 'positively bubbling over with enthusiasm', and over another quick meal told Schmidt again and again that things were going splendidly with the Russians. Molotov and he had discussed how to carve up Poland; he had checked with Hitler to see if Russia could have the Baltic ports of Libau and Windau. Within half an hour the reply had been there: *'Ja, stimmt.'* Yes, agreed. Now, confident there would be a pact that evening, Ribbentrop raced back to the Kremlin with von der Schulenburg and the head of the Embassy's legal department in tow; and once again, because the Reichsminister did not want a new face cropping up in the discussions, Schmidt was left behind to wait.

'Papa says that war is inevitable,' Niusia Zamecka wrote in her diary. 'I asked Papa why Hitler wants to attack us, and Papa said it's because he's a greedy bully.' It was as accurate and concise a description of the Führer as anyone could hope to make, and thinking it over, the ten-year-old Polish girl concluded primly: 'I only hope he knows that peaceful people don't think him very nice.'

It was about then that Colonel Beck relented at last. The Anglo-French mission could tell Voroshilov 'for certain that in the event of common action against German aggression, collaboration, and the technical conditions to be settled subsequently between Poland and the USSR are not excluded'. For the colonel this was an enormous step to take, but it was still far from what Voroshilov had wanted; and anyway it was too late. While Gauleiter Förster, by decree of the Senate, was being made Head of State in Danzig, Hitler had just set *Y-Tag*. Much calmer in speech and action than he had been in the morning, he summoned Ambassador Sir Nevile Henderson to receive his written reply to Chamberlain. It was suitably long, over a thousand words in translation, and it was uncompromising: responsibility for the existing political tension in Europe lay with Poland and Great Britain. 'Only after a change of spirit on the part of the responsible Powers can there be any real change in the relationship between England and Germany,' he declared. 'I have all my life fought for Anglo-German friendship; the attitude adopted by British diplomacy – at any rate, up to the present – has, however, convinced me of the futility of the attempt. Should there be any change in this respect in the future,' he concluded, 'nobody could be happier than I.' Naturally, though, he did not mention his latest decision: that at 4.30 a.m. on Saturday 26 August, in less than sixty hours, Poland would be invaded.

'How we did blackguard each other in the past!' Midnight in Moscow. With a jovial chuckle Stalin bade farewell to his visitors, and Ribbentrop found it easy to beam in response. For the past three years he had based his political work on the Anti-Comintern Pact, jointly signed by Germany, Italy and Japan. Now all that, of course, was out of the window, in the most radical about-face anyone could have conceived. Perhaps it should have felt like a betrayal, but it did not; on the contrary, to discover he was capable of making such a rapid, successful and fundamental switch was gloriously exhilarating.

At the same moment Sir Alexander Cadogan was at home, tired and confused. In the course of the day, 'the kind of lull that comes in the middle of a typhoon', Halifax has asked him: 'Do you think this means war?' 'Yes,' Cadogan had replied. 'I think it does, but I believe it doesn't.' All his staff had been recalled from leave; diplomats had been sent back to their posts. Now, sitting down to dinner, he thought wearily, 'These crises really are too tiresome. We can't go on living like this in Europe. There's no point in it.'

Harold Nicolson dined with Sir Archibald Sinclair, leader of the Liberal Party, and Sir Maurice and Lady Violet Bonham-Carter. Throughout the evening they discussed the meaning of the Russo-German agreement. Might Ribbentrop be kept hanging about, humiliated, like the Anglo-French military missions? Nicolson did not think so. 'I doubt whether Ribbentrop would have been such a fool as to go to Moscow,' he said, 'unless he was pretty certain that he would be exposed to no humiliating delays.'

Even then, Paul Schmidt was hearing from Ribbentrop himself just how swift and stimulating the negotiations had been. There had been a nasty moment early on, when, reading Ribbentrop's preamble to the German draft, Stalin had shaken his bearlike head and growled in obvious disagreement. Turning nervously to his interpreter, Ribbentrop learned that the Communist leader felt it was going too far to talk about friendly German–Soviet relations. 'He says his government could not suddenly present their people with a German–Soviet declaration of friendship after they had been covered with, er —' The interpreter hesitated. 'With, ah, pails of manure by the Nazi Government for six years.' With the flowery passage instantly struck out, everything had proceeded without a hitch, and at 11 p.m. the pact had been signed. For the next ten years, 'both High Contracting Parties obligate themselves to desist from any act of violence, any aggressive action, and any attack on each other, either individually or jointly with other Powers . . .' That would be made public; but the final protocol would remain secret. Poland's territories would be divided between Russia and Germany, and later they would determine whether or not any independent Polish State was permitted to exist.

After the signing of the pact, many toasts had been drunk, led by Stalin, and in the German Embassy the celebration continued into the early hours. In London Harold Nicolson left his dinner companions at 10.15 p.m. and drove home. On the way he saw something he had never seen before, a motorcyclist wearing a steel helmet. It was, he noted, 'a sinister sight', and though the night was 'very hot and still', he shivered.

12

Action will begin

ON THE MORNING of the 24th, Ciano visited his king in Sant' Anna di Valdieri, ostensibly to thank him for the Collar of the Annunziata. They hardly spoke of it; instead, the king wanted news of the situation. Ciano told him all he knew, including the four points agreed with Mussolini as an approach to the Germans. The king approved them, especially the third – the one about neutrality. Not only was he openly hostile to Germany but also he assessed Italy as being 'absolutely in no condition to wage war'. Ciano got it from the shoulder: the army was in a pitiful state, a military review and manoeuvres had revealed the unpreparedness of all their major formations, their frontier defences were insufficient; the king had inspected them thirty-two times and was convinced the French could go through them easily:

> The officers of the Italian Army are not qualified for the job. Our equipment is old and obsolete. To this must be added the state of mind of the Italians, which is distinctly anti-German: the peasants go into the Army cursing those 'damned Germans'. We must therefore await events and do nothing. Six months of neutrality will give us greater strength.

The king ended emphatically: if 'supreme decisions' had to be taken, he would be in Rome. He particularly wanted 'not to be left out'.

At the same time King George VI was travelling back from Balmoral to London, guided by a similar instinct: his place was in the capital, at the head of his people. By an equally natural instinct he wanted his wife the queen to stay in Scotland with their children, as safe as could be from any possible harm. Her mother-in-law Queen Mary wrote to her from the West Country: 'I feel deeply for you, I having gone through all this in 1914, when I was the wife of the Sovereign.' For the time being, Elizabeth obeyed.

Now that she was with her own children, Zofya Olscholwska felt more secure than for several days past. In the family estate of Moniaki, with a comforting sense of perpetual safety, everything was as it had always been. It was a beautiful, prosperous place. Eight thousand acres surrounded the house and its garden, studded with tall, old trees. The fields were full of hops, corn and beetroot. In the meadows cows munched steadily; astrakhan sheep and lambs bleated, and the family's herd of 140 horses ran and rolled under hot sun and clear skies. Ann, her sister, managed the household, and Zofya was able to do much as she pleased. She read, wrote letters, played tennis and played with her children, delighting to see them with their cousins in the sunshine. With Josephine, the fat, bad-tempered but excellent cook, she made preserves of strawberry, blackcurrant and redcurrant; and even Josephine's bad temper was welcome because it was so normal. She put the shattering memory of the refugee ship firmly to the back of her mind. Over the days the tensions from Gdansk and Gdynia faded; and if only Taddeus had been able to be with her too, all would have been perfect.

In another part of Poland, in a scene of equal innocence, Niusia had fallen in love 'with', she wrote in her diary, 'the most adorable little baby girl I have ever seen.' Irka the maid had returned after a successful confinement, 'absolutely glowing with pride, although she was shy at first'. Her daughter was illegitimate, but almost everyone was entranced. Niusia was fascinated by the infant:

> She has a few hairs on top of her head, navy blue eyes and she hardly ever cries. And when she does, the noise doesn't come out immediately. First, she waves her arms about, then she crumples her face, and only after that the sound comes out. Her hands are very tiny, and her toes are no bigger than peppercorns.

However, the infant's precise origin remained a mystery. Niusia's brother Jurek had told her how they grew inside their mother's stomach, which she found incredible. *Could Irka have eaten her own baby? No, that's too ridiculous altogether.* But now the observant girl noticed that Irka's tummy was much smaller than before. Still sceptical, she noted: 'It does seem that Jurek could have been right.' Only her grandfather was unimpressed. According to her mother, little babies niggled him. Leaving the others to coo, he made himself some sandwiches and went for a ride on Samson the horse.

So, in their different ways, the two families were able to ignore, or at least to be distracted from, the news that filled every newspaper in Poland and Britain: the text of the Nazi–Soviet Pact. The official Polish reaction was that it merely demonstrated Germany's basic weakness, and the government expressed complete confidence that if there was a war Poland would win with the help of France and Britain. But from Berlin Sir Nevile Henderson reported to Lord Halifax: 'I anticipate an ultimatum to Poland. Whether an eleventh-hour attempt of the Polish Government to re-establish contact will avail, I much doubt. But I regard it as the *last* hope, if any, of peace: if there is a last hope.' Harold Nicolson thought not. 'I see mighty little chance of peace,' he wrote to his wife Vita. 'It may be that Colonel Beck will lose his nerve and fly to Berchtesgaden. But even that would be a bad catastrophe.' And in the British Foreign Office, with the terms of the pact public knowledge, Sir Alexander Cadogan's advice to Lord Halifax was simple. In his judgment the only thing to do was to encourage Mussolini's peace moves. 'We can't urge the Poles to agree to Danzig's incorporation into the Reich,' he explained. 'But if Hitler will agree firstly that Polish rights must be safeguarded, and secondly that a settlement must be internationally guaranteed, then it would give us a basis on which we could approach the Poles.' Halifax agreed; so did Chamberlain; and before lunchtime a telegram was sent to Rome. Such speedy action was almost unheard of – 'almost Totalitarian!' Cadogan said with a quick smile. *But otherwise*, he thought, *everything is as black as black.*

As this was going on, a curious meeting was taking place in a country house named Karinhall. Field Marshal Hermann Goering, head of the German Air Force, was talking earnestly to a Swedish businessman named Birger Dahlerus. Goering's stepson was on Dahlerus's staff, which was how the two men knew each other. It was not the first time they had talked, nor was the subject new. But on 24 August, against a background of crisis, their discussions had a real intensity; theory was replaced by urgent reality. The idea was that Dahlerus, as a neutral with business interests and good connections both in Germany and Britain, could act as a go-between, an unofficial intermediary between Berlin and London, and perhaps pull off an agreement where professional diplomats had failed. It was a possibility, at least, and Dahlerus accepted Goering's invitation to Berlin. The portly Field Marshal squeezed himself behind the wheel of his neat little two-seater car, and the conversation continued as they drove.

From Threadneedle Street, home of the Bank of England, came a startling announcement at midday: until further notice the bank rate was increased from 2 to 4 per cent, the first rise in seven-and-a-half years. For many British people, both then and in later years, this seemed to be the moment when the crisis of 1939 became real; you could joke about gas masks and sand bags, but not about a doubled bank rate. Things must be serious indeed.

Lord Halifax lunched alone with King George. The king seemed 'very calm and steady'; and at 2.45 in the afternoon ('a Quarter before Three of the Clock') the House of Commons reassembled: 'a very full meeting,' noted Victor Cazalet, the Member for Chippenham. Immediately after the traditional opening prayers the motion was put that an Emergency Powers (Defence) Bill should be brought forward, 'a Bill to confer upon His Majesty certain powers which it is deemed expedient that His Majesty should be enabled to exercise in the present emergency', and that it should be passed through all its stages on the same day. Chamberlain spoke at length, summarising events since the House's last session. Sitting directly behind him Henry ('Chips') Channon, the American-born Conservative Member for Southend on Sea, was able to see Lloyd George and Churchill, 'those twin apostles of Russian friendship', looking 'old and dejected. Winston held his face in his hands'. Thinking of the Munich crisis of the previous September, Channon remembered 'all the excitement then' and wondered at the difference today. 'The House was calm, bored, even irritated, at having its holiday cut short by Hitler.'

The Prime Minister's speech set the mood of the House. 'Dignified and calm', thought Nicolson, 'but without one word which could inspire anybody . . . Exactly like a coroner summing up a case of murder.' Privately, Channon agreed: 'Clear and admirable, but with little passion or emotion.' So did Cazalet: 'A good but not very impressive speech' was his conclusion. Nevertheless the vote on the motion was almost unanimous. Recording the result, the ancient phrases and biblical cadences of the House's *Journal* seemed particularly suitable to the occasion:

> And the Question being put;
> The House divided.
> The Yeas to the Right;
> The Noes to the Left.
> Tellers for the Yeas,
>
> > (Captain Waterhouse)
> > (Captain McEwen:)   427
>
> Tellers for the Noes,
>
> > (Mr Stephen)
> > (Mr McGovern:)   4
>
> So it was resolved in the Affirmative.

Members worked at full speed, while in the Upper House Lord Halifax gave the peers an almost exact repeat of the Prime Minister's speech, and from the Admiralty came orders placing the Royal Navy at war stations. The French government, at this stage no less certain of its obligations than the British, confirmed its determination that in the last extremity France would stand by Poland. For ordinary people like Derek Silver all this combined to make 'a most jittery day'. Silver, twenty-two years old, was a journalist working in the Essex town of Chelmsford. He came originally from Tunbridge Wells in Kent, and (as he scribbled in his diary that night) 'feeling war to be pretty near, I wrote a more than usually passionate letter to my girl, who is away on holiday'. On hearing the news of the Nazi–Soviet Pact, Andrew Hole, the Plymouth schoolmaster on holiday in Sheffield, spent the morning stocking the house with food; it was, he thought, 'the most resigned-to-war news there could be'. And as Hole bustled around the shops of Sheffield a scene both farcical and frightening took place at Königsberg airport. The German delegation, led by Joachim von Ribbentrop, wished to return home at the first opportunity to present the signed pact to their Führer. In Moscow both Condors were prepared for the flight. The first was to take Ribbentrop direct to Berchtesgaden; the second, which left an hour later, was to take other members of the delegation, including Paul Schmidt, back to Berlin. From Moscow they arrived without hitch in Königsberg, where Schmidt assumed the same interval of an hour would apply. Deciding to take a stroll around the airport, he calmly watched Ribbentrop's plane take off, and then to his astonishment the Condor in which he had travelled immediately followed suit. Later he rather wished someone had been there to take a picture of him – so often he had been photographed in formal situations with VIPs – but there was no photographer at Königsberg. As the aircraft left without him, he just stood and gawked.

He had to get back. East Prussia was no good, he should be in Berlin. Quick – the train. No good. 'Rail connections with the Reich are suspended today.' Over to the Air Office – better luck: an empty Junkers 52 was leaving for Berlin at any moment, from the far end of the airfield. As fast as he could, he trotted towards it, gesticulating wildly; its engines were already running. He was glad to see them slow as he approached. Clambering aboard, they took off at once, whereupon the pilot asked him for his pass. 'As things are, one can't be too careful,' he explained apologetically, adding over the roar of the motors that many Lufthansa aeroplanes had come under Polish anti-aircraft fire recently. 'We're not so grand as those others,' he went on, nodding ahead towards the invisibly distant Condors. 'We get no fighter cover; but we fly out over the Baltic, where the Poles can't get us unless they chase us with fighters and then force us to land.' Just in case, Schmidt prepared his papers for destruction; but nothing happened and they arrived in Berlin only half an hour after von Ribbentrop. The Reichsminister's plane, scheduled for Berchtesgaden, had been diverted there because Hitler himself was already in the capital. 'This whole episode,' Schmidt wrote later, 'brought home to me how near war between Poland and Germany really was.'

Meanwhile work in the House of Commons continued at an abnormal pace. With the best will in the world, to process a bill through all its parliamentary stages took time, yet by nineteen minutes past ten that night honourable Members had completed their work: the Emergency Powers Bill had become an Act. They adjourned again, agreeing to reassemble a week later, on the 31st, or earlier if Mr Speaker was satisfied that the public interest required it. It had been a long, wearing day, and Cazalet and Nicolson joined Lloyd George and Churchill in the smoking room to talk over events. *Both very anti-Chamberlain*, Cazalet noted. 'He has let us into this mess,' said one of the older men angrily. 'We never ought to have given guarantees to Poland unless they had consented to allow the Russian army across their frontiers.' They had heard that Chamberlain had offered to resign if war came. Lloyd George was vehement: 'We must be able to tell the Prime Minister that he must go.' But perhaps the most remarkable event that day in Parliament was that Chamberlain did not go; the king had refused to accept his offer of resignation. And this refusal by His Majesty had an unexpected effect far away, about which the grumbling MPs knew nothing and could not guess: Hitler had expected that when his pact with Russia was made known Chamberlain's government would fall. When it did not, and the Führer learned the news the following day, he began to doubt the wisdom of attacking Poland, and hesitated for the first time in many years.

On the evening of 24 August, however, Hitler was being entertained, indeed enthralled, by von Ribbentrop's vivid description of business in Moscow. The pact was signed, sealed and delivered, and at that moment it seemed that nothing could go seriously wrong.

About the same time, Sir Alexander Cadogan was recording in his diary that he personally had not had much work during the day. 'There's really nothing to do. We've got to wait and hope. In one way, it's not so bad as last year. Then there was the awful question ought we to fight or ought we not? Now there's no question that in certain circumstances we must. It just depends on whether these circumstances – out of our control – arise.'

For others those circumstances arose within hours. Claud Kennerley, the Yorkshire doctor, had had a normal day's work. Throughout, he and his wife Eleanor had tried not to think too much about what the future might hold. By late evening weariness and the continuing insistent demands of normality helped to blot out speculation. They were going to bed when a phone call summoned the doctor to Listerdale Maternity Home where a woman was going into labour. 'All right,' he said, 'I'll be there in fifteen minutes or so. Goodbye.' Starting to dress again, he said to Eleanor, 'Funny how many of them choose the middle of the night to come into the world. You go to sleep, love. I'll be back as soon as I can.' A midnight birth was indeed nothing out of the ordinary, and Eleanor went calmly to sleep.

In Sheffield Andrew Hole and his wife could not sleep for worry. Around one o'clock in the morning, deciding to get up and make a pot of tea, he found that everyone else in the house was still awake. They all assembled for tea in his mother-in-law's bedroom, but it did no good; no one could think of anything to say that would make them feel any better. Andrew returned despondently to bed and lay awake. It was, he thought, 'a most suicidal night'.

At two in the morning the shrill ring of the doorbell awakened Eleanor Kennerley. Tottering downstairs, she opened the front door to a messenger – she was never sure later whether he was a courier or a postman – who asked her name, handed her an orange envelope addressed to her husband and sped off on a large motorbike into the darkness. Alone in the hall, she tore the envelope open and read the telegram: 'Report immediately in uniform to Drill Hall in Rotherham.'

Mobilisation. And Claud was not there. Closing her eyes with a sudden faintness, she had a brief, vivid mental image of him at work at that moment, encouraging the new mother, coaxing the infant into life – dear God, what kind of life? Reading the message again, as if the words might have changed, she found she was trembling all over. This was the reality of his Territorial Army training: he must go, and might never come back. And all she could do was all she had ever done, give him her help and support and love. Clutching the telegram to her, still shaking, she walked up the stairs and began to lay out his uniform.

Daylight that morning, Friday 25 August, revealed a cool but very humid day in Sheffield. Dark-eyed through lack of sleep, Andrew Hole read over some of the public announcements issued by the office of the Lord Privy Seal. Find out the name and address of your local Air Raid Warden, if you have not done so already. If an air raid comes, there might be warnings from police whistles as well as warbling sirens, and when the raid was over a single continuous note will sound. If there is a gas attack – *My God, they really mean it* – the alarm will be sounded on handrattles. For a moment he could not think what was meant by that, then realised they were the clacking wooden rattles football supporters wielded. It hardly seemed appropriate. The gas attack all-clear would be given by ringing bells. *And heavenly bells if you've copped it*, I suppose. There was that old favourite again: 'Take your gas mask with you. Those who ignore this advice may be running grave risks.' And blackout: remember that if your house is not blacked out when a 'no lights' warning is in force, you will not be allowed to have any lights on, because in that situation no lights at all are to be shown after dark. Black blinds and other curtaining materials are in short supply, but a heavy-weight beige material will do, and will help to keep a room looking cheerful. No doubt; and no doubt it was all sensible advice. But Andrew remained depressed.

The morning in Rome was cloudy and hot, and when Count Ciano visited Mussolini he found him in a 'furiously warlike' mood – the last thing Ciano wanted. More argument began, with Ciano using the king's opinions to back his own. Once again he managed to bend the Duce away from complete commitment to Germany; instead there would be 'non-intervention for the time being, pending a re-examination of our position and until such time as we have completed our preparations for war'. Authorised to send a message on those lines to Hitler, Ciano left the Palazzo Venezia happily: he knew that those conditions meant abstaining from any conflict for at least three years.

For Berliners the morning was warm and hazy with dust, the kind of muddy atmosphere that comes with prolonged dry weather, and Paul Schmidt was summoned to the Chancellery to provide Hitler with a translation of Chamberlain's speech in Parliament the previous day. The Führer smirked when he heard that the pact with Russia had come as 'a surprise of a very unpleasant character', but though he said nothing, his expression changed as Schmidt continued: 'In Berlin the announcement has been hailed with extraordinary cynicism as a great diplomatic victory which removed any danger of war, since France and ourselves would no longer be likely to fulfil our obligations to Poland. We felt it our first duty to remove any such dangerous illusion.' The translation finished, Schmidt was dismissed, and as he left he saw Hitler looking pensive and withdrawn.

In Washington DC this busy morning, Franklin Roosevelt still hoped for peace in Europe: he said so in a press conference, during which he announced also that he had written both to Hitler and the King of Italy. The Danzig dispute must, he believed, still be open to negotiation and arbitration; he had suggested that the arbitrator should not be the United States but some other American nation, and he awaited Herr Hitler's response.

On the German–Polish border the final moment of crisis was visibly approaching: 'incidents' multiplied throughout the day, all the way from harassment and insults to shootings on both sides. In Makeszowa, near Katowice, German soldiers took over the court house and railway station; Poles broke into and wrecked the Katowice offices of a German newspaper. More Polish reservists were being called up, and cars and horses requisitioned. Nevertheless foreign observers in the country assessed the national mood as still robust and optimistic; and in Rome Mussolini called Ciano back to the Palazzo Venezia to tell him that once more he had changed his mind. 'He fears the bitter judgment of the Germans,' the Count wrote, 'and wants to intervene at once. It is useless to struggle. I submit and go . . .'

But in the middle of the day, when all seemed set to topple over the edge, two simultaneous events brought sudden hope. At 2 p.m. Hitler was to have issued the executive order launching the invasion of Poland. Just before noon, however, he gave instructions that the order would be postponed until three, and at 12.45 requested the British Ambassador, Sir Nevile Henderson, to come to the Chancellery at 1.30. *Don't know what this means*, thought Cadogan when he heard of it. At the same time in south London the Swedish businessman Birger Dahlerus had landed at Croydon airport and was on his way to the Foreign Office: with Hitler's concurrence he had accepted Goering's proffered role of unofficial go-between, and in all secrecy Halifax had agreed to see him.

At the time that Henderson's interview with the Führer began, people in Broadgate, one of the main shopping streets of the city of Coventry, were interested to notice a bomber flying overhead. Such things were neither commonplace nor objects of terror. Craning their necks in the crowded street, they stared, pointed and discussed. And then there was what seemed to be an enormous explosion and a flash of light, followed by smoke and the crash of falling rubble. More than a dozen people were injured badly; five were killed. There was panic and the instant assumption that somehow, unknown to them, war had actually begun. In one sense it had, but not with Germany. With a small (but effective) bomb, the IRA had struck, hoping to profit from the national tension. They bombed Blackpool and Liverpool as well that day. As the bells of ambulances and fire engines clanged through the cities – bells which could soon become a daily, even hourly sound throughout England – Henderson was on the telephone from Berlin to Cadogan in London. His interview had ended at 3 p.m. with Hitler giving him a letter for the British government containing proposals to ease the international situation. Naturally it was of great urgency, and Herr Hitler, saying it was his last attempt to secure peace, had offered a German plane to take him to Britain next morning. Should he accept? Cadogan said he should, and went to tell Chamberlain and Halifax about it. But none of them knew that the conversation had been monitored by German intelligence, as happened almost routinely with calls from the British Embassy in Berlin. Another thing they did not know was that at two minutes past three, as soon as Henderson had left the Chancellery, Hitler issued an order to his High Command confirming the schedule for *Y-Tag*. Poland would be invaded at dawn the following day.

At 2 p.m. while Henderson and Hitler were talking, an 'ambiguous message' from the Führer was received in Rome. Accompanied by Hans Georg von Mackensen, the German Ambassador, Count Ciano hurried once more to the Palazzo Venezia to read it. 'Couched,' he said, 'in abstract language', it was not at all clear, but as far as he or anyone else could make out, it said that 'action will begin in a short time' and asked for '"Italian understanding"'. It was actually the kind of cue Ciano needed, and he used it to persuade Mussolini to write to Hitler. The core of the message was simple: 'We are not ready to go to war. We will go to war only if you furnish us with all the war supplies and raw materials we need.' *Not the kind of communication that I should have wanted to make*, Ciano thought, *but it is something, anyway*; and as soon as it was agreed he telephoned it personally to Ambassador Attolico for immediate relay to Hitler.

Throughout the day German naval and military reservists were being called up; throughout the afternoon units of the regular army were on the move. Lorry-loads of soldiers rumbled through Berlin – the roof-tops weirdly decorated with anti-aircraft guns – towards the Polish border. SS units already in place were put on stand-by alert, some changing rapidly from German to Polish uniforms in readiness for Operation Himmler, General Heydrich's plan which would justify *Fall Weiss*, the invasion of Poland. Everything was moving ahead smoothly: by 4 a.m. all that would be needed was the Führer's command, and blitzkrieg would begin – a smashing, lightning war so devastating that in all likelihood Poland would be crushed before France or Britain could move to its assistance. And after that, Hitler believed, they would not wish to move: for the sake of peace his domination of central Europe would be accepted.

He had planned every move hitherto on the assumption that in France and Britain the desire for peace was stronger than the fear of dishonour. Having won his way on every point – the occupation of the Rhineland, the remilitarisation of the Saarland, the Anschluss with Austria, the dismemberment of Czechoslovakia – the assumption seemed correct. Yet it was basically mistaken; it was not love of peace that had guided the western powers in their dealings with him so far, but fear of Communism. And now he was an ally of Stalin. Politicians in other countries could admit to an astonished professional admiration for the sheer dexterity of the coup, but for almost all of them it removed any lingering thought that Hitler could be trusted. He had never grasped this. Now, as he waited impatiently for a reply from London to the proposals he had given Henderson, it is likely that his final offer of peace was sincere: that is, to the extent that there would be no war if Britain was prepared to accept the sacrifice of Poland. 'The German–Polish problem,' he had said, 'must and will be solved.' In return he had proposed to discuss limitations of armaments, to guarantee west European frontiers, and even to guarantee the existence of the British Empire with German help 'in any part of the world where such help might be needed'. There is some evidence too that he was mentally preparing at least to delay *Fall Weiss* if a preliminary reply from London looked favourable, if London seemed ready to consider his bribe. A fully considered reply would be impossible in the short time available, but he assumed, again mistakenly, that Henderson would telephone the contents of the proposal to London at once, before taking the written version next morning, and that an initial reaction would come very rapidly. However, when telephoning to ask whether or not he should fly to England, Henderson had not divulged the details of the proposal: instead he had sent them by cable. They did not reach the Foreign Office until late in the afternoon and were preceded by another message, which Hitler would have dearly loved to have kept secret – the notes taken surreptitiously by a horrified general, of his ruthless speech in Berchtesgaden four days ago:

> Decision to attack Poland was arrived at in the spring . . . Our strength lies in our quickness and our brutality . . . Poland will be depopulated and settled with Germans . . . The fate of Russia will be exactly the same . . . Then will begin the dawn of the German rule of the earth.

And there was the date: 'The attack upon and the destruction of Poland begins Saturday, early.' There could only be one British reaction to this. At half past four on Friday afternoon Britain's informal guarantee to Poland was formalised into the Anglo-Polish Treaty of Mutual Assistance, binding the two countries together. Within minutes (not through diplomats but press agencies), the information reached Hitler. Paul Schmidt was with him, awaiting a visit from the French Ambassador Robert Coulondre. Hovering discreetly behind the Führer, he was able to read the report over his shoulder, 'and then I watched him sit brooding at his desk until the French Ambassador was announced'.

German radio carried the news of the treaty that evening. The young soldier Bernt Engelmann was having supper with his Uncle Franz and Aunt Käthe in their hotel in Bielefeld when they heard it. Uncle Franz was highly indignant. 'That's all we need!' he exclaimed. Loathing Communism, he had for years accepted Hitler's oft-repeated assertion that Germany and Britain were cousins and should be natural allies. 'Now our English friends have gone over to the enemy,' he added scathingly, 'and we're allied with the Bolshevists.'

Hitler's natural interpretation of the treaty was that it represented Great Britain's reply to his proposals. It did not. Chamberlain, Halifax and Cadogan did not discuss those until much later that evening, after dinner in No 10 Downing Street. Cadogan's reaction then, which the others shared, was impatience: 'They aren't proposals at all.' For all Hitler was really offering was the same as many times before, namely a free hand for Germany in the east in exchange for British freedom of action elsewhere. Nevertheless, the decision in No 10 that night was that they must be treated with some seriousness, if only to keep Hitler talking. Each day that peace continued could mean further chances of averting war altogether. Agreeing that they must prepare a preliminary draft before Henderson returned in the morning, they went back to the Foreign Office at 11.30 p.m. and continued work, not knowing that by then Adolf Hitler had been through one of the most humiliating evenings of all his years in power.

At half past five Coulondre had arrived. He was with Hitler for barely half an hour. During the interview, Schmidt noted, 'the Führer made very much the same statement as he had made four hours earlier . . . I had the impression that he was mechanically repeating what he had said to Henderson, and that his thoughts were elsewhere.' He clearly wanted to end the meeting quickly, and when he had finished his own statement half rose from his seat to indicate it was ended. But Coulondre (whom Schmidt, from ten years' acquaintance, rated highly as a diplomat) insisted on giving a reply. Lest there should be any misunderstanding, he said, 'I give you my word of honour as a French officer that the French army will fight by the side of Poland if that country should be attacked.' Raising his voice for emphasis, he added, also on his word of honour, that France would do everything possible for the maintenance of peace. Angrily Hitler interrupted: 'Why, then, did you give Poland a blank cheque to act as she pleased? It is painful for me to have to go to war against France; but the decision does not depend on me.' He dismissed the Ambassador. Already another was waiting outside: Bernardo Attolico, with the reply from Rome. The Italian squirmed with embarrassment as he produced Mussolini's letter to Hitler:

> In one of the most painful moments of my life, I have to inform you that Italy is not ready for war. According to what the responsible heads of the services tell me, the petrol supplies of the Italian Air Force are so low that they would last only for three weeks of fighting. The position is the same with regard to supplies for the army, and supplies of raw materials. Only the head of the navy has been able to acquit himself of culpable negligence; the Fleet is ready for action and supplied with sufficient fuel. Please understand my situation.

Please, Hitler might well have replied furiously, understand my situation: the British have just allied themselves with Poland; you, my own ally, have just defected from my side; and in ten hours I shall launch an attack which may trigger a major war. Certainly that was what he felt ('The letter,' said Schmidt, 'was a bombshell'), but he managed to hold his temper and contented himself with a frigid dismissal of Attolico. As Schmidt ushered the Ambassador out, Field Marshal Wilhelm Keitel, Chief of the High Command of the Armed Forces, was summoned in. Within minutes he came rushing out again, with momentous news: the advance on Poland was to be halted.

All communications from Berlin to the outside world were temporarily suspended. At the same time in London, Birger Dahlerus was with Lord Halifax. The British Foreign Minister was in optimistic mood. Knowing nothing yet of the moment by moment developments in Berlin, he explained to Dahlerus that his services as go-between would no longer be needed.

According to Nevile Henderson, Hitler himself had offered to reopen discussions. Looking back, it now seems a bizarre set of coincidences; yet on both sides lack of knowledge and misinterpretation combined to produce exactly the effect that Halifax wanted, a further delay. And while in France Prime Minister Édouard Daladier exhorted his people to be firm in the face of adversity, in Berlin Hitler, Ribbentrop and Goering began a conference with General Walther von Brauchitsch, Commander in Chief of the German Army, and Admiral Erich Raeder, Commander in Chief of the Navy. The session continued until the early hours of the morning. One of the first decisions, taken at 7.40 p.m., was to send a message to Mussolini requesting precise details of Italy's military needs. A few hours earlier Hitler had hoped that if he announced a delay in *Fall Weiss*, it would be with the added information that once again he was on the verge of a diplomatic coup: that Britain would talk, and that Poland was likely to fall bloodlessly into his hands. He did not know that even then the British Foreign Office was preparing to talk; and though there was no longer any possibility that Poland would have been sacrificed as he hoped, it remains deeply ironic that in this conference he was obliged to admit to his Commanders-in-Chief that *Fall Weiss* was cancelled because it was too risky an undertaking.

That evening in his barracks Bernt Engelmann learned that their expected 'mobilisation drill' had been postponed. One of his friends made a sarcastic, accurate comment: 'Adolf got cold feet.'

The final week

26 August–3 September 1939

13

To measure the unknowable

LATE IN THE EVENING of 25 August, Admiral Sir Reginald Plunkett-Ernle-Erle-Drax, head of the defunct Anglo–French Military Mission to Moscow, left the Russian capital by train with his British colleagues. At their departure courtesies on both sides, Russian and British, were minimal and perfunctory. Behind them they left a crushed and grieving man, their country's Ambassador, Sir William Seeds. Of all the British people involved he had had perhaps the highest hopes of a successful outcome to the talks; and although he had guessed the Russians might choose an alliance with Germany, when they actually did so he was shatteringly disappointed. Now, in a state of mental shock, he found himself 'left holding the beastly baby!' It was unbearable. Within four months he too quit Moscow, and left the diplomatic service.

At the peak of summer in that latitude the hours of darkness are short. As the Soviet train rattled and shook through the brief night towards the Finnish border, Admiral Drax, uncomfortable, disillusioned and bitterly angry, reflected on past days. The long sea passage through the Baltic was deemed too dangerous for his team's return route: instead they were travelling 700 miles overland to Helsinki, the capital of Finland; from there they would fly to Britain. They would be home the following day. The journey out had taken nearly a week. His mission had become a degrading, abject failure; and the sad thought came to him that his life would probably be remembered for that, if anything. True, his naval career had not been outstanding, yet he had played his part in some of the key battles of the Great War; he had always been a steady naval man; and he remembered that Nelson had once said something like 'Any fool can't be an admiral'. Well, well; but it was not much comfort. The real question was, could the mission ever have succeeded? If they had flown out, for example? If they had been more thoroughly prepared, particularly as far as the blasted Poles were concerned? Seeds thought so. Drax was more doubtful. The military aspects were logical, indeed obvious; even now he could only agree with Voroshilov's view. But he had not been ready for the extraordinary depth of mutual dislike between Russian and Pole, a dislike which completely overrode military logic. Today, at the formal termination of the talks Voroshilov, with passionate intensity, had suddenly exclaimed: 'Were we to have to conquer Poland in order to offer her our help – or were we to go on our knees and offer our help to Poland?' Unanswerable; yet that was the truth of it. What he, Drax, and General Doumenc – now on his way back to France to take up his command – had really been asked to do was not to negotiate a simple military treaty, but to overcome enormous national pride and centuries of reciprocal antagonism. *No wonder we failed*, he thought, staring glumly out at the fleeting, shrouded Russian landscape. *It was probably doomed from the start.*

'You remember all that stuff in the Great War about "gallant little Belgium"?' A thousand feet up the slope of Kinder Scout in the Pennine hills between Sheffield and Manchester, Andrew Hole and Jack Withers stopped for a breather.

'I wasn't alive then, but I know what you mean,' Withers answered. 'What about it?'

'It just occurred to me; there's no comparable feeling now about "poor little Poland". The papers aren't even trying to work it up.'

'That's probably why there isn't any such feeling,' said Withers sardonically. 'I doubt if our parents knew anything about Belgium except what the papers told them. And I don't really want to think about any of it, anyway.'

'Nor me.'

There was something about climbing high on a mountain or a hill that seemed to take one away from the cares of the world. Mussolini had felt that in the middle of the month, when Ciano came back from Salzburg: 'Perhaps we are closer to the Eternal Father up there, if He exists, but we are surely more distant from men,' the Duce had said. 'It is useless . . . This time it means war.' For lesser mortals, however, climbing brought a temporary but very welcome sense of release. Withers and Hole had left Sheffield that morning, Saturday, 26 August, simply to get away for a while from the stressful urgency bred by newspapers and wireless bulletins. It was a good morning for climbing; with a slight breeze from the south-east to keep them fresh, it was warm but not too hot; hazy, but not so much as to obscure the widening view. Slowly they continued upwards to the peak.

Derek Silver, the young journalist in Essex, was giving himself a similar kind of therapy. The day before he had cycled 62 miles around the county, noting with interest that the searchlights were in the positions they had been in all summer; there was only one he saw that could be towed. He had also spotted, and noted in his diary, approximately thirty fighters lined up around an aerodrome; but mindful of security he had been careful not to write down its name. Likewise today, 'much calmer', he rode from Chelmsford to London through Epping Forest, a distance of 35 miles or so, observing en route '——— squadrons lined up ready for action at —— aerodrome', and in the capital was glad to find everything 'normal and cheerful'. The mood of the people was generally cheerful – indeed reports that Hitler had made an offer contributed to that – and the football season had opened that day; but many odd things were happening as well. Outside Buckingham Palace the wooden sentry boxes were being replaced by curious conical steel shelters, looking like giant bells with doorways, each with a protective shield of sandbags. With back-breaking toil, more sandbags were being piled outside shops, offices and public buildings. The National Gallery in Trafalgar Square was closed for 'picture storage', said apologetic posters. In Canterbury and York medieval stained glass was being removed from cathedral and minster to safer housing, while in London (and most cities) alternate kerbstones were being painted white, and white lines were being painted on trees and lamp-posts, to assist night-time drivers in the event of blackout. (Silver subsequently discovered that one Essex farmer painted white stripes on his cows for the same reason, although he did not explain why he thought cows and cars might be in the same place after dark.) The trenches in Hyde Park, dug with furious haste during the Munich crisis, were being repaired; and, moored at various points, a growing number of barrage balloons floated 2000 feet above the city. Some had been in position for 'experimental purposes' since the middle of July. People had become accustomed to them and were reassured by the sensible nature of the additional precautions; and so for that day at least, they could feel 'normal and cheerful' in a London increasingly filled with signs of abnormality.

At ten o'clock in Rome the Chiefs of Staff of the three Italian armies and Antonio S. Benni, an industrialist who was also Minister both of Communications and of Public Works, met at the Palazzo Venezia to see Ciano and Mussolini. Ciano had already heard of Hitler's postponement of marching orders. Now, he explained to the visitors, 'Berlin is showering us with requests for the list of our needs.' He paused before entering the Duce's room. 'May I remind you, gentlemen, we need the whole truth on the extent of your stocks – none of your usual criminal optimism, if you please.' There was a chorus of indignant protest, and feeling half depressed, half cynically amused, the Count realised they had all come prepared to put the best possible gloss on the situation. They filed in and he closed the door. In two hours they filed out again, more than a little dazed. Ciano had put them all through the wringer and at last had extracted an accurate list. Alone with the Duce, he remarked, 'It's enough to kill a bull – if a bull could read it.' Mussolini could hardly bear to acknowledge the extent of Italy's weakness: 17 million tons of basic materials and 17,000 vehicles. Reluctantly he helped draft a letter to

Hitler explaining why their needs were so vast and concluding: 'Italy absolutely cannot enter the war without such supplies.'

At ten minutes past noon the letter was telephoned to Ambassador Attolico in Berlin. Ulrich von Hassell saw him in the German Foreign Office, 'obviously deeply worried'. There was a pervading sense of uncertainty: 'Everything is up in the air; orders terribly confused. The Reichstag is to meet within a few hours, nay, minutes; thrice called into session and dismissed.' Simultaneously the German plane bearing Sir Nevile Henderson was approaching London, and Birger Dahlerus was fidgeting in the British Foreign Office, awaiting Lord Halifax. After their first meeting the day before, in which Halifax had shown such optimism that he felt Dahlerus was not really needed, the Swede had called Field Marshal Goering, and learned that in his judgment war might break out at any moment. That was the message Dahlerus had just passed on, adding his personal opinion that Goering was the only man in Germany who could prevent war, and offering his services once more. A personal message from Halifax to Goering saying that England's desire for peace was genuine would, he believed, work wonders. Frank Roberts (later Sir Frank Roberts, Ambassador to Moscow and Bonn) was then on the Foreign Office German desk, and assessed Dahlerus as well-mannered, possessed of some charm, sincere and honest, but naïve. 'We knew definitely that Goering did not want war,' he recalled in after years. 'Goering had too many of the good things of life, and he wanted to keep his lifestyle, not gamble it all on a war.' This time Halifax was sufficiently impressed to relay Dahlerus's offer to Chamberlain. The Prime Minister swiftly approved; and before lunchtime Dahlerus was being driven to Croydon airport, the letter in his case. As Roberts observed, Goering was a devil, but at least he was a less warlike devil than Hitler.

Sir Nevile Henderson arrived at No 10 about one o'clock. There he found Cadogan, Halifax and Sir Horace Wilson, the Permanent Head of the Civil Service, 'jiggering about with words', as Cadogan put it, while they tried to agree on a draft reply to Hitler. Since Henderson had nothing essential to add to Hitler's message they adjourned for lunch, meeting again at 2.30 when Wilson and R. A. ('Rab') Butler, Under-Secretary for Foreign Affairs, were given the task of improving the draft. Settling himself in the garden of No 10 with the Prime Minister, Cadogan remarked, '*What* a party!' and 'tried to put ginger into him. He, I think, quite receptive.'

General Sir Edmund Ironside lunched at Chartwell with Winston Churchill. On the whole their conversation was optimistic. Ironside was just back from Poland, and brought very favourable reports of the Polish army; he had watched a divisional attack exercise under live barrage, and though there had been casualties, morale seemed high. Churchill, for his part, was 'full of

Georges', Ironside wrote in his diary. 'I found that he had become very French in his outlook and had a wonderful opinion of the whole thing he saw.' Optimistic as they were, neither became carried away; all that was possible, in Churchill's words, was to try hard 'to measure the unknowable'.

At that time Bernt Engelmann's little radio team, consisting of himself, his friend Erwin (who had spoken of Hitler having cold feet) and a loathsome creature named Barczustowski (who, despite his Polish name, was a fanatical Nazi), were sitting in their communications car with nothing to do except listen to all the available news bulletins. Years later Engelmann remembered how 'the British, and even Mussolini and the Pope, were trying to find a successful solution to the conflict over Poland ... "I hope they succeed," said Barczustowski in a subdued voice.'

Perhaps wiser, certainly freer, than the young German soldiers, Andrew Hole and Jack Withers were by then lounging on the top of Kinder Scout, as far as possible from any news bulletin. The views of moors and Pennines were magnificent. 'Capital, capital,' Withers said with satisfaction. 'And what marvellous air ... This was a first-class idea, truly it was; you've no notion, it makes me feel – well, ordinary again. It's a wonderful feeling.'

'I know,' said Hole. 'It's just the same for me. I'd never thought of it before, but feeling ordinary can be a real luxury. Goodness, it was worth the climb.'

Withers laughed. 'But then comes the climb down, eh?' He was remembering that yesterday, after hearing that an offer had come from Hitler, Andrew had said, *Can this be the first recognition that Britain can't be shaken?* and had assessed the three possible alternatives for the future: *Either we climb down; or war; or they climb down.*

It was a measure of Andrew Hole's relaxation that he laughed too. 'No, no, it won't be us who climb down, not us, Britain, I mean. As for us, you and me,' jumping to his feet, he pulled Withers up as well, 'we'll have to be the Grand Old Duke of York!'

With the youthful, even boyish mood upon them as they walked down the hill, they could not resist singing the nursery rhyme:

> Oh, the Grand Old Duke of York,
> He had ten thousand men,
> He marched them up to the top of the hill
> And he marched them down again,
> And when they were up, they were up ...

The song would have found an echo very far away. Echoes too of Europe's profound abnormality had penetrated to Schoharie County in New York State, midway between the Catskills and the Adirondacks. There two other young men, Ernest Kroll and Heinz Lindt, were vacationing for the same reason as Hole and Withers: the need to escape the constant influx of unsettling news, the need to climb back to normality. As their names suggest, both were of German origin: Lindt was a refugee from the Nazi regime. Both worked for another refugee, Otto L. Bettmann, one-time curator for prints at the Berlin State Museum, who now owned the Bettmann Archive, a New York picture agency. Both, the day before, had travelled the 120 miles up river from New York City to Catskill in the *Governor Clinton*, a great oval wedding cake of a ship belonging to the Hudson River Day Line; had bussed a further 40 miles to Livingstoneville; and had checked into the Schoharie Rest, a small hotel run by a Mrs Seidel, also of German origin. Finally, this morning of the 26th, both had got out of the hotel as fast as possible. Mrs Seidel, motherly and thoughtful, had one blind spot: while serving their supper she would keep on relaying news of Europe from her wireless in the kitchen. 'And what do you think of that, then, Herr Lindt?' she would ask. But neither Herr Lindt nor Herr Kroll wanted to think about any of it, and hence now found themselves walking in the rolling Schoharie hills. They had been told the Hudson was nicknamed the Rhine of America; the Schoharie Rest was just like a Rhineland *pension*; and Mrs Seidel's questions made Heinz, a stocky, blond Alpinist, homesick. But the hills beguiled him. With eager professionalism he took picture after picture while Ernest (who would become a noted poet) wrote down those things the shutter could not capture. Years later Ernest recalled how 'with his photographer's eye for detail' Heinz 'found cows on a hilltop consorting with clouds enough to make him forget the absence of mountains'. It was balm to the spirit. In order to enjoy a full week's holiday free from European politics, they had only to ramble during the day, and to evade Mrs Seidel's well-meant questions at night.

'And when they were down, they were down . . .' At 2088 feet the peak of Kinder Scout was just 88 feet above the clear-weather daytime flying level of London's barrage balloons; yet the return to ground level, the level of everyday fear, did not affect Andrew Hole at once. On the way back to Sheffield he saw soldiers boarding trains at Dore Station, and felt interested rather than worried. As it had been for Londoners, Saturday for him had been a 'cheerful day, not bothering about war'. But after a short time his anger at Poland returned. *It's infuriating*, he thought, *that we let a decent country like Czechoslovakia go, if we are to fight for a lousy dictatorship.*

While *The Times* hinted that it might not come to that and there could yet be some compromise over Danzig, more reservists were called up in France. Cars, horses and various useful blocks of French property were requisitioned;

and in Scotland Queen Elizabeth gave in to instinct. 'If things turn out badly,' she told a lady-in-waiting, 'I must be with the King.' Many of their subjects, advised to evacuate London, would feel the same: if you are going to be bombed, it might as well be at home under your own rubble. She travelled south that afternoon.

Meanwhile with growing disbelief, Ribbentrop was reading Mussolini's list of Italian requirements: 7 million tons of petroleum, 6 million of coal, 2 million of steel, another million of timber . . . Before finishing he stared frigidly at Attolico and asked when the Duce wished delivery of the items. Attolico, who, as much as Ciano, wanted to keep Italy out of war, answered on his own initiative. With a look of surprise, as if it were the most obvious thing in the world, he said: 'Why, at once, before hostilities begin.'

Outside, the city was baking under a clear blue sky; with the temperature in the high 70s Fahrenheit, many Berliners had gone to cool off and relax a little by the lakes. Attolico's request was so clearly impossible that for a few moments he thought Ribbentrop might explode in front of his eyes. Yet somehow the German controlled his reaction. The requirements could be met, but unfortunately, at such short notice, not immediately in full. No doubt the Führer would wish everyone to do their best. If His Excellency would care to wait, he could have the Führer's reply very soon. Attolico waited, and considering the circumstances the reply was a model of restraint. At eight minutes past three he telephoned it to Rome: 'Duce, I understand your position,' were Hitler's words, 'and would only ask you try to achieve the pinning down of Anglo-French forces by active propaganda and suitable military demonstrations, such as you have already proposed to me.' But after the Ambassador was gone the corridors echoed with loud abuse of the Italian nation; and at twenty-two minutes past three General Franz Halder, Chief of Staff of the German Army, noted in his dairy: 'Attack starts 1 September.' *Y-Tag* had been retimed.

Sir Alexander Cadogan was even then redrafting the draft reply on which Wilson and Butler had worked. '*Quite* awful,' he said to himself as he corrected the worst errors. But it was not as if this was simply a chatty letter to a friend. Any diplomatic communication had to be scrutinised line by line and word by word, because at the best of times it was at the very least embarrassing if one's intention – the national intention – was misunderstood, and these were hardly the best of times: there was no room for ambiguity or anything which might be open to misinterpretation; yet without retreat one had to avoid confrontation. It was a very narrow path, with the edge perilously close. And time was marching on; the re-draft would have to go to the Cabinet at six o'clock. Cadogan was sure they would still not like it. *Let them fight their own battle*, he thought, and rushed home for a quick dinner.

For the second time in a year, Henderson joined the Cabinet session at half past six. It was not common for an Ambassador to be part of those discussions, and he enjoyed the privilege; he was also rather relieved to be away from the Berlin Embassy. Many British nationals fleeing the German capital had put their belongings there for safe keeping, and Henderson's First Secretary, Sir George Ogilvie-Forbes, had been left in charge of what he complained was looking more and more like a furniture depository.

While the British Cabinet meeting was going on, Mussolini and Hitler exchanged messages once more. Over this and the next few days, said Paul Schmidt, 'verbal or written contact with ambassadors in Berlin and statesmen in London, Paris and Rome continued almost without intermission. It was a sort of long-distance conference by telephone and telegraph . . .' The latest message from Rome was a grovelling apology and self-justification. Mussolini explained that Attolico's stipulation of immediate delivery had been an absurd mistake: naturally he did not expect anything from Germany for a year at least. Until then, of course and most unfortunately, he could do nothing to help: 'I leave you to imagine my state of mind,' he wailed, 'in finding myself compelled by forces beyond my control not to afford you real solidarity at the moment of action.' Never mind, said Hitler: 'I respect the reasons and motives which have led you to take this decision.' His ally had ratted on him; very well, Germany would go it alone. Asking for psychological support from Italy, through the press or other means, he added that during the winter or at latest in the spring, he would attack in the West, with forces at least equal to those of France and Britain, so (with a piece of refined sarcasm) it would be very helpful if the Duce could send over some Italian labourers to assist with industry and agriculture.

In London the Cabinet learned much of interest. Halifax's assessment, with which his colleagues agreed, was that Sir Nevile Henderson should not be sent back at once, nor should their reply go that day, 'this might create the impression we could be rushed'. Tomorrow would be time enough. Hitler's present offer used the same old techniques: trying to divide Britain from the French and the Poles, it pointed out that with the Russo-German Pact, Poland's friends could not and therefore should not help her. Hitler clearly wanted to settle the Polish question; equally clearly he wanted to avoid a quarrel with the British Empire. The question was, which did he want the more? They had heard he meant to attack Poland any moment, but sending Henderson over by special plane did not seem to tally with that. Without identifying him, Halifax mentioned Dahlerus obliquely; Henderson expressed the views that the message sent through the 'neutral person' was not open to misinterpretation, that there must be a secret protocol attached to the pact with Russia, and that this year was quite unlike last in as much as, compared with his feeling about the Czech leadership, Hitler was quite well disposed towards Colonel Beck in Poland. In short, there was still everything to play for. Inspecting the draft reply to Hitler – and rejecting it on the grounds that it should be stiffened up: Cadogan was right – the single most interesting thing they learned was the answer to the question of timing. If Britain had to declare war, when should it be done? Lord Chatfield, speaking with a report from the Chiefs of Staff, had the answer: 'If an ultimatum is not to be issued until all essential preparations for war have been completed, the earliest date for the ultimatum will be Thursday, 31 August.'

Five days to go.

Derek Silver spent the evening in London at the Proms, where he noticed among the audience a corporal in RAF uniform. In Berlin Ulrich von Hassell, the ex-diplomat and secret anti-Nazi, passed his evening in the White Room of the Imperial Castle, attending the last night of the International Congress of Archaeologists. 'In view of the situation,' he wrote, 'it was grotesque. Englishmen, Frenchmen and Poles had already been recalled. Boring concert . . . my thoughts wandered elsewhere.' There was a banquet afterwards, during which he and Johannes Popitz, the Prussian Minister of Finance, shared a table with Bernhard Rust, the Prussian Minister of Education. 'He played the host loudly and often tactlessly. A silent exchange of glances with Popitz at one moment almost cost us our self-control.' Von Hassell did not say whether he and Popitz felt angered or amused by Rust, or both; but Popitz was another covert opponent of the Nazi regime, who in 1944 would be executed after the attempt on Hitler's life.

Hitler went to bed early that night, worn out. In Bielefeld the young soldier Bernt Engelmann was also in bed by 11 p.m., but before midnight he was awakened and up again: his unit had been alerted and must move at once. At half past midnight Hitler too was roused: Birger Dahlerus was there to see him with Field Marshal Goering. Stumbling into wakefulness, the Führer presented a weird picture to the Swede, who, before this midnight meeting, had never encountered him in person. A glassy-eyed stare gave way to an amiable greeting, followed by a well-practised monologue on the desirability of peace with England, which developed into a passionate indictment of the Poles. Dahlerus was brave enough (or naïve enough) to interrupt with a remark about British and French armed preparations and their ability to blockade Germany. Walking to and fro, Hitler did not appear to register this at all; but then he stood stock still and as if hypnotised began to repeat: 'If there should be a war, then I will build U-boats, build U-boats, build U-boats, U-boats, U-boats –' It came out louder and louder: 'I will build aircraft, build aircraft, aircraft, *and I will destroy my enemies!*'

Dahlerus turned in astonishment towards Goering, and what he saw astonished him even more: the Field Marshal beamed at him benignly as if nothing unusual was happening.

14

What's the use of worrying?

AT 1 P.M. on Sunday 27 August a Lufthansa flight brought (as British newspapers put it) a 'strange man' into Croydon airport. His arrival was notable, because there were no civilian flights arriving from Germany; all normal air communication between the two nations had been stopped. Of medium build, clean shaven, dark-suited and carrying only a small briefcase, the man, or one very like him, was seen arriving two hours later at the German Embassy, from which he did not emerge until 6.15 p.m. Thereupon a reporter from the *News Chronicle* approached him with a simple question: 'Can you tell me who you are, please?' The courteous journalist was thrown by the reply, 'I do not know who I am.'

For some reason the reporter got the stranger's times and locations in London wrong, but there is no doubt as to his identity. *Ich weiss nicht, was ich bin; ich bin nicht, was ich weiss* – I know not what I am; I am not what I know. Perhaps, when giving that cryptic answer, Birger Dahlerus had the old German poem at the back of his mind. The past twelve hours had been enough to tax anyone, and he, an amateur, was dabbling in things of world-wide importance, where a handshake might bring peace, or a wrong word a global war.

Newspapers could only speculate on his identity and purpose, implying in their articles that he must be part of some secret international negotiation. They were right, but outside the Cabinet scarcely a soul in Britain knew for certain; indeed, apart from Chamberlain and Halifax, not even the Cabinet had known until the middle of the afternoon. As far as the general public was concerned the full weight of Anglo-German diplomacy was borne by Sir Nevile Henderson. It was the same in Germany: 'There is news everywhere,' von Hassell wrote, 'but it is not easy to verify. This day may go down in history as the day of a very great decision. Whether there will be a world war or not will ultimately depend on what Henderson brings back today from London.'

Andrew Hole made a solitary entry in his diary that Sunday: 'No climb-down from Germany yet.' On Hampstead Heath Derek Silver watched troops filling sandbags. The sky over the whole city was dotted with barrage balloons. In their respective capitals, Halifax and Hitler were both at work, the former still struggling with the draft reply to the latter, who in turn was replying to a message from the French Prime Minister. Édouard Daladier, reminding Hitler of the Great War, lamented the possibility that France and Germany might fight again. If they did so, he predicted that a second war would be longer and more deadly than the first. Hitler agreed. 'As an old front-line soldier, I know, as you do, the horrors of war,' he said sympathetically, and in a blatant attempt to separate his possible opponents, added that there need be no quarrel between France and Germany: the entire present situation was the fault of Great Britain, because of the encouragement it was giving to Poland. Without that, he was sure the Poles would have been reasonable. But the same morning, as Dahlerus was flying to London, Hitler refused to accept an offer from two Polish diplomats of similarly secret, semi-official negotiation. In additon he forbade Ribbentrop's staff to listen to any further offers like that; he forbade military, naval and air attachés to leave Berlin until further notice; and he ordered the beginning of rationing. 'The higher-ups are in a "state of mind", and the people in the throes of great unrest and anxiety,' von Hassell observed. 'Mobilisation goes on apace. War weddings for weeping couples. Ration cards, scarcity of foodstuffs – all that even before war begins.'

Dahlerus met Chamberlain for the first time at 2.15 p.m. Halifax and Cadogan were present. The three Englishmen listened carefully but, Dahlerus sensed, with scepticism, as he did his best to persuade them of his own view that 'Mr Hitler himself is not in favour of war.' Much later – when the war was over – he wrote that he already considered Hitler 'patently unstable'; today, however, he limited himself to saying that 'his temper is at times uncontrollable'. Chamberlain asked the Swede what he personally thought of the Führer. Dahlerus hesitated before answering: 'I shouldn't like to have him as a partner in my business.' Otherwise grim throughout the conversation, the Prime Minister did smile a little at that.

'He didn't add much to what we know,' Cadogan commented afterwards, adding that though the Cabinet was due to meet at 3 p.m., 'we didn't finish with D till 3.40'. Halifax put the same thing another way to his colleagues: telling them of the current efforts, he said regretfully that Dahlerus 'was not a man who came very quickly to the point'. Nevertheless he had brought with him at least one new piece of information: Hitler had specifically demanded that Danzig and the existing Corridor should become part of the Reich, with a corridor for the Poles to Gdynia. Dahlerus had also made a suggestion which they had accepted: he should return to Germany that day ahead of Henderson. That had required a telephone call to Goering, who had spoken to Hitler, gaining his assent; and if nothing else, it won an extra day.

A further item for the Cabinet's information was that during the session with 'Mr D', Halifax had been asked to receive a telephone call: Ciano had been on the line from Rome, recommending British acceptance of Hitler's present proposals (which Chamberlain indicated they might well do) and repeating Italy's wish to co-operate in the search for peace. What none of them in London knew was that Ciano was positively seething with indignation, because the first he had known about Hitler's proposals to Britain was from the British. 'We are entirely in the dark,' he fumed to Mussolini. 'Hitler proposes to the English an alliance or something like it. And this was naturally without our knowledge.' The Duce's assessment was that it had happened because Hitler must feel a successful Italian intervention would raise Italy's prestige at the expense of Germany. With a snort of contempt, Ciano dismissed that idea outright: 'For me there is a simpler explanation, namely that the Germans are treacherous and deceitful. Any alliance with them becomes a bad alliance after a while.' He liked talking to Halifax; the English Foreign Secretary was always courteous and cordial. What a contrast with his German counterpart! 'Could there ever be a more revolting scoundrel than von Ribbentrop?'

In Poland Colonel Beck had reached a difficult decision; he was willing to consider the possibility of an exchange of German and Polish populations in the disputed areas. Nevertheless, being suitably cautious, he also ordered Polish mobilisation. Meanwhile in London, as 'C', the head of the Secret Intelligence Service, passed to the Foreign Office a report that General Halder and Admiral Raeder were both convinced that Britain would fight and had warned Hitler of the danger of a double-fronted war, 'Mr D' was hidden in Cadogan's room in the Foreign Office. In the waiting room Cadogan was talking to the French Ambassador Charles Corbin, and denied all knowledge of a 'mystery man'. 'C' had also produced a spy he wanted to send back with Henderson. 'Arranged that,' Cadogan noted laconically. As for the draft reply to Hitler, Leslie Hore-Belisha found it 'obsequious and deferential', a judgment with which his Cabinet colleagues agreed, sending it back to the Foreign Office for further work. In Cadogan's view, 'Cabinet did nothing'.

Cabinet rose at 4.30 p.m. An hour later in the Chancellery in Berlin, Adolf Hitler was in conference. 'A secret meeting,' Ciano wrote, with 'the Deputies of the Reichstag . . . I don't know what he said, nor has Attolico been able to tell me.' What he said, as noted by one of his audience, was simple and crucial: his minimum and maximum demands. Colonel Hans Oster scribbled them down: 'Minimum demands – return of Danzig, settling of Corridor question. Maximum demands – "depending on military situation".'

Rather less than three hours after that (according to the *News Chronicle*), at twenty minutes past seven, 'the mystery stranger's plane left Croydon for Heston'. Cadogan had insisted that Dahlerus should not leave Britain by the same route as he had entered the country, and in an effort to maintain secrecy had the Swede ferried first to the smaller airport. He reached Berlin's Tempelhof airport well before midnight and went direct to Goering with news of his activities during the day. The Field Marshal passed on the information privately, and at half past one in the morning, telephoned him with Hitler's reaction. The Führer was delighted that Britain wished for a peaceful settlement. Should it take the form of a treaty, or a pact? The suggestion that Danzig and surrounding issues should be settled by direct negotiation between Warsaw and Berlin was acceptable. In summary, said Goering, 'If Henderson's note corresponds with your report, we should reach agreement.'

Within half an hour Dahlerus was briefing Ogilvie-Forbes at the 'furniture depository', the British Embassy in Berlin. After a few hours' sleep he breakfasted on the morning of Monday, 28 August with Goering. The Field Marshal's subordinate commanders were hopeful that war could be avoided; but Goering did not agree. As far as he could tell, the Führer and von Ribbentrop still wanted open conflict in Europe.

A letter from George Bernard Shaw, querulous, but articulate as ever, was published in *The Times* that morning. Hitler was now under Stalin's thumb; Stalin's interest in peace was overwhelming. 'And everyone except myself,' the playwright complained, 'is frightened out of his or her wits. Why? Am I mad? If not, why? Why? Why?'

He did have some measure of the British people. Back at work in Essex, the indefatigably observant journalist Derek Silver noted that some of the printing firm's staff were taken off their regular work and put to filling sandbags, while in Sheffield Andrew Hole decided the time had come to alter his holiday plans, and with a group of friends took a trip to Leeds now, instead of later. Stopping on the way in 'a very miserable café' they noticed 'a very pathetic young woman obviously longing for company . . . We were all frightfully hilarious, ate twice as much as we'd expected to, and made crude and contemptuous jokes about Goebbels and Goering.' Looking grateful, the young woman cheered up considerably. At the same time in Edinburgh, Jim Latimer, a medical student aged twenty-four, noticed how petulant his golf-addicted grandfather had become. 'Having business worries,' young Latimer noted clinically, 'and in addition is "socketing" his mashie shots. Very dramatic manner of condemning Hitler, with a wonderful air of personal indignation.' During the day a family argument developed on the advisability of war, with Jim's parents and grandfather trying to balance the horror of dead children and babies against the loss of honour. On the whole they thought the loss of honour was worse. With youthfully easy philosophy, Jim wondered what the bother was. War, in his view, was the greatest calamity in the world; but the world had carried on regardless for millions of years. Even if he and they did not do so individually, he was sure the race would survive to fight another day. So, to the exasperation of his elders he ended his argument by borrowing a line from a song from the Great War, their war, 'what's the use of worrying?'

It was, Harold Nicolson noted, 'a lovely hot day'. He bathed, wrote an article for the *Spectator*, and pondered. The one o'clock news said that the Mediterranean and Baltic were closed to all British merchant shipping; in Germany all private train traffic, and even private post, was prohibited. He could remember clearly the same month, twenty-five years ago, when the Great War began. Now he marvelled at the contrast: 'Then we were excited . . . There was a sense of exhilaration. Today we are merely glum.'

During the afternoon Latimer sat sunning himself in his parents' Edinburgh garden, reading a book called *Privileged Spectator* – a curious title, under the circumstances. One day, when he was much older, he would be able to look back in memory and understand that, like millions of other people, he too had been a privileged spectator, present on the eve of the greatest upheaval in the history of the world. Yet at the time, again like those millions of others, each in their individual way, he could only see what was immediately around him: in his case, the old stone wall of the property, its lawn, trees and trim flowerbeds, and beyond, the roofs and chimneys of the Scottish capital. He did not know then, while he read, that Chamberlain was again visiting the king; that Arthur Greenwood, deputy leader of the Labour Party, visited No 10 four times in the course of the day; that staff in the War Office practised an air raid alert, scurrying to the cellars; that the price of gold suddenly and sharply increased; or that Sir Nevile Henderson was on his way back to Berlin. Of course, none of that was particularly secret: Latimer heard some of it on the news that evening and saw more in the papers next day. One reporter, seeing Sir Nevile go, wished him good luck. With a wave of his hat, the Ambassador replied, 'Thank you; I shall need all the good luck I can get.' .

There were other events, small private ones, which Latimer never knew at all, simply because like his own life they were not worthy of public record or announcement: for example, the activities of the Hawkers, Gerald and Betty; and of the Richters, Richard and his mother. Gerald Hawker was seventy-two years old but still worked as a consulting engineer. From his office in central

London he called his wife Betty, at home in NW11, and suggested they might take a little trip out of town to Claygate, near Esher in Surrey. Together they caught a train at 4.25 from Waterloo. At the same time, Richard Richter was pacing up and down the continental arrivals platform at Victoria, awaiting, with considerable agitation, the arrival of his mother from Vienna.

On the way to Claygate, Hawker explained to his wife what was on his mind: memories of the Great War. If things went wrong again with Germany, the capital might not be a very safe place to be, and he felt they ought to investigate the possibilities of a bolt-hole out of town. Claygate sounded very suitable: it was said to be attractive, and was fourteen miles from the heart of the city. With a direct railway link it was close enough to be convenient for work, and far enough to be safe. Arriving at Claygate punctually at 5 p.m., they spent an interesting three-and-a-half hours inspecting five different houses, before returning to town on the 8.42. They stopped for supper at Lyons' Corner House in the Strand, compared notes and agreed that the rooms offered by Mrs Ashdown in Gatehouse Lane were far and away the nicest. The rent was reasonable, and they could move in whenever they chose; so, well satisfied with their outing, they returned to NW11.

Richard Richter, meanwhile, was doing his best to drive safely and listen to the chilling tale his mother had to tell, of her summary arrest and imprisonment by the Gestapo. Slipping from English to German and back to English again, she did not notice that even after three years in England, and though he had a perfect command of the language, Richard's accent was still quite heavily German. But then, he had little chance to say anything, for she had scarcely stopped talking since their emotional meeting in London. There seemed to have been even less reason for her release than there had been for her imprisonment; a few days ago, an Indian maharaja, or someone who appeared to be a maharaja, had visited the prison and seen that among the female prisoners there was one British national. Perhaps he had had something to do with it. It sounded a wild idea, but no more so than anything else; and for both Richard and his mother the important thing that afternoon was that she was safe in England. But he could hardly square his own happy memories of the Austrian capital with his mother's description of it since the Anschluss, and as he drove her to his little house in Kenilworth, he decided that one day he would go back to Vienna, and, if it were possible, find out who in the Embassy had reported her to the Germans.

On Monday, 28 August 1939 these were just two of the many episodes in other private lives that John Latimer, drowsily reading in Edinburgh, never knew of at all. And years passed before he learned from history books what else happened in secret between public people that same sunny afternoon.

The Cabinet had met at twelve to finalise the reply to Hitler. To help them they had in front of them Dahlerus's report, forwarded by Ogilvie-Forbes. It was extremely encouraging: Hitler would accept international guarantees for Poland, and was willing to negotiate directly with the Poles. Knowing that, Cabinet agreed the final text of their reply; Chamberlain described it as dignified and firm, yet quite unprovocative. As soon as the session was over Sir Alexander Cadogan was ushered in to draft a momentous telegram, which Lord Halifax telephoned direct to Warsaw at 2 p.m. It asked if the Poles would accept direct negotiations with Berlin. Remembering how obdurate they had been about the Russians, their answer could be crucial. (As it happened, this day was Admiral Drax's fifty-ninth birthday; he spent it at home, quietly, still coming to terms with the failure of his mission.) For two hours, while Ambassador Kennard hastened to see Colonel Beck, the diplomats, politicians and civil servants in London waited in suspense, until at 4 p.m., just before Henderson's departure, the reply came back. It was a simple affirmative: Beck was willing to negotiate.

But just about then, General Franz Halder, Chief of Staff of the German Army, received via General Walter von Brauchitsch, Commander in Chief, a most important document from the Führer – his schedule for the invasion of Poland.

At 9 p.m. Henderson arrived in Berlin and was whisked to the British Embassy, where, among the stacks of unfamiliar furniture, his First Secretary had a message waiting for him. 'Must be at least a dozen sets of dining-room things alone,' said Ogilvie-Forbes ruefully. 'If it goes well with Herr H. tonight, we could have a party – no trouble in finding somewhere to sit, if one doesn't mind climbing a bit.' Henderson did not appear in the mood for levity. Asking for a half-bottle of champagne, the message and dinner, he began to prepare himself for what he suspected might be an ordeal. Ogilvie-Forbes put the mood down to pressure of work. The nervous and mental strain they had all been under for so long was certainly more than sufficiently trying; but he did not know, for Henderson had kept it secret from everyone, that the Ambassador was in constant physical pain. After a recent medical operation, he had been diagnosed as suffering from terminal cancer. Henderson ate and drank hurriedly, reading the message. It was the full text of the reply:

> Everything turns upon the nature of the settlement and the method by which it is to be reached. On these points, the importance of which cannot be absent from the Chancellor's mind, his message is silent, and His Majesty's Government feels compelled to point out that an understanding on both is essential if further progress is to be achieved.

The British government would not be bribed at Poland's expense: 'could not, for any advantage offered to Great Britain, acquiesce in a settlement which would put in jeopardy the independence of a State to whom they have given a guarantee.' In a paragraph added at the last minute, the Note proposed direct negotiations between Poland and Germany, explaining that the Polish government had given its definite assurance of willingness to negotiate, and it concluded:

> A just settlement of these questions between Germany and Poland may open the way to world peace. Failure to reach it would ruin the hopes of better understanding between Germany and Great Britain, would bring the two countries into conflict, and might well plunge the whole world into war. Such an outcome would be a calamity without parallel in history.

That's telling him, thought Henderson. *Could any reply be more precise or straightforward? It makes it easy for Hitler to avoid war, if he really wishes to do so.* Such was the British point of view; from the Axis side, as Count Ciano noted, things looked somewhat different. When he saw an outline of the text later that night, one of his thoughts was that 'the British action has induced Poland to become more conciliatory. This is probably the key to the whole situation.' Even so, his basic reaction to the Note was one of relief: *Not bad; in fact it leaves the door open to many possibilities.*

During Henderson's meal another message was brought in: the Führer wished to see him as soon as possible, and suggested ten o'clock. Henderson put off the meeting until half past; more haste, less speed. In fact at ten, another call was made, this time from Ribbentrop to von Mackensen, German Ambassador in Rome. Reports which Ribbentrop wanted to quell at once had reached Berlin of rumours in Italy that Germany was about to back down. On the contrary (von Mackensen was told) 'the armies are on the march'. And Henderson, making his final preparations to see Hitler, did not know that his colleagues in the British Foreign Office had just received more information from Dahlerus: all German forces would be positioned ready to attack Poland by the night of 30–31 August, only two nights away.

At 10.30, fortified by his half-bottle of champagne, the Ambassador arrived outside the Reich Chancellery. He was driven the short distance through pitch-dark streets – the blackout in Berlin. There had been a small crowd outside the Embassy; a much larger one waited outside the Chancellery. Both crowds were silent, and in the darkness the drum-roll from a guard of honour sounded unnaturally loud.

*

When they heard of it a little later, even those in the diplomatic service who did not particularly care for Sir Nevile agreed that he had managed the interview skilfully. His hosts had gone out of their way to set him at ease – even Ribbentrop was polite, and Hitler, looking well, 'was absolutely calm and normal,' Henderson reported. 'No fireworks or tirades of any kind.' Ribbentrop was present throughout the hour-long interview, and Paul Schmidt, translating, was surprised at how quiet the Führer was; he never even came close to losing his temper, and actually appeared to be interested in the British proposal.

There was only one aspect of Henderson's report which did cause concern in London. While he had been there the day before, he had put up the idea of a non-aggression pact between Britain and Germany. With the Prime Minister and Lord Halifax, Cadogan noted, 'I managed to kill this.' But Henderson still thought it a feasible idea. In the interview with Hitler he emphasised repeatedly that the whole British nation supported the Prime Minister's stand, that the time for a final decision had arrived, 'and it rested with Herr Hitler . . . Herr Hitler must choose between England and Poland'. Accepting that, Hitler expressed ('in moderate terms') his view that the Poles were incapable of being reasonable. Ribbentrop then intervened; could Henderson guarantee that the Prime Minister would still have unanimous British support if his policy was one of friendship towards Germany?

'There is no possible doubt whatever that he could and would,' Henderson answered, 'provided Germany co-operated.'

In that case, Hitler inquired smoothly, would England be willing to accept an alliance with Germany? 'I said,' Henderson wrote in his official account, 'speaking personally, I did not exclude such a possibility provided the developments justified it.'

That was way beyond his brief: it was neither the time nor place for an accredited Ambassador, acting as spokesman for his country, to express personal opinions. 'A treaty, Yes,' wrote Sir Robert Vansittart, the British Government's Chief Diplomatic Adviser, when he read the account. 'An alliance, No. An alliance means a military alliance if it means anything. And against whom should we be allying ourselves with such a gang as the present regime in Germany? The merest suggestion of it would ruin us in the United States.' Halifax agreed the notion was preposterous: 'An alliance raises all the difficulties in most acute form that we felt yesterday when discussing the "non-aggression pact" idea.' A stern warning came swiftly to Henderson, telling him not to allow the subject to crop up again. But it had come up, and even if the answer was only a personal one, it had not been rejected out of hand; as far as Hitler was concerned, that was the important thing. When the interview ended at 11.30 p.m., in a mood of self-congratulation, he immediately summoned his own Cabinet to tell them how well his plans seemed to be working. An alliance with Britain was not impossible; if it took place it would be a coup on a par with the Russian pact, probably splitting the western allies and certainly greatly reducing the risks concerning Poland. Further, he had worked the British into persuading the Poles to negotiate; and one had only to recall Austria and Czechoslovakia to see where such negotiations would lead. Schmidt should not have been surprised at the Führer's even temper; everything appeared to be falling into place.

At the same time in Warsaw, Sir Howard Kennard was finding sleep difficult. While Henderson had been with Hitler, he had been with Colonel Beck. The Colonel would not accept his advice. Poland continued to mobilise.

15

And still we wait from day to day

IN ST JAMES'S PARK in central London on the morning of Tuesday 29 August, three people were to be seen walking, and talking most earnestly together. One of the gentlemen was immediately recognisable, because of his tall, lean, rangy figure; the less familiar lady at his side was correctly assumed to be his wife. The second man was much shorter and slightly built, yet had an air of authority, and seemed to be leading the discussion. Sitting down together on a bench, they were joined presently by another couple. Again the newly-arrived lady must be the wife of the gentleman with her; and again there was no mistaking his handsome, famous face. The five strolled on together.

No one outside the quintet could hear their conversation, which was evidently private; no one had the temerity to follow them, and if anyone walking in the opposite direction passed them, a respectful greeting was courteously returned, and the discussion paused until the passer-by was out of earshot. It was another day of high humidity, but the sun ascending had burned off a morning fog and, though it was still early, was once again edging the temperature into the 70s. Grateful for the pleasant weather, Sir Alexander Cadogan, the Prime Minister and Mrs Chamberlain, and Lord and Lady Halifax continued to talk over Birger Dahlerus's report.

The Swedish go-between had telephoned at 7 a.m. after being briefed by Goering at a quarter past one in the morning on Hitler's reaction to the British note. Apparently the Führer 'was in fact only considering how reasonable he could be', and was about to extend an invitation to the Poles for discussions in Berlin. Dahlerus, enthusiastic and eager now his efforts seemed to be paying off, gave a strong recommendation that they should accept. Yet in the Foreign Office, the feeling that Dahlerus might not be entirely trustworthy was spreading; and ironically that was one view with which Ribbentrop would have agreed – he thought Dahlerus might be a British agent.

*

'The only bad news that I can see is the cricket – Surrey beating Middlesex. I ask you!'

'Well, I didn't ask you, and I think cricket's a stupid game anyway.'

Tempers were fraying in the Woodward household in east London. At breakfast Mr and Mrs Woodward had not disguised their worries about the future, and it rubbed off on their sons Ed and Jack. Although they were grown men – Ed was twenty-one and Jack nearly nineteen – they had been bickering like boys.

Ed's show of disdain for events outside cricket grounds maddened Jack. He hated to sound frightened, but he tried to ram home the reasons for his fear: 'You know what I saw? Blue lights in the train, that's what. They're so dim you can't even read.' He shrugged his shoulders. 'OK, nothing much. It just gives me the willies, that's all.'

'Scared by blue lights?' His brother sneered. 'You read too many ghost stories, that's your trouble.'

'Ed –' Torn between impatience and apprehension, Jack's voice was almost pleading. 'You like to pretend you're as thick as a plank, but you must have grasped it. If there's war, who d'you think's going to be doing the fighting? Among others.'

'Soldiers, of course. And sailors and pilots. Who d'you think, cloth-head?'

'I've got to go. But I'll tell you who I think – you and me. We're the right age. I'll bet you a quid we're both soldiers inside a year. G'bye.' Angry with everything, he slammed the door.

Ed stared after him and smiled. 'That's a quid you'll owe me then, little brother,' he said to himself. 'I'm going to join the navy.'

Andrew Hole began digging an air raid shelter in his mother's garden that morning. The soil was heavy clay, and it was back-breaking work. *A year ago*, he thought as the sun climbed and he toiled and sweated below, *she wouldn't have a stone moved*. The Scottish medical student, Jim Latimer, was in a thoroughly bad temper. Somehow he had got a bad sore throat, which he regarded as a professional insult. His morning was spent in Aberfeldy trying to get his car fixed; during the afternoon he had to go visiting with his parents in Perth; and in the evening, to his utter disgust, he had time for only nine holes of golf. His father read in the paper that his lucky number that day would be six, 'so he backed the sixth horse in every race at Birmingham, thus backing six losers'. Jim found some sardonic pleasure in that. His Dad had rendered him utterly speechless at one point with the suggestion that the best way out of the present pickle would be for Hitler to rent Danzig and the Corridor from the Poles. Though he did not say it out loud – he had learned it was not worth arguing – it was beyond young Latimer's grasp how dim some people could be. But with his sore throat, and 'everyone twittering the same thing over and over again', Tuesday, 29 August was altogether 'an aggravating day'.

Derek Silver, the Essex journalist, found that inexplicably his jitters had completely vanished. From Chelmsford he wrote to his girlfriend in Tunbridge Wells, saying with complete confidence that he would see her the following Sunday, 2 September. Another young journalist, twenty-four-year-old Michael Dowering, returned home with his wife to Surrey after a holiday in Eire 'to find,' as he wrote in his diary, 'everyone very het up – apparently a crisis on.' Three months ago he had reckoned 'on good authority' that Hitler would attack Poland on 5 September. 'Heaven knows what all the fuss is about . . . If we knew then, why are people getting so worried now, we ought to be fully prepared!' He was one who vehemently did not support the Prime Minister. 'Presumably it was that —— Chamberlain's fault for openly asserting that there was no reason to expect a crisis in the near future.' That, he seemed to remember, had been a week or two before they left on holiday. 'And now there is a crisis. He knew there would be one all along.'

The seventy-two-year-old consulting engineer Gerald Hawker went to his office at 10.30. There was no work to do, but 'my very capable secretary, Gladys Flight, strongly advised our getting out of London at once, because evacuation of children was expected at any moment'. He decided she was probably right – she usually was – 'so phoned my wife to this effect. Had some trouble to get her to agree because of our elder daughter Brenda being left alone in our home.' Fortunately Brenda was quite happy to go and stay with a friend, so Hawker was able to telegraph and write to their prospective landlady in Claygate, Mrs Ashdown, telling her they would arrive that evening. In Sheffield Frank Peters, a thirty-five-year-old clerk, was:

> waiting to hear what our Government will tell Hitler, and wondering if he will explode or climb down in view of the determined opposition. Will Mr Chamberlain say much in the House? I don't think so – only the usual vague talk. Getting a bit tired of the big headlines in the papers and the crisis news . . . Not seen much about 'No war this year' in the *Express* lately. No explanation yet . . .

He finished with suitable scepticism: 'but I am prepared to be reminded of their ability to foretell events if this blows over'.

Another normal morning in abnormal times. 'Nothing much,' Cadogan concluded. 'Further messages from Dahlerus, who seems to think that things are going well.'

Harold Nicolson heard the same thing from another Member, General Sir Edward Spears, who in turn had it from Count Edward Raczynski, the Polish

Ambassador to London. Far from being desperate, Raczynski was reported as saying 'things are going very nicely', and when the House reassembled early in the afternoon it was with a distinct air of optimism. There had been no attack over the past weekend, as most people had expected, and Henderson being shuttled back and forth seemed a hopeful sign. So, though anti-gas doors were being fitted in the House of Commons and sandbags piled against its basement windows, Members only found them amusing. 'The House is more cheerful than it has been for weeks,' Nicolson wrote when the short session was over. 'I think also they are proud of themselves for having behaved so well, so calmly, so unitedly today.'

They had indeed, even Winston Churchill and Anthony Eden. They were photographed entering the building together. Their shared strong opposition to Chamberlain's previous policy of appeasement towards Germany was internationally known; because of it, in Germany, and sometimes in Britain too, both had been repeatedly denounced as warmongers. Eden, the Member for Warwick and Leamington, had been Lord Halifax's immediate predecessor as Foreign Secretary, but after fiery arguments with the Prime Minister over foreign policy, had resigned in February 1938. The event had distressed Churchill deeply: 'There seemed one strong young figure standing up against long, dismal, drawling tides of drift and surrender, of wrong measurements and feeble impulses,' he had written. 'Now he has gone.' The photograph of the two men taken that afternoon was to be used in the *Tatler* the following week, with the caption 'Not a War Cabinet – unfortunately.' In fact by the time the magazine came out on 6 September Churchill was in the Cabinet, as First Lord of the Admiralty, and Eden, as a major in the Territorial Army, was in uniform. But on 29 August they did not attack the Prime Minister, as they had done so often before: his twenty-one-minute speech, explaining developments since Members had last met, was so eloquent, balanced and firm that scarcely anyone wished to criticise it.

His first words were designed to avoid any false optimism: 'The catastrophe is not yet on us, but I cannot say that the danger of it has yet in any way receded.' He warned that the press should exercise the utmost restraint: 'it is quite possible for a few thoughtless words in a paper, perhaps not of particular importance, to wreck the whole of the efforts which are being made by the Government'; and he apologised for being unable to give more than an outline of communications with Hitler. Honourable Members would understand that 'when issues so grave hang precariously in the balance, it is not in the public interest to publish these confidential communications'. Describing the national mood as one of calm, united confidence, he went on to list some of the preparations in hand: air defence in a state of instant readiness, key points protected, the whole of the fighting fleet ready to take up war dispositions at a moment's notice, the merchant fleet under Admiralty control and the Civil Defence regional organisation on a war footing. Evacuation plans for schoolchildren, mothers with young children, expectant mothers and the blind were prepared and had been practised. He added more ominously that preliminary steps had been taken in hospitals to prepare for the reception of casualties. All this, he believed, contributed to and justified 'the general absence of fear, or, indeed, of any violent emotion' in the country; and he ended with a stolid but stirring declaration:

> The British people are said sometimes to be slow to make up their minds, but, having made them up, they do not readily let go. The issue of peace or war is still undecided, and we still will hope, and still will work, for peace; but we will abate no jot of our resolution to hold fast to the line which we have laid down for ourselves.

Moods were dictated as much by location as anything else; in spite of Ambassador Raczynski's optimism, Danzig itself was a place of high tension. There was good reason: no traffic was permitted through the Free City; on the other side of Poland's southern frontier German troops were entering Slovakia, while to the east Russian troops were moving into position. And from what the Poles had heard, the British and French were weakening in their determination to stand by them. Polish mobilisation became general, over the protests of Ambassadors Kennard and Noël; and yet Zofya Olscholwska and her large family in Moniaki were completely undisturbed in their perfect rural tranquillity, while Niusia Zamecka was happily preparing for the next term at school. She had a new satchel and pencil box, and a new black overall with a white collar, two pockets and a belt. 'Next weekend we are going back to Warsaw,' she wrote. 'The trees are tired after the long hot summer and gossamer is floating in the air. The autumn has crept in and our holiday is almost over.' The only disappointment was that her father would not allow her to take her bicycle. 'I've tried to convince Papa that I could ride my bike in Warsaw's parks, but Papa said no. Papa can sometimes be as stubborn as Samson, the difference being that one can bribe Samson with sugar lumps.' And so, being a philosophical child, she spent the afternoon with her mother pickling pears and apples.

Gerald Hawker got home at five and settled down to sunbathe in the garden until seven, when he was called into his house to be presented with dinner. It did not take long: within an hour and a half he and his wife Betty were at Waterloo in good time for the 8.42 to Claygate. Regarding the move as no more than a temporary precaution, it disturbed them very little, and they were not surprised to find Mrs Ashdown ready to welcome them; she had, of course, received his letter of that morning, as well as the telegram, and everything was ready for them.

Jack Woodward's evening was spent with some friends digging up a wasps' nest in a wood and putting up with the jibes of other ramblers, who helpfully pointed out that their air raid shelter would have to be a lot deeper if it were to be any good. By then it was known in London's diplomatic circles that Mussolini had recommended Hitler to accept the British note; and in Berlin, still quivering with indignation, Sir Nevile Henderson was writing the official report of his latest meeting with Adolf Hitler. He had waited the whole day for a summons to the Chancellery, with only a single worry. While every indication was that Germans and Poles were feeling well-disposed to each other, the only diplomatic representative in Berlin who had not asked to see him that day was Josef Lipski, the Polish Ambassador.

Henderson had come to the Chancellery at a quarter past seven, expecting the Reich Chancellor to be as calm and sensible as he had been the night before. Instead, with Henderson completely unprepared for the change, Hitler reverted to the manic vituperative mode of diplomacy he generally favoured. Its immediate cause was the report in German newspapers of the deaths that day of five or six more Germans at Polish hands – reports which may or may not have been true, but which he at the very least feigned to accept. Gone was the semblance of sweet reason; in its place a shouting fury. Henderson did manage to extract a grudging acceptance of direct negotiation with Poland, but the Führer said plainly he was sure such talks would fail, expressing at the same time his deep resentment of British interference. It was when he bawled at Henderson that he, quite clearly, 'did not care how many Germans had been slaughtered in Poland' that the Ambassador lost his temper too. 'I proceeded to outshout Herr Hitler,' wrote Henderson in cold rage, aware that he was claiming something few could do, and honestly furious: although he was not pro-Nazi, he was more pro-German than pro-Polish. 'I told him I would not listen to such language from him or anybody. Such a statement was intolerable and an example of all his exaggerations. I added a good deal more, shouting at the top of my voice.'

The message reached Cadogan about 10 p.m. *Looks pretty bad*, he thought, and promptly took it round to Lord Halifax. Together they went on to No 10, and with the Prime Minister read in more detail Hitler's reply, an outpouring of abuse against Poland. 'Barbarous atrocities which cry to heaven', 'persecution of the German population of Poland', 'the murder of Germans settled in the country, or their compulsory evacuation in the most cruel circumstances', 'a state of affairs which is intolerable to a Great Power'; such was its general tone. 'I glared at Herr Hitler the whole time,' said Sir Nevile, with a touch of pride. But it was Hitler's final demand which, by its departure from normality, really irritated the British politicans. He was still willing to negotiate directly with the Poles; yet he insisted that a Polish plenipotentiary should come to Berlin for the purpose by the end of the following day. In London they agreed with Henderson's remark: the phrase sounded like an ultimatum.

There are two conflicting accounts of the immediate aftermath of that stormy, undiplomatic interview. According to one, as soon as Henderson had left the Chancellery, Hitler had something like a nervous collapse, and had to be given immediate medical attention. The other says that his mood changed instantly, that he declared gleefully that Poland would be finished within two months, and that a great peace conference would follow. Whichever is true – perhaps both, with a different time order – it is worth remembering the testimony of Hitler's translator, Paul Schmidt. The reply to the British note, with all its inflammatory accusations against Poland, had been written by Hitler and translated by Schmidt the night before.

That, of course, was not known in London then. Chamberlain, Halifax and Cadogan sat up late working on a reply to the outburst. 'Between us,' Cadogan noted, 'we knocked up a fairly hot draft by 12.30.' They continued working on it for a further two hours.

And still we wait . . . Far across the Atlantic ocean, Eleanor Roosevelt could not forget Europe. 'And still we wait from day to day,' she wrote, 'hoping and praying for peace. I feel that every day that bombs do not actually burst and guns go off, we have gained an advantage.' But nearer to the heart of events, though no less concerned, Count Ciano closed his diary for 29 August with a portentous note: 'The two armies are now within rifle range, and the slightest incident may cause a clash.' And at 2 a.m. on Wednesday 30 August, Sir Nevile Henderson was informed from Great Britain that Hitler's demand for the arrival of a Polish plenipotentiary that day was unreasonable. There would be no pressure from Britain on the Poles to comply.

Cycling to work on Wednesday morning, Derek Silver followed a route he had devised a few weeks ago – not the shortest, but one which took him past a newsagent's. He liked to get any news as soon as possible. This morning the newspaper hoardings carried only two words: 'Hitler replies.' He assumed rightly that that meant the reply was not to be made public (otherwise it would have said 'Hitler's reply') and he did not stop. In the office he got on with his usual first job of the day, ploughing through all the national daily papers for material he could use in his weekly provincial one. It was a smooth morning's work with no sense of crisis. Outside, half a dozen men were still engaged in a leisurely way (they could hardly be called busy) filling sandbags

183

with earth and piling them against the machine room wall. Feeling the need for a smoke, he went out to join them; smoking was banned indoors, but not outside ('yet!'), and they all chatted and joked about A R P.

The conversation continued inside when, back at his desk, he found that another reporter, Chris Marley, had just got back from holiday in Cornwall. Silver asked him what signs there were down there of military activity.

'Oh, practically none to speak of,' was the surprising answer. 'Of course, every single village has its A R P on the go, and most of them an Auxiliary Fire Service too; and naturally Plymouth's absolutely full of sailors. But that's about it, as far as visible signs go – no doubt it's all very hush-hush and underground, and we just don't get to see it. After all, if we could see it, so could everyone else.'

'But even if we could see it, we wouldn't have to write about it,' Silver remarked. 'Look at these, the *Herald* and the *Mail*. They've both got a story about Hornchurch R A F station. And both say what type of aircraft is held there. I think it's shamefully irresponsible.'

Glancing at the articles, Marley nodded. 'Frankly, I wouldn't have noticed it myself. Silver's unerring eye for security breaches strikes again. You'd be an utter beast if you were in charge of that kind of thing; but you're right. Talking of underground, though, I saw some wonderful caves on the Cornish coast. If they were furnished, they'd make the most perfect air raid shelters imaginable. What d'you reckon to a little story about that?'

'It's a good idea, but you'd better not write about it.'

Marley frowned. 'Why ever not? Saboteurs might go and blow the caves up?'

'Not that. I don't suppose there's a single place in Essex that could claim to have a self-respecting cave. If Joe Bloggs reads that he can make himself into a caveman and keep his wife and aunty safe, he'll fill up the car with tinned peaches, rush off to Cornwall, and we won't have anyone left in the county to buy our papers.'

A R P was also the first topic in Donald Richardson's office. Working in London, he was a solicitor in local government, and in common with more and more of his colleagues and friends, was undertaking warden's work in the evenings. He had been on duty until 8.30 the night before. However, there was little time to gossip; he had to go to Bow Street Police Court to prosecute a minor villain. Over there, he found that apart from sandbags round the door, the court looked quite normal inside and out; the only reminder of the outside world was when the magistrate referred briefly to the police having more than enough work at the moment. The right attitude, Richardson thought, nodding to show his agreement with the Bench. He did not think this would be a difficult prosecution, but every little thing helped.

In the Stock Market, reports that Hitler had studied Chamberlain's note with care led to a flurry of optimistic dealing; and at 10.45, less than two miles away in Downing Street, Birger Dahlerus was ushered discreetly into Number 10.

His latest secret concerned the conversation he had had with Goering in the early hours of the morning. It added two notable items of information to Henderson's report. The first was an explicit delineation of the geographical areas in which Hitler was most interested: Goering, in anger or panic, had dramatically pulled out an atlas, torn the appropriate page from it, and coloured in the relevant parts. Danzig was specifically included; Gdynia, however, was left out, to remain a Polish port whatever happened. The second item was that Hitler was willing to accept a plebiscite on the matter: depending on the result, either the existing Corridor would become German, with a Polish right of passage across to Gdynia, or the existing Corridor would remain Polish and the existing German right of passage to Danzig would stay in force. But Danzig itself must become German.

Chamberlain, Halifax and Cadogan were uncertain whether to believe Dahlerus. 'Says Hitler may offer a plebiscite,' Cadogan noted cautiously. But he added that if it were true, 'this throws a new light', and with his colleagues decided that a few questions to the Field Marshal would be in order.

Andrew Hole's diary was simple: 'Digging shelter in sweltering heat most of the day.' By lunchtime in Bow Street, Donald Richardson had secured the conviction he was after. Without a second thought for the man now facing sentence, he had coffee at Lyons and went on with a colleague to a nearby restaurant that catered especially for chess players. He found the game kept him in mental trim, but that lunchtime he was disappointed: he and his friend were checkmated into a long and tedious conversation with 'a garrulous old gentleman who insisted on talking about the crisis', and who did not appear to notice how fidgety they were, until their lunch period was over.

Harold Nicolson also lunched with a talkative gentleman, but he found it fascinating: Sir Ivone Kirkpatrick, now based in the London Foreign Office, had been First Secretary at the British Embassy in Berlin from the time that Hitler first came to power until last year, and had met the German leader many times. Nicolson and their companions, Lady Colefax and Lady Cunard, asked him eagerly what the man was like.

'Socially, and when he is host in his own house, he has a certain simple dignity,' Kirkpatrick answered. 'Like a farmer entertaining neighbours. None of Mussolini's showy vulgarity. But when one begins to work with him, or when one sees him dealing with great affairs, one has such a sense of . . . evil arrogance, that it is almost nauseating. In fact,' he confessed, 'some of the interviews I have seen have made me physically sick. You've probably heard people speak of his eyes being hypnotic. Certainly they're a very bright piercing blue, and when one actually meets him, they're virtually his only truly noticeable facial feature – photographs don't capture that quality. Otherwise I wouldn't say they're hypnotic at all.' He thought carefully and continued, 'They do look like the eyes of a mystic sometimes; but they dart with evil and treachery and malice. He is always laying down the law, and has a maddening way of talking – sharp, syncopated sentences – and gesture – he ends either with a sharp pat of his palm on the table, or a half-swing sideways in his chair, crossing his arms like Napoleon and staring at the ceiling in a suffering, detached way. He's terrifically impatient.'

'Impatient, yes – but a sense of actual evil? What gave you that feeling?'

'I'll give you one example; I could give you fifty. You recall when Roehm was murdered? The head of the *Sturmabteilung*, the Stormtroopers – it's just over five years ago now. Hitler ordered that, of course, and flew from Godesberg to Munich to make sure it was done; and one of those who was with him on his return told me how he had been in the very highest spirits, describing the whole business to his secretary in minute detail, even mimicking the gestures of fear that Roehm had made.' Kirkpatrick shook his head at the memory. 'No: he is not just a simple sadist, but something far worse. I don't think I am overstating it when I say he is actually evil. I have never encountered that before, and I hope never to do so again. It is a very, very strange experience.'

There was a silence around the table. Kirkpatrick smiled slightly: 'I'm sorry. Hardly lunchtime conversation. Let me tell you something else a little more cheerful. Less sinister, at any rate. Even some of the highest Nazis can be amazingly disloyal to him at times. For instance, when Henderson was going in for some important conversation with him, the man – I don't remember the name offhand, but it's irrelevant – the man who took Henderson to Hitler's study whispered to him as he opened the door.' Leaning forward, Kirkpatrick spoke in a hushed, conspiratorial tone, with a mock-German accent: '"For God's sake don't let him get away with it!"'

At 2.35 Betty Hawker took the train from Esher to London for an afternoon's shopping. From another direction Jack Woodward, the not-quite-nineteen-year-old civil servant, was travelling up to work. During the crisis his department was working in shifts, and he was on from 2.45 to 8.45. A small girl in the train was chattering enthusiastically to her mother: 'Did you have blue lights last time, Mum? . . . I'm glad we've got black stuff for our windows . . . The shelters in the park are deeper than ours . . .' Chilly with apprehension, he tried not to listen, but there was no getting away from it; and when he stepped out at the station he saw with a thrill of fear that armed guards were posted on every platform.

Gerald Hawker sat contentedly in his landlady's garden all afternoon, writing letters and reading *The Golden Bough*, an abridged edition, for he was not an ambitious reader.

In Chelmsford, cycling out to cover the funeral of a local worthy for his paper, Derek Silver admired the white lines that were being painted down the centre of the roads to help drivers in the blackout. *Going to mean pleasant night-cycling without lights*, he thought. *Also strikes one that white lines everywhere are going to cut out a lot of guesswork in careless and dangerous driving police court cases.* It seemed odd no one had thought of it before, but then crisis made people think a lot of new things. One such turned up at the office that afternoon: a thick green-covered book of about a hundred pages, labelled in large letters SECRET.

'The vindication of Silver, dear boy!' Chris Marley chuckled. 'It's D-Notices, hundreds of 'em, listing all the things we can't write about. Plane types and locations, locations and numbers of troops, you name it – no doubt caves as well somewhere. Makes you wonder what we can write about, without boring everyone to tears.'

Flicking through the pages and nodding with satisfaction, Silver remarked: 'It also makes you think why every newspaper, national or local, sounds so undisturbed. What was it Chamberlain said, "the general absence of fear"? Of course that's how it seems. You can only judge the nation's mood by the papers, and what it amounts to is that we aren't allowed to say anything which could benefit the possible enemy, which includes reporting fear and frightening people more than they are already.' Closing the heavy book and dropping it on the desk with a thump, he added: 'Just as well too, in my opinion.'

Frank Peters, the Sheffield clerk, would have disagreed strongly. 'Hitler's reply has come and ours has gone back,' he wrote. 'When do we get to know something? A year of crisis has left me feeling very calm. My wife made herself ill with worry last year, and is determined not to do so this time.' For him the most serious consideration was that 'if war comes, there is likely to be an immediate slump in our income. That is of more concern to us than bombs.'

George Bernard Shaw's letter of Monday, (Everyone is frightened out of his wits . . . why? Why? Why?) received an epigrammatic reply in *The Times* that morning: 'Who is frightened out of his wits? Who? Who? Who?' If there was one feeling which everyone shared, it was not fear so much as plain impatience with the seemingly endless waiting. 'A waiting period of that kind is often very trying', Chamberlain had said in the House, and he was right. In Walton-on-the-Naze on the Essex coast, not far from Silver's office, a young tea merchant named Ross Mackay described it: 'Everyone is feeling the strain, even in this out-of-the-way seaside town which never gets het up about anything.' During the morning, while helping to overhaul his van in the local garage, 'people talked of nothing else, and every newcomer offered his own theory. The optimists and the pessimists seem to be about even, while there are few middlemen. All are at one in wishing something would happen to ease the tension . . .'

At a quarter to three, just as Jack Woodward was beginning his shift, Chamberlain had sent a brief message to Hitler: not a reply, but merely to let the Reich Chancellor know that the continuing exchanges were welcome, his most recent interview with Henderson was being considered 'with all urgency', and an official reply would follow shortly. By then Birger Dahlerus had telephoned Goering from the Foreign Office. The Field Marshal could not be definite; however, repeating his hope of a plebiscite, he also hoped that Hitler's next proposal would not be in the form of a diktat, but a genuine offer. The only point on which he was certain was that a Polish plenipotentiary must come to Berlin that day. Both Cadogan and Halifax repeated emphatically that this was unreasonable. From Warsaw, Ambassador Kennard supported them in this judgment: in an early morning telephone call, before Dahlerus had arrived in London, he had expressed his certainty that 'it would be impossible to induce the Polish Government to send Colonel Beck, or any other representative, immediately to Berlin . . . They would certainly sooner fight and perish than submit to such humiliation.' Kennard had received a copy of the Hitler–Henderson interview demanding an immediate plenipotentiary, with instructions from London not to pass it on to the Polish authorities, and Joseph Kennedy, the American Ambassador to London, sent to Washington his own assessment that Chamberlain was more worried of getting Poland, than of Adolf Hitler, to reach agreement. He was right to an extent: there was concern in London that revealing the demand to Warsaw might result in a Polish reply so unco-operative that Hitler could feel at liberty to proceed as he chose. In that sense, the Poles were being protected from themselves. But there was still more to it: they were being protected from Hitler as well. Before passing on his demand, the British wanted to be absolutely certain that he was actually going to negotiate seriously, and was not merely manoeuvring for advantage so that he could give invasion a public justification.

By keeping the Führer's demand secret from the Poles, rightly or wrongly the British believed they were doing two things at once: firstly deferring war, and a war deferred might yet be a war avoided altogether; and secondly standing by the bottom line of their guarantee to Poland. If negotiations were to take place they must be real, without the threat of force, and with Poland treated as a nation equal to Germany.

For weeks past, Hitler's most secret intelligence service, the *Forschungsamt* or Research Office, had monitored, recorded and reported every telephone conversation between London and the British Embassy in Berlin. But despite their skill, which was of a very high order, they, and consequently the Führer, did not know that his demand had not been forwarded to the Polish government. In choosing this unilateral method of standing by its guarantee, the British government was accepting a very great risk and a very grave responsibility: for in Poland mobilisation carried on as if the demand had never been made, while in Germany news of that continuing mobilisation could only be viewed as a challenging refusal. And yet it did cause Hitler to hesitate. General Halder's diary for the 29th reads: 'Basic principles: Raise a barrage of demographic demands ... 30.8 – Poles in Berlin. 31.8 – *Zerplatzen*.' [The word means burst or blow up.] '1.9 – Use of force.'

On the 30th, however, again on information from Commander-in-Chief General von Brauchitsch, Halder noted that the Führer had amended the strategy: 'Make all preparations so that attack can begin at 4.30 a.m. on 1 September. Should negotiations in London require postponement, then 2 September. In that case we shall be notified before 3 p.m. tomorrow [31st] ... Either 1 September or 2 September. All off after 2 September.'

By half past four on 30 August every Polish city was plastered with posters summoning all men up to the age of forty to report for enlistment. At half past five, after receiving reports of German sabotage in Poland, another message came from London to Berlin: Germany must exercise complete restraint if Poland were to do so as well. At ten minutes to seven, the text of His Majesty's Government's reply was sent to Henderson. 'We understand,' it began, 'that the German Government are insisting that a Polish representative with full powers must come to Berlin to receive German proposals.' Nineteen of the twenty-four hours' notice given in the demand had by then elapsed, and this was to be the first official intimation to Berlin that a plenipotentiary might not arrive. When this reply was presented, it seemed scarcely credible, as if the British government had been sound asleep.

But it could not be presented yet. Lord Halifax was, in fact, asleep – he had gone to bed at five in the afternoon, exhausted – when the French Ambassador Charles Corbin came to the Foreign Office 'with,' Cadogan noted, 'an objection from his Government to a passage in our Note to Hitler. And Van [Sir Robert Vansittart] blew up. By desperate efforts managed to compose the differences and get PM's approval. Home about 8 – mad with fatigue. Things must now take their course . . . I can't help feeling Germans are in an awful fix.'

There was a marked and sinister change in the tenor of German news broadcasts during the evening. In place of the previous night's main subject, Anglo-German peace efforts, almost every item spoke of alleged atrocities on German people in Poland – rapes, murders, burnings, beatings – while the police looked on indifferently and the government made belligerent preparations. The same propaganda process had been used before the destruction of Czechoslovakia, and many Germans accepted it as gospel; but even so, by no means all were eager for a war of revenge. A couple of nights earlier Ulrich von Hassell had been to the cinema and seen a newsreel in which weeping women and children were shown, describing their sufferings in Poland. *A disgusting example of how human misery is exploited for propaganda purposes*, he thought, and noticed how the other spectators remained 'completely passive; there was only very weak applause at the showing of military pictures, not taken up by the bulk of the audience.'

'Today,' wrote Harold Nicolson on the evening of 30 August, 'when war seems a matter of hours, the absolute gloom of a week ago seems to have changed into determination, the gloom of anticipation melting into the gaiety of courage. It is as though we had taken our fill of apprehension and sadness and can absorb no more.' Other Britons, writing their diaries at the same time, backed this up. Jim Latimer, his mother and his aunt all took part in their golf club's weekly competition, and did rather well; his mother won the scratch prize, his aunt the first handicap, and he himself the second handicap. Andrew Hole went to the theatre to see Shaw's *Geneva*, and after listening to a Bach promenade concert on the wireless, Derek Silver went to the cinema, timing his arrival 'just right – getting in just as the frightful Kay Francis sobstuff second feature (*Comet over Broadway*) ends, and the news comes in.'

Even those ordinary folk who, with their own eyes, could see physical evidence of the times, seemed less inclined than ever before to be worried. Donald Richardson, the London solicitor, went walking with his wife on Ealing Common after supper, and, noticing a searchlight, strolled over to have a look at it. They 'found it surrounded by a fair-sized crowd, seemingly in almost holiday mood. A poor devil of a sentry marching up and down the fence was being ragged by schoolboys, who had laughing support from the crowd. When the sentry said "Keep back", a woman's said, "Listen to the voice of officialdom!"' Feeling sorry for the sentry, Mr and Mrs Richardson turned for home, where she went to bed early and he played draughts with his brother until eleven o'clock. Silver's film, *Stagecoach*, was over by then. 'Well up to expectations,' he jotted.

Walked home with my head full of its grand theme tune and got in just in time to hear 11 p.m. news summary. This tells of much mobilisation going on (reservists called up in France; cars, cycles commandeered in Poland; precautions in Switzerland), but while this warlike activity goes on, all seems much calmer on the diplomatic front. And so calmly to bed to write this.

He could scarcely have been more mistaken.

16

I hear the wings of the angel of peace

AT MIDNIGHT on 30 August 1939, in a room where Bismarck used to work in the German Foreign Office, Joachim von Ribbentrop sat at a small table, almost shivering with excitement. His face was pale, his lips set, his eyes unnaturally bright. Opposite him, speaking mostly in German, sat Sir Nevile Henderson; between them at the end of the table was Paul Schmidt, the sole spectator, translating whenever Sir Nevile's command of the language failed him. Beginning with the message that it was unreasonable to expect a plenipotentiary so swiftly, Henderson had just finished reciting the communications which he had sent in writing during the course of the day.

Ribbentrop's reply ignored it all. 'The time is up,' he said bluntly. 'Where's the Pole your government was to provide?'

Henderson did not give a direct reply; instead he handed over a letter from Chamberlain to Hitler, stating that Poland had been asked to prevent frontier incidents. Sir Nevile added that Germany should adopt a similar policy.

'The Poles are the aggressors, not we!' Ribbentrop retorted hotly. 'You've come to the wrong address.'

As calmly as he could, Henderson gave his government's suggestion that the Germans should follow normal diplomatic procedure and send their proposals through the Polish Ambassador.

Folding his arms, Ribbentrop shouted across the table: 'Out of the question, after what has happened! We demand that a negotiator empowered by his government with full authority should come here to Berlin.'

Schmidt saw Henderson's hands begin to tremble, and thought he was frightened; he was not known in Berlin as a brave diplomat. But then, as the Ambassador began to read the official British reply, Schmidt noticed his face was flushed red: the tremble was not from nerves but anger. As he read, Ribbentrop's frown deepened. He interrupted repeatedly, 'Ridiculous! Absurd!' and at the recommendation that troop movements should cease, burst out: 'That's an unheard-of suggestion!' Unfolding and refolding his arms, he stared at Henderson in direct challenge and shouted: 'Have you anything more to add?'

'Yes,' said Henderson in German, his own temper barely under control. 'As a verbal addition to the written reply, my government possesses information to the effect that Germans are committing acts of sabotage in Poland.'

Utterly enraged, Ribbentrop roared at him: 'That's a damned lie of the Polish government's! I can only tell you, Herr Henderson, that the position is damned serious!'

Henderson reeled in shock; then he too lost his temper completely, and, wagging his finger like a schoolmaster, shouted back: 'You have just said "damned". That's no word for a statesman to use in so grave a situation.'

For a moment Ribbentrop stared at him in disbelief, then jumping to his feet, he bellowed, 'What did you say?'

Henderson jumped up too. The two men leaned on the table breathing heavily and glaring furiously at each other. Schmidt gulped. 'According to diplomatic convention,' he wrote later, 'I too should have risen; but to be frank I did not quite know how an interpreter should behave when speakers passed from words to deeds.' Thinking that at any moment it might well degenerate into a fist-fight, 'I therefore remained quietly seated and pretended to be writing in my note-book.'

The least that can happen now, he thought, *is that the Foreign Minister of the Reich will throw His Britannic Majesty's Ambassador out of the door*. He did not find it in the least bit amusing.

After a good deal more glaring and heavy breathing, however, there seemed to be an improvement. Peeping up warily, Schmidt saw 'the two fighting cocks' were sitting down again, their composure evidently somewhat restored. Ribbentrop then began to read through Hitler's proposals to Poland, a list which became known as the Sixteen Points. He did so in German, naturally, and Sir Nevile, proud of his ability with the language, did not ask for an interpretation. But he was not as good a linguist as he thought. To him, it seemed Ribbentrop gabbled through the list; later, both Ribbentrop and Schmidt denied this, Schmidt adding that the Reichsminister actually elaborated on the outline of some of them. Henderson's lack of complete comprehension was unfortunate; but the real surprise, both for him and Schmidt, occurred when he asked for a copy to transmit to London. Schmidt wondered why he asked – to provide a copy was normal diplomatic practice – and could hardly believe Ribbentrop's answer. 'Sorry, no,' the Reichsminister said, with an inappropriate smile. 'I cannot hand you these proposals.'

Henderson obviously thought he had misheard and asked the question again, only to receive the same reply. Throwing the document on the table, Ribbentrop said, 'Anyhow, as the Polish envoy has not appeared, it's out of date.'

Schmidt 'suddenly saw the game', and believed ever after that the proposals had only been put up for show, that there never had been any intention they should actually be used. They were generous; the Poles might have actually accepted them. He desperately wished he could intervene, but was unable to; an interpreter putting his own view could only create confusion. Grinding his teeth, he saw a chance of peace 'deliberately sabotaged' before his eyes. *So this is what Hitler and Ribbentrop have been discussing*, he thought, and gazed at Henderson, mentally willing him to ask for an English translation, which Ribbentrop could not have refused; Schmidt would then have translated slowly enough for Sir Nevile to take full notes. But the Ambassador was not telepathic. The moment passed.

For many people it was a long and almost sleepless night. Henderson returned to the Embassy convinced that the last hope of peace had vanished. He had put it to Ribbentrop that if the proposals were out of date, they had in fact been an ultimatum. Ribbentrop heatedly dismissed the allegation as nonsense, whereupon Henderson suggested that the Reichsminister should at least contact Josef Lipski, the Polish Ambassador to Berlin, direct. Ribbentrop's reply 'in the most violent terms', was that 'he would never ask the Ambassador to visit him. He hinted that if the Polish Ambassador asked him for an interview it might be different.'

With that – the slenderest of hopes for Henderson – they parted. As soon as he reached his own Embassy he called Ambassador Lipski over to see him, while his First Secretary, Sir George Ogilvie-Forbes, informed Birger Dahlerus of the ghastly interview with Ribbentrop. By half past one in the morning of Thursday 31 August, Lipski was at the British Embassy, and Dahlerus was in consultation with Hermann Goering. The Field Marshal had just been appointed head of a newly formed Ministerial Council for the Defence of the Reich, a War Cabinet. Now, listening to the Swede's reprimand ('This is no way to treat the Ambassador of an Empire like Great Britain,) he protested that the German proposals were extremely liberal, 'formulated to show how extremely anxious the Führer is to reach an agreement with Great Britain'. Very well, said Dahlerus, give them a copy.

By 3 a.m. Lipski was back in the Polish Embassy, having had Henderson implore him to seek Colonel Beck's immediate permission to receive the Sixteen Points. Ambassador Kennard had already been in contact with Beck at midnight to give him the text of the British reply, and on Halifax's instructions to ask for the earliest possible opening of discussions between Poland and Germany. Lipski, by telegraph to Warsaw, was able to add details of three of the Sixteen Points, the only three of which Henderson was fully certain. He also despatched the Embassy Counsellor, Prince Lubomirski, to Warsaw to request permission for an interview with Ribbentrop. At four in the morning Henderson dropped into bed, confused and exhausted. At 5.35 Kennard reported to London that more delay was unavoidable: Beck insisted he must consult with his government, and could only promise that a formal reply would be sent to Berlin by noon. Less than an hour later, at 6.30 a.m., German troops were ordered to take up their positions.

On the last morning of August 1939 Count Ciano's first note was uncharacteristically brief: 'An ugly awakening.' Ambassador Attolico had telephoned him at nine o'clock, 'saying that the situation is desperate and that unless something new comes up there will be war in a few hours'. The Count went quickly to the Palazzo Venezia thinking: *We must find a new solution.* By then Sir Nevile Henderson had already conducted three separate interviews, of which the third had been with Attolico. The first, at 8 a.m., was with Henryk Malhomme, First Secretary of the Polish Embassy. Lipski himself had been too busy to come. In a voice filled with sadness, Henderson's opening words to his visitor were: 'Malhomme, I do not like war.' They had known each other from previous years working in Belgrade, and their meeting this morning was sad and friendly, Henderson still fuzzy from lack of sleep, Malhomme deeply concerned about the outcome of the next few hours. Above all, it emerged that the British Ambassador wanted to tell a Pole exactly what he felt about Poland, especially since he had come to believe that many of them regarded him as a Nazi sympathiser. He was not. On the contrary, he said, he knew Poland well because of his passion for hunting; he liked the people and the country; he had done and would continue to do everything in his power to avoid a war which must end in Poland's destruction. But if he failed, Malhomme recorded, 'he would like me, when the war was over, to repeat his motives to my compatriots'. Despite the frightening augury for his own immediate future, Malhomme was touched by the un-British display of emotion and promised he would do as Henderson asked. As if neither wished to proceed with the day, their farewell handshake was noticeably long.

Over breakfast Henderson's second visitor was another old friend, Ulrich von Hassell. Because of his curious position, an ex-diplomat opposed to the Nazi regime but still well-connected, he could be used by those still within the administration who shared his dislike of Nazism. On this occasion he emphasised he was only there in a private capacity, without orders; Ernst von Weizsäcker, Ribbentrop's Under-Secretary, had asked him if he could influence the British Ambassador at least as far as getting Lipski to announce before noon the intention of sending a plenipotentiary. Henderson had already done as much as he could towards that, as he explained, adding that the chief difficulty lay in Germany's methods: 'particularly', von Hassell noted, 'the way in which we expected the English to order the Poles around like stupid little boys.' To this the German answered that the Poles' persistent silence was also objectionable. It did not occur to Henderson, but this was a remarkable thing for von Hassell to say. He was a cultured, educated, experienced man, yet even he accepted that one part of current Nazi propaganda. He put it down to Slav behaviour; no doubt Henderson remembered that kind of thing from his time in St Petersburg, before the Russian Revolution. That touched off the Englishman's fragile emotions again. 'Ah,' he said nostalgically, 'I wish those times would only come back.'

'Times in which you almost strangled your own ambassador?' In an effort to make a joke, von Hassell was remembering an occasion one night, when, thinking he had disturbed a burglar, Henderson had tackled his boss. *Now*, von Hassell thought, seeing Sir Nevile smile with a mixture of sadness and anger, *he is in a mood to strangle others*.

As if reading his thoughts, the Ambassador said with finality, 'It would be easy, you know, to reach an understanding between England and Germany if it were not for the calamitous Ribbentrop. With him, it will never be possible.'

The 'ugly awakening' to the last day of August extended far beyond Rome. Derek Silver's landlady declared herself 'quite shocked' at the sight of so many sandbags in Chelmsford. 'All round the 'ospital, they are, Mr Silver,' she said. 'And the police station, and the drill 'alls, and even the grocers are putting up thick wooden shutters over their windows, so you can't see a thing they've got inside. Not that they've got so much as usual,' she added reflectively. 'People do seem to be buying a lot. Makes you rather feel it's . . . a bit serious, doesn't it?'

In London the solicitor Donald Richardson was having a good deal of trouble calming down his father-in-law, 'rather jittery on the subject of mustard gas, some idiot having taken the trouble yesterday to explain in detail the way it works'. As far as possible Richardson reassured him, using his judicial skills of argument to invent an 'authoritative (but highly inaccurate) account of how little danger there really is . . .'

In Chartwell, his house near Westerham in Kent, Churchill was working that morning on his *History of the English-Speaking Peoples*. The four-volume work, commissioned in September 1932 for £20,000, was scheduled for publication in 1940. Other events intervened, and the first volume eventually appeared sixteen years late. While he was out of office, writing and lecturing formed his sole source of income (by October 1988, incidentally, the equivalent of £20,000 was £536,618) and he knew intimately how hard such work could be. But these days, sleeping with a gun under his pillow and a guard at his door, 'it is a relief,' he admitted, 'to be able to escape into other centuries.'

In Berlin, however, there was no escape from the pressures of the morning, intensifying moment by moment. Henderson passed on von Hassell's assessment to Attolico, and at 9.15, soon after the Italian had left the British Embassy, sent it to London as well: 'On the best possible authority . . . If nothing happens within the next two or three hours, i.e. possibly by midday, German Government will declare war.' It was received in London at 9.30 just as von Hassell, through the agency of Olga Riegele, Goering's sister, was talking to the Field Marshal. His assertion, startlingly at odds with Ribbentrop's, was that if the Poles had not definitely refused to come, the proposals remained on the table. Von Hassell hurried back to Henderson (He was greatly interested), and then reported to von Weizsäcker, who promised to keep him up to date.

The next two crucial hours were quite simply weird: a graphic demonstration of the rivalry and opposition that lay between Goering and Ribbentrop. At 10 a.m. Birger Dahlerus appeared at the British Embassy, bearing with him the typed copy of the Sixteen Points he had received from Goering. 'Tired and depressed', Henderson listened to him, and, deciding he could be used to pressurise Lipski, sent him with Sir George Ogilvie-Forbes over to the Polish Embassy. Lipski was not impressed. His staff were already packing up the Embassy; he himself was irritated at having Dahlerus, whom he had never heard of before, introduced into the business. Finding it difficult to credit Sir George's explanation that the Swede was a neutral who had the confidence of the British Cabinet, the British Embassy and the German government (and just as difficult to keep track of Dahlerus's excited ramblings); he asked him to go and dictate what notes he had to a secretary in another room, then told Sir George that the German plan breached Polish sovereignty. It was, he declared, 'a trap, and acceptance was quite out of the question'.

At eleven o'clock, after consulting with Mussolini, Ciano telephoned Halifax 'to tell him that the Duce can intervene with Hitler only if he brings a fat prize: Danzig. Empty-handed, he can do nothing.' Halifax refused, saying the most urgent problem was to get the Poles and Germans to agree to talk to each other – could the Count help with that? Ciano said he would try.

But at the time that conversation was going on between Rome and London, Ernst von Weizsäcker, in the presence of Ulrich von Hassell, was being told by Ribbentrop in no uncertain terms that Sir Nevile Henderson should *not* be given a copy of the proposals. He himself would telephone Henderson to say the Poles could have the proposals if they sent a plenipotentiary.

Forbidding von Weizsäcker to have any further dealings with Henderson, Ribbentrop added that Hitler had ordered any overtures to be rejected.

Thus, as midday on 31 August approached, the situation in Berlin was more than a little confused. (As Ciano put it later that evening, 'There is something obscure about the whole German attitude.') Ribbentrop and Goering, two of the most important men in the country, were operating without mutual liaison in exactly contradictory ways. Officially, that is, as far as the Führer and his Foreign Minister were concerned, the Poles still did not know the detailed proposals, which might or might not be out of date, and which therefore might or might not have been an ultimatum, and they would not know them officially unless they first agreed to send a plenipotentiary. Unofficially the Poles did now have a good idea of the proposals, but they would not budge unless they were told them officially beforehand. Von Hassell noted:

> That was proof for Weizsäcker that Hitler and Ribbentrop wanted war; they imagined their proposals had furnished them with an alibi. This seems nonsensical to me if the proposals are not given to the Poles. Ribbentrop further stated that during the next half hour it would be decided whether the proposals should be made public. If this is really under discussion it is altogether incomprehensible why the proposals should not be given to Henderson, unless they want war.

And from von Weizsäcker he heard the British point of view, as told to the Italians: 'The only question now was one of honour: whether we asked Lipski to call, or whether he came of his own accord.'

Twelve noon came and went without any reply from Warsaw to Berlin, or any apparent change in the impasse. The Ribbentrop–Goering clash was not the only difference of opinion on one side; when Henderson urged the British Foreign Office to put direct pressure on the Poles, Kennard's advice was a firm contradiction: 'H M Ambassador at Berlin appears to consider German terms reasonable. I fear that I cannot agree with him from point of view of Warsaw.' By half past twelve the Foreign Office had from Henderson a copy of the detailed proposals, and at the same time received a telephone call from Dahlerus, speaking from Henderson's office. Sir Horace Wilson took the call, and, as the Swede babbled excitedly on, was horrified to hear a German voice repeating his words.

'You'd better give this information to Henderson,' he interrupted, but Dahlerus took no notice, saying that Lipski had described the proposals as out of the question.

'Don't get ahead of the clock,' Wilson exclaimed in agitation. He could still hear the eavesdropping German voice. 'If there's anything to say,

Henderson should say it in the ordinary way.' Still Dahlerus ignored him, announcing that the Poles were not going to give way and that it was obvious they were being deliberately obstructive.

'Shut up!' Wilson yelled. But even that did not stop Dahlerus. Wilson slammed the receiver down. It was the only way to end the grotesque indiscretions, and fuming with rage he promptly sent a stern telegram of warning to Henderson.

Within minutes the Foreign Office telephone shrilled again. Ciano was on the line from Rome with a new suggestion: what about a peace conference hosted by Mussolini, to take place on 5 September? André François-Poncet, the French Ambassador to Rome, was sceptical but thought it a good idea; Sir Percy Loraine, his British counterpart, welcomed it with enthusiasm; Lord Halifax was favourable but said he must ask the Prime Minister. Simultaneously (the time was 12.40) Colonel Beck was talking to Lipski from Warsaw. More experienced than the amateur Dahlerus, he used a code for his message, which was that Lipski should request an interview with Ribbentrop: Poland was 'favourably considering' Britain's request to open direct negotiations. A formal reply would come soon. Meanwhile, and this was secret, for the Ambassador's knowledge only, Lipski should not begin any concrete negotiations, and if asked to do so, should refer back to his government.

At 1 p.m. Lipski duly applied for the interview. To his mystification, Ribbentrop did not seem particularly surprised to hear from him, or particularly eager to see him. Some time in the afternoon would do; he would be told when. Uncertain, and more suspicious than ever, the Ambassador wondered what prompted this unexpected lack of interest. It was a very long time before he knew the terrible double truth. The Research Office had not, this time, made the error of letting themselves be overheard. In spite of Beck's code, his entire message including the secret section had been intercepted, decoded and delivered to Ribbentrop, before Lipski's call at one o'clock; and an hour earlier, at noon, Adolf Hitler had issued an order whose title would become infamous – Directive No 1 for the Conduct of the War.

Donald Richardson, the London solicitor, did something he had never done before; he went to see a film at lunchtime, the latest one by Will Hay, and overstayed his lunch hour by fifty per cent. The sense of guilt at such irresponsible behaviour lessened his enjoyment of the film, but when he returned to the office he did not know whether to feel relieved or cross – no one had noticed his absence.

Jack Woodward, the young civil servant, was at work – his shift that day was from noon to 7 p.m. He was unable to forget the latest things he had overheard on the way in, as two old ladies gossiped morbidly.

'They're clearing out all the 'ospitals . . . Doctors won't 'alf 'ave a time . . . They're digging an underground passage from the railway to the 'ospital . . . They've remembered everything, nothing left to chance . . . If a train's 'it they can take 'em into 'ospital quicker – poor fings might lie on the track for hours.' He could not help thinking that soon he too might be one of those 'poor fings'.

In Edinburgh, Jim Latimer was recovering from 'the shock of my life'. Feeling something wriggling in his pocket, he had put his hand in without looking and pulled out a live and very angry wasp. In Surrey, after a walk to Oxshott, Gerald and Betty Hawker were returning to Mrs Ashdown's well satisfied with their choice of bolt-hole. 'This place is a *beauty spot*,' wrote Gerald with pleasure.

In Essex, the journalist Derek Silver had just heard a shocking announcement on the 2 p.m. news. Evacuation of three million mothers and children from 'the menaced areas' would begin tomorrow. The added information that this did not mean war was regarded as inevitable reassured him somewhat. However, telephoning the local education department, he found both that they were preparing to receive evacuated children and that their own children would not return to school as expected on 4 September, but would remain on holiday until further notice. The railway station too advertised a 'heavy curtailment' of normal services over the next four days; but 'far more unpleasant than the crisis', his main job that afternoon was to visit the father of a twenty-one-year-old RAF man whose bomber was believed to have crashed into the North Sea.

At Walton-on-the-Naze on the coast of that sea, the decision to start evacuating the cities caused great commotion. 'Visitors have left in crowds while the going is good,' Ross Mackay wrote, 'and we may now expect thousands of children who will be everything from thrilled to bewildered.' Business was brisk: 'it takes little effort to sell tea just now. Nearly everyone is buying extra.' He saw his first ARP rehearsal, 'four inhuman objects in gasproof clothes', and concluded in wonder: 'Walton has never taken anything so seriously.'

In a peaceful cemetery far away Niusia Zamecka knelt down beside her mother and aunt at the foot of her grandmother's grave. Fresh crimson gladioli fanned out from its centre, with two bunches of white and yellow dahlias. Close by were three new graves, one quite small. Niusia asked her mother who was buried in the little grave. There were pink ribbons on its bouquets and wreaths, and her mother said it must have been a little girl. Niusia was shocked: she had always thought that only old people died. 'I should hate to be dead,' she wrote, 'when there is so much to live for. Every new day is as exciting as a birthday present. In fact, the more I live the more I like it.'

'Grandmama dead' – the code words had stung Alfred Helmut Naujocks to action, ending his fourteen-day wait at Gleiwitz. As Niusia and her mother made arrangements with Father Jakob for the christening of Irka's infant daughter, SS Sturmbannführer Naujocks and Heinrich Mueller, head of the Gestapo, were carrying out the arrangements long planned by General Heydrich. The canned goods were ready; a dozen 'condemned criminals' dressed in Polish military uniform, here administered with fatal injections and subsequently shot. All was in order.

At 4 p.m. the OKW *Oberkommando der Wehrmacht*, the High Command of the Armed Forces, issued instructions for the great assault, and the executive order was confirmed:

The Supreme Commander of the Armed Forces   Berlin
OKW/WFA Nr. 170/39 g. K. Chefs. L1   31st August 1939
MOST SECRET
Senior Commanders only   8 copies
By hand of Officer only   COPY NO 2

Directive No 1 for the Conduct of the War

1. Since the situation on Germany's Eastern frontier has become intolerable, and all political possibilities of peaceful settlement have been exhausted, I have decided upon a *solution by force*.
2. *The attack on Poland* will be undertaken in accordance with the preparations made for 'Case White', with such variations as may be necessitated by the build-up of the Army which is now virtually complete.
   The allocation of tanks and the purpose of the operation remains unchanged.

   Date of attack: 1st September 1939. Time of attack: —

   This time also applies to operations at Gdynia, in the Bay of Danzig, and at the Dirschau Bridge.
3. *In the West* it is important to leave the responsibility for opening hostilities unmistakably to England and France . . . Attacks on the English homeland are to be prepared, bearing in mind that inconclusive results with insufficient forces are to be avoided in all circumstances.

[signed] Adolf Hitler.

In the draft orders the time of attack was left blank. When the orders were issued, it was inserted in red: 0445.

In Danzig large crowds had turned out to admire and gawk at the cruiser, in port for a courtesy visit. A long banner strung over the fronts of warehouses welcomed her: *Wilkommen, Schleswig-Holstein.* At 5 p.m. Captain Karl Dönitz, head of the U-boat arm of the Reich navy, moved from U-boat command headquarters east, in Swinemünde, to a plain wooden barracks on the outskirts of Wilhelmshaven, designated his western command headquarters 'if *Fall Weiss* should develop into a major war'. In the German capital, seeing that Hitler was in a noticeably genial frame of mind, Admiral Albrecht approached him diffidently and ventured his opinion that England must inevitably be drawn into the conflict. He never understood the Führer's reply: *'Ich höre den Friedensengel rauschen'* – 'I hear the wings of the angel of peace.'

There were few sandbags in Berlin, and no evacuation: the atmosphere was no different from any other day of the past four weeks. Had it been otherwise, an event taking place at the same time in another part of the city would have been inconceivably surreal: Goering, Henderson, Dahlerus and Ogilvie-Forbes were having tea together. Dahlerus had already treated Goering to a slap-up meal at the Hotel Esplanade, where the brandy was of such outstanding quality that the plump Field Marshal insisted on removing two bottles for later use. Dahlerus's current brainwave was that Goering should meet a Polish representative somewhere in Holland. Goering, whose gastronomic content served to remind him what personal loss might be at stake, hoped it might be possible, and Henderson agreed that he would submit the proposal to the Foreign Office. Privately though, the British Ambassador considered that if Goering could spare so much time right then, it could only be a bad omen. He would not bother to send the message.

The discussion was still going on at 6.30, when Ambassador Lipski was at last permitted to see Ribbentrop. Once again Paul Schmidt was present, and in all his years as a diplomatic interpreter the meeting was the shortest he had ever attended.

'Have you authority to negotiate with us now on the German proposals?' Ribbentrop asked.

'No,' Lipski replied, as the Reichsminister had known he must.

'Well then,' said Ribbentrop, 'there is no point in our continuing this conversation.' And that was that.

At the same moment a message was sent from High Command to U-boats waiting on Atlantic stations. Hostilities with Poland would begin at 4.45 a.m.

but 'attitude of Western powers still uncertain', so there were to be 'no attacks against English forces except in self-defence or by special order'. Very soon after, Lipski got back to his Embassy and tried to call Warsaw. He could not: the line had been cut.

'A calm twilight,' wrote Harold Nicolson, 'under which the garden stretches itself at ease. The flag hangs limply on its flag-staff. It is odd to feel that the world as I knew it has only a few hours more to run.'

'But why?' With the Duce's agreement, Count Ciano was talking to Sir Percy Loraine, and committing a deliberate political indiscretion. 'Why do you want to start the irreparable? Can't you understand that we shall never start a war against you and the French?' There had been no reply at all from London about the idea of a peace conference; this was the only way the Italians could think of to transmit their determination to keep out of things while appearing, as Hitler's allies, to make ready. Loraine, almost in tears, gripped Ciano's hands in his: he had guessed that two weeks ago, he said, and had so informed London; but he was delighted to hear it direct from the count. 'He shook my hand again,' Ciano wrote, 'and left happy.' At 7 p.m. – nine minutes after sunset in Britain – London cut its communications with Italy.

Exactly an hour later, German-speaking people listening to the broadcasts from Gleiwitz were horrified out of their evening routine by the sound of gunfire from their wirelesses. There were shouts, crashes and more shots, and through the commotion, for three or four minutes, a voice yelling in Polish. Heydrich's nasty little stunt was going according to plan: scattered outside the radio station, the customs house at Hochlinden and other border points, lay a dozen drugged and dying men in Polish uniforms.

Returning home on the blue-lit train, there was nothing for Jack Woodward to do but, despite himself, listen to the girls in his carriage: 'They've got whisky, brandy, meat extracts and everything down in our basement . . . If it weren't so serious, it wouldn't half be funny.' He thought with dread of the sudden popularity of air raid shelters. *Haven't seen any lying around in gardens the last two days* . . . Andrew Hole, true to his name, had spent the day getting further into the intractable Sheffield clay. Four feet down, he had had enough, but because there had been no word from Germany published throughout the day, and considering there was no obvious reason for delay, he felt more hopeful than before. After a bath he went out with his wife to see some friends.

Donald Richardson could not get home from London, the evacuation traffic was so heavy; so in spite of his guilty trip to the cinema at lunchtime, he went to see another film, *Double Crime on the Maginot Line*. Coming out he saw three news-vendors doing a good trade and bought a paper. There was nothing new, but 'somehow,' he wrote, 'it seems as if anything might have happened in the interval, it seems so long'.

Derek Silver was very alarmed by the evening paper placard, 'Mobilisation order', and breathed a great sigh of relief when he found it applied only to reservists. His chatty landlady told him she had been that day to see a wealthy friend who had spent five pounds on sandbagging her house. Neither woman had stored any extra food – 'Well, you'd be too young to remember, Mr Silver, but there was plenty to eat in the last war.'

At 9 p.m. all radio stations in Germany interrupted their scheduled programmes and broadcast, word for word, the Sixteen Points. The broadcasts omitted to mention that one-and-a-half million fully armed German soldiers were in forward positions on every one of the common borders with Poland, that tank units were with them, and that every German military airfield was alive with final preparations. To William Shirer, an American journalist resident in Berlin, and to all his foreign colleagues, the Sixteen Points sounded eminently reasonable. Within minutes they were being received in Great Britain, and there the reaction was the same, or stronger. Derek Silver thought so, although 'still we are kept in the air as to the next step'.

Andrew Hole and his wife returned home to find a sight they found 'horribly ominous'. By the light of hurricane lamps, neighbours were continuing to build his mother's air raid shelter. But when they heard the broadcast of the Sixteen Points, 'though we knew it might be false, we embraced it with joy'.

The world turned, and darkness spread from the east. Each in its different mood, the nations of Europe slept. Niusia slept in happy innocence; in happy ignorance, Zofya Olscholwska slept. In Devon, tired from the work on the farm, Kit Dennis slept; in the orchard below her window, Mary the lamb slept; in London, wrapped in the security of an unshakeable faith, the cycling pilgrim Francis Vanek slept peacefully. In the distant Shetlands, on the remote island of Foula, fragrant, well-banked peat fires smouldered and the Smith family, Willie, Lizzie and their three daughters, all slept, and dreamed of wind and work and heather, and salt sea spray.

The world turned, and darkness was on the face of the deep. Sunset came to eastern America, and night beckoned. In the Schoharie Rest, with an ideal escape from Mrs Seidel's well-meant inquisitions, Ernest Kroll and Heinz Lindt read aloud to each other from the works of Alphonse Daudet and William Shakespeare's *A Midsummer Night's Dream*: 'the perfect text,' said

Kroll, 'for August nights in the country.' In Oakland, in the state of Maine, Vacationland, Barkeley Goodrich snuggled down under his blankets in the big old bed on the cottage porch, wondering hazily if the thunder would come rumbling across the East Pond again. Not many miles away little Libby Tufts was sound asleep already: at eleven years, two months and three days, to be awake at a quarter to midnight was utterly beyond her.

Strangely enough, the small town in which she slept was named South Poland. A quarter to midnight on Thursday 31 August, 1939 in South Poland, Maine, USA, was a quarter to five the following morning in the country of Poland. And there, at that moment, the darkness was shattered.

17

Time limit?

AS HE REACHED HIS OFFICE in the Horse Guards on Friday 1 September, General Sir Edmund Ironside could hear Big Ben striking ten o'clock. Inside the room the telephone was ringing. It was Winston Churchill, calling from Chartwell. 'They've started,' the familiar gruff voice announced. 'Warsaw and Cracow are being bombed now.'

'Great God in Heaven! Thank you for telling me, Winston. Goodbye.'

Without hesitation, Ironside telephoned the War Office to speak to General Lord Gort, Chief of the Imperial General Staff. Gort was an officer of exceptional gallantry: during the Great War he had been mentioned in dispatches nine times, and, in addition to the Military Cross and DSO with two bars, had won the Victoria Cross. But today, complaining to Ironside that he was off to a meeting, he did not believe what he heard. 'Well, it's true,' Ironside repeated testily. 'You'd better tell Belisha.' Gort did so, and within minutes Leslie Hore-Belisha, the Minister for War, was seen rushing to 10 Downing Street. A sudden thought came to Ironside. Telephoning Churchill, he asked him how he had got the news. 'From the Polish Ambassador, an hour and a half ago,' Churchill replied. 'He was absolutely definite. I'm afraid you don't need to doubt it.'

Ironside assured him he had had no such doubts, and hung up. But as he gazed out of the window, he said to himself, 'How could the War Office possibly be ignorant of this?'

It was a hot, misty morning in London. West of the Horse Guards Parade, St James's Park, Green Park and Hyde Park stretched into the haze, two and a half miles of almost uninterrupted urban garden. In another Hyde Park, some three thousand miles further west, at the precise moment of Churchill's call to Ironside, Eleanor Roosevelt was awakened by the telephone. For her, the time was 5 a.m. 'It was my husband in Washington,' she wrote a little later, 'to tell me the sad news that Germany had invaded Poland and that her planes were bombing Polish cities. He told me that Hitler was about to address the Reichstag, so we turned on the radio and listened until six o'clock.'

'. . . *Dieses möchte ich der Welt erzählen* . . .' In spite of the hiss and crackle of static interference, the harsh, metallic voice from the Kroll Opera House in Berlin came over clearly:

> I should like to say this to the world. I alone was in the position to make such proposals . . . For two whole days I sat with my Government and waited . . . I can no longer find any willingness on the part of the Polish Government to conduct serious negotiations with us . . . I have therefore resolved to speak to Poland in the same language that Poland for months past has used towards us . . . This night for the first time Polish regular soldiers fired on our own territory . . . We have been returning the fire, and from now on, bombs will be met with bombs.

Among all the lies and distortions, the Führer said one thing that day, and one thing only, which was true: 'I now want to be nothing but the first soldier of the German Reich. Therefore, I have once more put on that uniform which was once most sacred and dear to me. I will not take it off again until victory is secured – or I will not live to see the outcome.' It was intended to sound heroic, and perhaps to some it did; but few Germans stopped to think what it actually meant. After leading the nation into war, Hitler acknowledged with those words that he could not stomach the possibility of defeat. If that came, he would be dead, leaving Germany to sort itself out without him.

Outside the grandeur of the Opera House, under a sultry sky overcast with low grey clouds, the streets of Berlin were almost deserted. All newspapers had been rushing out extra editions since early morning, but to his surprise William Shirer noticed that hardly anyone was buying them. The Berliners seemed not to be interested, or even to care, and it occurred to him they might just be too dazed – *dazed*, he thought, *by waking up to find themselves in a war which they had been sure the Führer would somehow avoid. They cannot quite believe it, now that it has come.* He was right, so right indeed that elsewhere in Berlin, and also in Düsseldorf, his thoughts were being echoed almost exactly. Ulrich von Hassell heard Hitler's speech in his hotel room and dismissed it in one word: 'weak'. Throughout the capital he found 'only official enthusiasm over the closing of the border . . . The feeling that war is really here has not yet penetrated the public mind. They are for the most part apathetic, and still look upon it as a sort of Party project.' Similarly, after listening to Hitler's broadcast, the young soldier Bernt Engelmann drove with an army motorcycle courier named Pliechelko into Düsseldorf. 'No crowds had gathered,' Engelmann wrote later:

> We saw no trace of rejoicing, certainly none of the wild enthusiasm that Germans had shown when war broke out in August 1914. Here and

there small groups of people clustered around the newsstands, talking quietly among themselves, depressed and anxious. No one waved to us soldiers or pressed bouquets into our hands . . . 'They don't believe it yet,' Pliechelko said. 'They probably thought everything would turn out all right this time, too.'

Zofya Olscholwska's reaction was identical. That section of the Polish population fortunate enough to live in the heart of the country, away from borders and cities, heard the appalling news over the wireless. The one at Moniaki had a huge horn-shaped loudspeaker, like the one on the HMV advertisement; and like the little dog, she and her family huddled around, ears cocked in fixed, disbelieving attention. As the announcement ended, someone wailed: 'How could it have been so easy for them?' 'Thank God Taddeus is on his way to Britain,' said someone else; and Zofya, suddenly feeling she might vomit, remembered that her husband was travelling via Riga in Latvia, and that to get there, he was flying in a German plane.

Niusia's first hint of the invasion was at ten minutes to ten. She was returning from the privy when she heard aeroplanes and, looking up, saw two machines circling each other:

> I thought it was manoeuvres. Then I heard some machine-guns and everybody came out of the house to see what was happening. Grandpa said, 'My God! It's war!' and rushed indoors to switch on the wireless . . . Everybody was stunned. With ears glued to the loudspeaker we were trying to catch the fading words. The battery or the accumulator, or both, were packing up. When we could no longer hear even a whisper from the wireless set, Grandpa turned the switch off and looked at our anguished faces. He knelt down in front of the picture of Jesus Christ and started to pray aloud. We repeated after Grandpa, 'Our Father, Who art in Heaven, hallowed be Thy name . . .'

It was the same in Britain too. 'Few people really thought it would happen,' wrote Ross Mackay. 'Everywhere people stood in groups discussing it. Schoolchildren arrived by the trainload, all very subdued. The wireless confines itself to news bulletins and instructions to the people, with gramophone records in between. The Country has mobilised . . .'

After his elation the night before on learning of the Sixteen Points, Andrew Hole had no feeling left. He and his wife spent the morning 'packing up for the duration – a queer job; too busy to be emotional; bunging all the valuable china into boxes in the cellar'. For various reasons, some people did not hear the news at once. Harold Nicolson was sitting in a deckchair at Sissinghurst Castle, deeply engrossed in reading, when his wife Vita came walking quickly down the path. 'It has begun,' she said, and told him all she knew, including the fact that Parliament was recalled for 6 p.m. He noticed it was exactly 10.45. Plenty of time to finish his book. He carried on reading, and Miss Macmillan, their secretary, brought him his gas mask.

Donald Richardson, the London solicitor, found all normal work in his office had ceased, so he had a not very successful go at *The Times* crossword and finished reading a novel. But then rumours began to circulate; and when at last he was able to contact his wife she was weeping so much she could not speak. Half-heartedly, he finished off his routine work 'and waited for orders, and waited and waited . . . After being for more than half an hour alone in my own office, I feel as though I have completely lost touch with events outside, yet I have the greatest reluctance to look at a paper or listen to the wireless. War seems absurdly remote for *me*.'

In spite of being a journalist, Derek Silver missed it as well. On the way to work he passed a *Daily Mail* placard as usual, but all it said was 'Hitler's 6 a.m. proclamation'. He did not know the Führer had made a broadcast to the Wehrmacht just before then, and since war was not mentioned he ignored the placard. Twenty empty buses were waiting at the station for evacuees; trestle tables were set out with tins of biscuits; but otherwise there was nothing unusual. By five to twelve he had been sitting in the Police Court for an hour and a half, taking notes on a case of such interminable dullness that for preference he began reading a volume entitled *Cheddar Gorge: A Book of English Cheeses*. Then the office boy from a rival paper came in with a note for his boss, who was chairman of the bench, and whispered to Silver something that sounded like 'Thames . . . bombed'. For an instant his stomach turned over, but the boy repeated more clearly, 'Eight towns in Poland bombed.' With worldly-wise relief Silver whispered back: 'Tell it to the Marines. Just exaggerated frontier incidents. They've been having frontier incidents all week and we aren't at war yet.' 'We're not now, but we soon will be,' the boy hissed in return. 'It's real – it's on the wireless now.' He left the court, and, hastily packing his papers together, Silver hurried after him.

In fact the Marines had been among the first in Britain to know. Sandy Powell was one, seventeen-and-a-half years old, six foot three with a 48 inch chest. In Whale Island, the naval gunnery school in Portsmouth, he was on parade at 8.30 a.m. with about a hundred other men of C Company, when the adjutant, Captain Pickton-Phillips, informed them of the invasion. 'The Germans,' Pickton-Phillips added, 'have two or three days to get out of Poland. If they do, well and good; if they don't, I have no doubt you are all ready.' They were: remaining rigidly at attention, not one Marine showed any reaction until the parade was dismissed.

During his phone call just after ten o'clock, Ironside must have misinterpreted Lord Gort's reaction and the Minister of War's hasty departure for No 10, because as early as half past five Leslie Hore-Belisha had received the first terse intimation, 'Germans are through.' At 7 a.m. Sir Alexander Cadogan had been awakened by a telephone message; at nine he had picked up Lord Halifax from Eaton Square and gone to Downing Street. At 10.30 Count Edward Raczynski, the Polish Ambassador, was the first foreign diplomat to see Halifax. Even he had no written evidence, only telephoned information, but, he said, 'The Polish Government considers this to be a case of aggression under Article 1 of the Anglo-Polish Treaty of Mutual Assistance.'

'I have very little doubt of it,' Halifax replied. Soon after, he summoned Theo Kordt, the German Chargé d'Affaires, for an interview. It was completely unproductive: Halifax did not know exactly where Poland had been invaded, and Kordt, who was certainly not going to tell him, suggested his information might be mistaken. At 11.30 the Cabinet met, as the Prime Minister said in his opening address, 'under the gravest possible conditions. The event against which we have fought so long and earnestly has come upon us. But our consciences are clear, and there should be no possible question now where our duty lies.'

Before noon, therefore, both in the Polish Embassy and the Cabinet Office in London, it was taken virtually for granted that within a very short period Britain would fulfil its guarantee to Poland. But instead another international conflict began, bloodless yet as fraught with danger as the undeclared war which had been raging since dawn; and Chamberlain's government found itself on the brink of overthrow.

'In all the break-up of the office routine, there is a distinctly holiday-adventure feeling apparent with everyone,' Donald Richardson wrote. He wished he could share the mood. 'Behind it all, at least as far as I am concerned, however, there is a cold fear that keeps popping into my heart – chiefly,' he noted wryly, 'through my ears. All yesterday and today my hearing has been keenly on the alert, however absorbed I may have been in any job, and at least once an hour I hear a backfire, or what seems like gunfire, and my whole being leaps at it . . .'

At noon in Berlin, Goering took Birger Dahlerus to see Hitler in the Chancellery. Along with a ridiculous suggestion that Marshal Smigly-Rydz should come at once to Berlin – as if the Polish Commander-in-Chief might not be sufficiently busy, and in any case he would not contemplate an action which would be tantamount to surrender – Sir Nevile Henderson had also informed London that after the Opera House speech, Hitler had begun to address his generals, but had broken down and been unable to finish. He had recovered somewhat by the time he received Dahlerus, and opened the interview by thanking the Swede for all his efforts. But then, blaming Britain for their failure, he began once again to grow passionately excited. Poland, he declared, would be crushed and annihilated as a nation. If Britain still wished to talk, he was willing to do so, but – and gesticulating violently – he began to shout, 'If England wants to fight for a year, I shall fight two years . . . If England wants to fight for three years, I shall fight for three years . . .' Crouching low and clenching his fists, his voice rose to a shriek: 'And if it is necessary, I shall fight ten years!'

Another shriek echoed through Chelmsford market, a terrible, high-pitched wailing scream that did not stop. Seeing the crowd, Derek Silver pushed his way through. 'Press!' he called out. 'Excuse me, Press!' A man looked at him in surprise as he elbowed past. 'Nothin' 'ere for the papers, mate,' he said. 'It's only a pig 'avin' its teeth off.' Sure enough, struggling against ropes and the firm grip of several men, a large pig was being crudely operated on, its front teeth being cut off with a hacksaw. To Silver's amazement, the crowd seemed to be enjoying the spectacle. He backed off with distaste, and, as the tortured animal's cries pursued him, muttered to himself: 'Well, war shouldn't bother them too much.'

In the dining room of the Schoharie Rest, Ernest Kroll and Heinz Lindt tucked into an extra-hearty breakfast: it was the last morning of their holiday, and Mrs Seidel wanted to stoke them up for the journey back to New York. Through the closed kitchen door the sound of the wireless came only as an ominous vibrating hum. Whatever it was saying, it was sure to be bad news, and they did not want to hear. 'I expect she'll tell us anyway when she brings the pancakes in,' Ernest muttered sombrely. For once, however, she did nothing of the sort, but bustled around in a motherly way, making sure that they had every comfort possible, and bringing them packets of sandwiches for the downriver boat trip. But there was evidently something on her mind. 'Look,' she said, 'why don't you boys stay a little longer? When will you have such a good time again?' Sincerely wishing they could, they bade her farewell with affection: for all her gossipy ways she was a kind-hearted woman, and they would both remember her and the Schoharie Rest with fondness. Yet work called; their week was up, and Otto Bettmann was running his photographic archive with the help of only one secretary. Mrs Seidel took them to the bus stop. From there they retraced their route to Catskill, boarded the *Governor Clinton* and, sitting on the vessel's open top deck, steamed sedately down to Manhattan.

That was where they learned the news they had been avoiding. Descending the gangplank, they heard newsboys shouting, saw them holding up placards with huge black headlines: HITLER INVADES POLAND. Heinz stopped.

Ernest could see he had tears in his eyes. 'Now it's just a matter of time,' said Heinz, his voice choked. 'Hitler will come here.'

Ernest could still hear those words the following morning when he reported for work at the Archive. Herr Bettmann was already there, and he greeted his employee with a weird smile. 'Kaput,' he said, 'Europe is kaput.' Using the surname with which Hitler's illegitimate father was born, he went on: 'Nobody would stand up to that Schickelgruber. Ach, that Chamberlain! Now we shall all have to pay the price. America too. America will be alone – without the will – without even the strength – to stop the Nazis.' Rubbing his hands one inside the other to stifle a shiver, he sighed deeply and said: 'Why did not someone stand up in the beginning to that Schickelgruber?' It was by then only the second day of war between Germany and Poland, but with sinking apprehension, Ernest Kroll realised that at least two people in America had already mentally surrendered.

But would there actually be a war between Britain and Germany? If so, when – why not immediately? These were the questions unexpectedly exercising the British Cabinet during the afternoon of Friday, 1 September. The first hesitations were expressed in the Cabinet by ministers whose names were not recorded, but who argued that their information was insufficiently firm to allow the irrevocable step of declaring war. Birger Dahlerus had been on the telephone to Cadogan, requesting permission to come to England again and return to Berlin with General Ironside as a mediator. He would not accept Cadogan's refusal, demanding that the suggestion be put to the Cabinet. Their answer was robust: 'out of the question. The only way in which a world war can be stopped is (1) that hostilities be suspended and (2) German troops should be immediately withdrawn from Polish territory.' So much for that one. The Cabinet's agreed communication to Germany said much the same, with the added observation that if the conditions were not instantly met, the British 'will without hesitation fulfil their obligations to Poland'.

It was Chamberlain who pointed out that the conditions might not be met. The only remaining option would be to declare war. The governments of Britain and France had already agreed that such a declaration should come from both simultaneously. But as Germany's blitzkrieg smashed more and more deeply into Poland, it transpired that although the French Cabinet, meeting at the same time as their British counterparts, had decided on immediate mobilisation, the French Parliament was not going to be recalled until 3 p.m. next day, Saturday, 2 September. The implications of this were considerable. Only Parliament could pass a war budget, without which war could not be declared; and only Parliament could permit the inclusion of a time limit in any warning, since that would amount to an ultimatum.

Thus, when the House of Commons convened at 6 o'clock on Friday evening, the Prime Minister's speech, firm as it was, fell short of expectations. It was a dramatic, twilit scene: the lights were dimmed, the blackout curtains were tightly shut, and as Chamberlain and Arthur Greenwood, deputy Leader of the Labour opposition, entered together, they were loudly cheered by all Members. In the Distinguished Strangers' Gallery, the Polish and Russian Ambassadors found themselves sitting side by side, as, in the dim chamber below, the Prime Minister described what measures had been taken so far. When he told the House that the Sixteen Points ('which Hitler claims to have been rejected') had never even been communicated to the Poles, there was an audible gasp on all sides, and in ringing tones, Lady Astor exclaimed, 'Well, I never did!' But when he read out the text which in a few hours Sir Nevile Henderson would give to Hitler, one Member cried out: 'Time limit?' There was none.

'He is evidently in real moral agony,' Harold Nicolson wrote, 'and the general feeling in the House is one of deep sympathy for him and of utter misery for ourselves.'

In Chelmsford, hearing reports of the speech, Derek Silver found in it 'a loop-hole of hope . . . We are giving Hitler a last chance to turn back.' But he reflected, 'every hour we waste is an hour gained by him in his invasion'. Close by, children dancing on sheets of corrugated iron were making a great racket which did not stop until they were driven indoors by rain. Thereafter there was no sound except hammering as people nailed up blackout curtains.

Later in the evening in London, walking through 'a perfectly black city', Harold Nicolson began to wonder why no time limit had been given; and within twenty-four hours the House's attitude to Chamberlain had swung completely around.

'Aren't we a very old team?' At half past midnight on the morning of 2 September, Winston Churchill was wide awake and writing a letter to the Prime Minister. As a matter of course under the exceptionally threatening circumstances, the entire Cabinet had resigned in order to allow Chamberlain to form a much smaller, more compact War Cabinet. Churchill had at long last been invited to rejoin, and although he would be without portfolio, that is, a specific area of responsibility, he accepted with pleasure. By midnight though, he had heard nothing more from Chamberlain. His letter began in a semi-jocular way, a complaint against old age. The six Cabinet members he knew of, including himself, aggregated 386 years – 'an average of over 64! only one year short of the Old Age Pension!' – and he wished to urge the inclusion of some younger men, particularly Anthony Eden. But far more seriously, by the time he wrote his letter he had heard that, even though the

Poles had been under heavy attack for thirty hours, there was talk in Paris of sending yet another note to Germany. 'I trust you will be able,' he wrote, 'to announce our Joint Declaration of War at latest when Parliament meets this afternoon . . . I really do not know what has happened during the course of this agitated day; though it seems to me that entirely different ideas have ruled from those which you expressed to me when you said "the die was cast".'

Many others were awake in Britain, among them Donald Richardson, too frightened to sleep, 'one could not dream it could be so dark in London'; and Derek Silver in Chelmsford. With a sudden intimation of mortality, he had become very preoccupied with the thought that he and his girlfriend had never made love. 'In view of the situation', he wondered if he might broach the subject, and then realised he would have to buy a contraceptive, something he had never done before. The thought of future embarrassment blended with a tingling anticipation and, feeling a sudden need for fresh air, he switched his light out, opened the blackout curtains and the window, and returned to his virginal bed.

The uncertain hours of darkness passed in peace for Britain, while for Poland the war continued. Sunrise on Saturday came at 5.12 a.m. London was soon warm and humid: it would be a close, muggy day. During the morning Lord and Lady Halifax went walking again with Sir Alexander Cadogan, grateful for the extra security of their new environment – the king had given Halifax a key to the gardens of Buckingham Palace. Absently they admired the purple autumn crocuses blooming on the lawns, but as Cadogan wrote later in the day, there had been 'no answer from Germans. We are simply waiting.'

So too, in Berlin, were Ambassadors Henderson and Coulondre. The night before, both had presented their countries' notes to Ribbentrop, though not simultaneously, as they had wished: the Reichsminister would not allow it, and had seen first Henderson at 9.30 and Coulondre half an hour later. Henderson's staff had already moved from their houses to a hotel adjacent to the Embassy and had burnt ciphers and confidential documents, while he had asked the American Chargé d'Affaires to be 'good enough to take charge of British interests in the event of war'. But so far there was not a hint of a reply from either the Chancellery or the German Foreign Office.

Donald Richardson awoke to a magnificent sense of safety, mainly because neither he nor, it seemed, anyone else had expected there would be quite so many barrage balloons. On his way to work he counted a hundred and fifty floating over the city. Thrilled to imagine how many more there were that he could not see, he determined not to have another empty anxious day like yesterday, and since there was no legal work to be done, persuaded his boss to let him act as doorman for the Town Hall. As he pointed out, many people were coming in unidentified, and 'any ill-disposed I R A man could blow the place to bits with impunity'.

He was kept happily busy the whole day long, sorting out hundreds of callers, mostly people wanting gas masks. A high percentage were foreign refugees; others wanted to volunteer for the forces. One old man of at least eighty tottered in 'to see if he was wanted'. A very old lady in nurse's uniform, charming to look at and charmingly mannered, 'stoutly declared she had been right through the last war and was ready to face the next: "I may not be young, but I'm still active."' But others were less cooperative, such as the woman who accepted A R P night duty, then refused because, although it was more than six hours before her duty began – plenty of time to get home independently for warm clothes – no official car could be provided for the task. Then there were the pathetic ones, the most difficult to handle: the crippled man with a crippled wife and a six-days-old baby, just sent home from the maternity hospital to make way for casualties, and somehow left out of the evacuation scheme; and another young woman, 'her face showing long suffering', asking about evacuation plans for her parents, both aged over eighty. 'Sorry,' he had to say, 'nothing doing yet.' 'Never mind,' she replied. 'I'm sure there's not going to be a war.' Good for you, he thought, and wished her luck.

The British Parliament was going to meet at 2.45, expecting to hear of firm decisions taken in conjunction with France. It was at half past one in the afternoon of 2 September that the real trouble with the French government began, an hour and a half before their Parliament met. Their general staff had advised them that forty-eight hours was still needed to complete evacuation and general mobilisation; their Foreign Minister Georges Bonnet therefore insisted that if an ultimatum was given to Germany, it should not be less than that time, and should begin from noon on 3 September. Lord Halifax told Sir Eric Phipps, British Ambassador to Paris, that the apparent delays and the French government's attitude were causing 'some misgiving here', and added: 'We should be grateful for anything you can do to infuse courage and determination into M. Bonnet.' No sooner was that done than another telephone call came from Count Ciano which, though well meant, only increased British nervousness about the French. Ciano explained that he had approached Ribbentrop again with a suggestion for a five-power peace conference; that Ribbentrop had rejected it with the assertion that Britain and France had, in their notes of the night before, made an ultimatum to Germany; that Ambassador Attolico had raced around to those countries' embassies and received confirmation that no ultimatum was involved; that Hitler had then been willing to consider a conference, and would reply by noon on 3 September; and finally, that the French government had already agreed to the proposal. (Indeed, in his diary the Count wrote privately that he had proposed the conference as a result of French pressure, and that judging from Bonnet's tone of voice when told of progress in Berlin, it 'produced lively satisfaction in Paris'.) Now, he wondered, what did the British think of this?

The short answer was not much. Sir John Simon, Chancellor of the Exchequer, was due to speak on Chamberlain's behalf in the Commons with a prepared statement saying that no reply had come from Germany, that Britain was unwilling to wait longer and that as soon as the French Parliament had finished its session an ultimatum would be sent. He was just going into the Chamber to say this when Halifax, rushing over from the Foreign Office, managed to stop him with a breathless warning to 'make no statement at all about the international situation.'

'I never remember spending such a miserable afternoon and evening,' Halifax wrote later. 'From 3 to 5.30 we were telephoning to Bonnet, who I suspect had committed himself rather further than he was willing to admit to the conference.' It was an appalling quandary. 'You seem to me,' Halifax told Bonnet cogently, 'to believe that one can resuscitate a corpse with holy water!' When a message from Colonel Beck to Bonnet became known in London, the French Foreign Minister's attitude seemed even more extraordinary: for the day before Beck had told him plainly, 'We are in the thick of war as a result of unprovoked aggression. The question before us is not that of a conference but the common action which should be taken by the Allies to resist.'

That was precisely the British government's view, yet the immediate decisiveness and essential co-operation expected from France were missing. However much anyone in London might want peace, it was never again to be peace at any price: everyone from Chamberlain down was firm on that. The alliance with Poland would not be sold out. But by the same token the alliance with France could not be ignored; the agreement for joint action must be honoured. Britain could not make a unilateral declaration; yet if a conference was undertaken while German troops were still in Poland, how wretchedly timid it would appear! If it was even suggested, Chamberlain's government would certainly fall; and all the while, though Bonnet appeared to ignore it, their mutual ally was under attack.

The Cabinet met at 4.15 in what Halifax delicately described as an 'extremely difficult mood'. The weather matched them: inside and outside the Cabinet Room the air was hot and humid, with intermittent rumbles of distant thunder. Halifax summarised the communications with Ciano and Bonnet, and gave the provisional conclusions he and Chamberlain had agreed

– to allow the Germans until noon or possibly midnight next day for their reply, which must accept an armistice; and to insist as a precondition for a conference that German troops must be withdrawn from Poland. But hardly anyone in the Cabinet would support those ideas. A heated argument began as one Minister after another demanded no further delay. Malcolm MacDonald, Secretary of State for the Colonies, remarked bitingly, 'The Germans can make up their minds quickly enough on occasion, and have been known to ask other people to make up their minds in a very short time.'

Chamberlain realised he had severely misjudged his Ministers' frame of mind. A personal message from the Polish Ambassador and a telegram from Warsaw strengthened them further; the message, which Chamberlain read out, was a plea for an immediate honouring of Britain's obligations. He read the telegram aloud as well: 'Battle today over the whole of the front has increased in intensity and has acquired a very serious character. Our troops are opposing strong resistance. The whole of German air force is engaged against Poland. Villages and factories bombarded. The engagement of German aircraft by allied forces of greatest urgency.'

That settled it. Prime Minister and Cabinet together agreed that Hitler would be informed he could have until midnight that night to decide on all the questions facing him, and the Cabinet accepted that Halifax and Chamberlain would work out the communication's precise wording in conjunction with the French. Members of Parliament would be informed that evening.

Packed and tense, the House of Commons was waiting for Chamberlain; exactly like a court, thought Harold Nicolson, awaiting the verdict of the jury. At 7.35 the Clerks entered and took their places; two minutes later Mr Speaker came in and Honourable Members stood in silence. It was not a pleasant silence. At 7.42 Chamberlain and Greenwood came in together, and at 7.44 the Prime Minister began to speak.

'We expected one of his dramatic surprises,' Nicolson wrote afterwards, 'but none came.' His speech lasted only four minutes; he sounded ill. 'Amazement turned into stupefaction,' wrote General Spears, 'and stupefaction into exasperation.' Cabinet members saw and shared the House's reaction. 'Our own people were flabbergasted,' wrote Euan Wallace, the Minister of Transport, 'and the Opposition infuriated.' Nicolson put it simply: 'It was evident when he sat down that no decision had been arrived at.' No ultimatum; no time limit; not even any agreement yet with Paris. Elsewhere, in unhappy anger, Cadogan was writing his notes: 'We couldn't budge the French. Awful evening.' In the House, every Member felt with Nicolson the same surge of fear: 'Was there to be another Munich after all? Then Greenwood got up.'

The Deputy Leader of the Opposition was not accustomed to the kind of reception he was given. Nicolson described it: 'His own people cheered, as was natural; but what was so amazing was that their cheer was taken up in a second and greater wave from our benches.' And in 'an astonishing demonstration' (one which ever since has usually, and wrongly, been attributed to Leo Amery), 'Bob Boothby cried out, "*You* speak for Britain" . . . Greenwood almost staggered with surprise.'

But he did speak for Britain: 'There is a growing feeling, I believe, in all quarters of the House that this incessant strain must end sooner or later – and in a sense the sooner the better.' This was the kind of thing the House had hoped to hear from Chamberlain:

> I am gravely disturbed. An act of aggression took place 38 hours ago. The moment that act of aggression took place one of the most important treaties of modern times automatically came into operation. There may be reasons why instant action was not taken . . . That delay might have been justifiable, but there are many of us on all sides of this House who view with the gravest concern the fact that hours went by, and news came in of bombing operations, and news today of an intensification of it, and I wonder how long we are prepared to vacillate?

They cheered him to the rafters for that.

> If, deeply though I regret it, we must wait upon our Allies, I should far have preferred the Prime Minister to have been able to say tonight definitely, 'It is either peace or war' . . . There shall be no more devices for dragging out what has been dragged out for too long. The moment we look like weakening, at that moment dictatorship knows we are beaten. We are not beaten. We shall not be beaten. We cannot be beaten; but delay is dangerous . . . I cannot see Herr Hitler making any deal which he is not prepared to betray.

The tension, said Nicolson, became acute: 'Here were the PM's most ardent supporters cheering his opponent with all their lungs. The front bench looked as if they had been struck in the face . . . We feel that the German ships and submarines will, owing to this inexplicable delay, elude our grasp. The PM must know by now that the whole House is against him.'

*

Time limit?

In a pub in Portsmouth, Sandy Powell sat drinking with a group of other neatly uniformed Marines. The room was crowded, and most people were talking together, but quietly; there was none of the usual raucous Saturday evening jollification. Even the piano in the corner was closed; no one felt like playing, or singing. The morning in Whale Island had been spent cleaning kit, washing, pressing, polishing, blancoing, and the afternoon in sport. The mood then had been mixed, some of them getting edgy, others talking big. Now, deeply aware that this was likely to be their last run ashore for some time, the young Marines wanted to get drunk, but could not. Instead, as they drank, they discussed the possibilities ahead of them: which ships they might be with, where they might have to go, whether anyone would be lucky enough to get some cushy number. One young man, an expert footballer, expected to be asked to stay and continue playing for the corps. But all were subdued. Eventually, although time had not been called, Sandy said: 'Well, lads – reckon I'll thin out. Church parade in the morning.' Although he was not yet eighteen, his six-foot-three made him a dominating figure anywhere, and standing in uniform he seemed to fill the whole pub. 'I'll come too,' said another. One by one they downed the last of their pints, and headed for the door; and as they did so, one of the civilians called out 'Good luck!' and raised three cheers for the Marines. In a sudden tremendous outburst of encouragement, everyone picked it up, clapping and banging their glasses. The young men grinned and waved, and stepped out into the dark.

At the Tunbridge Wells Repertory Theatre there was a play on that evening called *Idiot's Delight*. Saying he thought it sounded appropriate, Derek Silver's girlfriend's brother took his own girlfriend to see it. Derek had other things in mind, which did not include extra company. He had cycled the 50 miles from Chelmsford that morning, pausing on the way to buy for the price of a shilling his first contraceptive sheath; and he took his girl to see the film *Jesse James*. A few hours later, somewhat despondently, he wrote that it 'went all right, with hand-holding accompaniment'. But that was all. Coming out of the cinema into a pitch-black town centre was strange. Cloudy and raining, it was very, very dark – their first experience of full blackout. Huddling close together under one umbrella, they hurried for home, and around midnight went to bed – each in their own bed, alone.

As a further mark of the serious situation, the cricket club at Walton-on-the-Naze cancelled its scheduled Saturday match. All day long Ross Mackay had expected a declaration of war to come at any minute, but when nothing had happened by 9 p.m. he wondered if there might still be time to go to London and see his family. Night driving under blackout regulations was difficult – car headlights had to be shaded with layers of newspaper, leaving a small slit which gave barely more than a glow – so he decided to go at dawn.

In London, because the evacuation traffic had quietened down, Donald Richardson was able to get home for the first time in three nights. It was only a temporary place, but his wife was there, and travelling out in the darkened Tube he felt rested and content; yet when he reached home and saw her, for a few minutes he was suddenly completely overcome. Holding her tight, he wept and shook with emotion. It was, he said, 'a horrible reaction . . . Although having done very little for the past three days (or perhaps because of that), the tension must have been deeper than I knew. I felt as though I were on leave from the front.'

Sir Alexander Cadogan was half-way through dinner when the summons came from Downing Street. He was wanted there 'at once: at once'. He drove as quickly as possible, which was not easy, for in addition to the hazards of the blackout it was raining. At No 10 he found the Prime Minister and Annie Chamberlain dining with Lord Halifax and Sir Horace Wilson, and gratefully joined in the meal. 'PM told me about the House and the trouble with his own colleagues,' he wrote later that night. It was a terse enough description: the Prime Minister's speech in the Commons, given without warning to Ministers, had overturned the agreement with them, and afterwards Chamberlain had faced open revolt.

One of the rebels, Sir Reginald Dorman-Smith, the Minister for Agriculture and Fisheries, later recalled: 'It didn't seem real. We were on strike.' This was literally true: as soon as the session was over Dorman-Smith and thirteen other Ministers gathered in one room and decided they would not move from it until war was declared. It was not a large room, and with fourteen angry men in it 'as we waited, we got scruffier and sweatier'. Eventually the Chancellor of the Exchequer, whose room it was, and who was one of the rebels, decided they must confront the Prime Minister. They did so with force, and, following the verbal challenge with a letter, returned to Sir John Simon's room.

Again, as thunder grumbled over the capital, Cadogan's diary summarised events in No 10: 'We got Corbin [the French Ambassador] and telephoned to Daladier, and then to Bonnet. But couldn't move them. Finally agreed we must act . . .' Britain would declare war independently of France. The ultimatum would be delivered next morning at nine with a deadline of 11 a.m. 'My suggestion,' Cadogan noted in brackets in his diary. It was becomingly modest for a man who had just stipulated the moment when Britain's war against Germany would begin.

Nevertheless it was as well a decision was reached (assuming, of course, that it was stuck to) because while the Cabinet rebellion was going on, a backbench rebellion was growing too. Its focus, of course, was Churchill. Through the day he had waited at his flat in Morpeth Mansions expecting a call from Chamberlain. None had come, and after the inadmissible further delay announced by the Prime Minister in the House, Churchill's parliamentary supporters gathered in his flat to debate their own next move. They knew his national popularity, the degree of support his stance of consistent anti-appeasement enjoyed: should he now bolster the Prime Minister, or stand against him? Either could split the country.

The rebellious Cabinet Ministers were summoned to No 10. When they arrived in the Cabinet Room ('really scruffy and smelly,' Dorman-Smith remembered) they found Cadogan on the telephone to Bonnet, with a secretary – the only other person who could speak French really well – listening and taking notes. Outside the thunderstorm gathered force. Dorman-Smith never forgot the scene:

> Cadogan was saying that naturally, we would like to go in with the French at the same moment, but Paris was saying that if you start war now, we cannot get our young people out of Paris . . . They were horrified and terrified at our determination for an immediate ultimatum and said, 'Are you going to have all our women and children killed?'

> Throughout the meeting, the Prime Minister was completely calm,

> But now, facing a sit-down strike, he had no alternative. The climax came most dramatically. The P M said quietly: 'Right, gentlemen, this means war.' Hardly had he said it when there was a most enormous clap of thunder and the whole Cabinet Room was lit up by a blinding flash of lightning . . . the most deafening thunder-clap I've ever heard in my life. It really shook the building. I felt in a different world.

On the other side of London Donald Richardson jerked upright in bed, eyes wide, staring into the darkness. Outside came another shattering crash. Even through the heavy blackout curtains, the livid flicker of lightning was visible. He tottered to the window, drew the curtain aside and stood for some minutes gazing at the downpour before returning, trembling, to bed. He noticed his pyjamas were damp – he was sweating as if he had a high temperature, but he was icy cold. His wife did not waken. He lay as still as he could.

18

All that beautiful Sunday

THE NIGHT'S HEAVY RAIN had washed the air clean: it could not have been a more lovely morning, and it was Sunday, the day of rest. In her bedroom at Winsor Farm near Plymouth in Devon, Kit Dennis hummed quietly as she brushed her hair. Elsewhere in the house her mother, gloves already on, was choosing a hat; her father, his gold watch ready and waiting to be slipped into a waistcoat pocket, was struggling with a stiff white detachable shirt-collar; downstairs her sister Margaret, whose turn it was to stay at home and cook lunch, was at work in the kitchen; outside, even though it had been completely cleaned the day before as usual, her brother Henry was giving the family car a final polish, to make up for not going with the others. A last pat of the hair, a straightening of a hat, a satisfied jingle of a watch-chain: the Dennises were ready to leave for church.

At the other end of the country, on the island of Foula in the Shetlands, the kirk had fallen into some disrepair, but there was a Church of Scotland chapel, run by (as they called him) a missionary. Often they would gather too in the Smiths' house, the schoolhouse, where Lizzie would lead their singing with the school piano. The service in the chapel took place at noon. This morning, however, Nanette and her sisters were told they would not be going: at eleven o'clock there was to be an important broadcast on the wireless, all the way from London. They could play in the garden until then.

In Nottinghamshire in the Midlands, Oscar Baker and his sister Margaret were already on their way to worship at St Philip Neri's, the nearest Roman Catholic church. The five-mile walk from their village usually took nearly two hours, and they always set off early. It was particularly fortunate that they did so today, for to their astonishment they were stopped, though only briefly, by three soldiers who asked where they were going.

In Bradford in the West Riding of Yorkshire, Elspeth Harmes was also walking early to St Stephen's. It was only a few months since she had been confirmed, and her regular attendances at the Victorian Gothic building were as much to do with the leading choirboy, Eric Jones, as with the forceful, forward-looking character of the vicar, Donald Foster, an outspoken pacifist.

His Sunday evening 'talking parties', loosely structured debates for young people, stimulated her immensely. She knew she had acquired a reputation for questioning anything to do with established thinking, a reputation which she rather liked and which he encouraged. As for Eric, it was simple: he and Elspeth were in love, and had been so for eight years.

At nine o'clock in Whale Island, 'C' Company's church parade began, every Marine – Sandy Powell among them – spotlessly turned out in peacetime No 1 kit, complete with pith helmet. From the parade ground they marched with faultless rhythm out through the main gate, a sturdy, deliberate public show, to worship.

At the same moment in Berlin, Sir Nevile Henderson marched as deliberately up the front steps of the German Foreign Office. Neither Hitler nor the Reich Foreign Minister Joachim von Ribbentrop was prepared to receive him: the task had been delegated to Paul Schmidt, and that morning of all mornings the hard-pressed interpreter had overslept. He was very nearly late for the momentous appointment. As his taxi hurtled over the Wilhelmsplatz he could see the British Ambassador entering the building by the front door. Schmidt raced around to a side door and ran to Ribbentrop's empty office. Just as nine o'clock struck, Henderson was announced.

Although he shook hands, he refused to sit down. Standing in the middle of the room, he said – and Schmidt could hear the deep emotion in his voice – that he had come on the instructions of his government to present an ultimatum to the government of Germany. Both he and Schmidt remained standing as he read it out loud. It was not long.

> More than twenty-four hours have elapsed since an immediate reply was requested to the warning of September 1st, and since then the attacks on Poland have intensified. If His Majesty's Government has not received satisfactory assurances of the cessation of all aggressive action against Poland, and the withdrawal of German troops from that country, by eleven o'clock British Summer Time, from that time a state of war will exist between Great Britain and Germany.

Two hours to go. With a hollow sensation in his stomach Schmidt listened to history happening and gazed sadly at Henderson. They had always got on so well together. The Ambassador finished his short speech and presented the document to him; then, with some words of personal regret which Schmidt sincerely reciprocated, Henderson formally bade him goodbye.

Sandy Powell was in good voice and, before sitting to hear the padre's address, joined in the three hymns with vigour. The prayers were different from usual: normally they were for the health of the King and Royal Family, the prosperity of the Empire and so on. Today there was an extra one, for peace. Shifting his gun to a more comfortable position (for church parade, they only wore side-arms, but they kept them on all the time), he knelt and joined in. Couldn't do any harm.

Others in Britain did not get to church that morning at all. In South Wales Tom Elliott never had any intention of going; he had fixed with some friends to spend the time playing nap, their favourite card game. In North Shields Lionel Tomlinson had come home in exasperation: although the business needed it, he could do no fishing today, not because of it being Sunday but because it had become virtually impossible to persuade a full crew to go out at all. Further up the river, Molly McAndrew would normally have gone to St Lawrence's in Byker, but not today; Ernie, her fiancé, had got his converted lifeboat *Monarch* ready for a day out on the Tyne. While they were chugging contentedly downstream, Mike Warbreck-Howell and his family were half-way through a major house move from one side of the Pennines to the other: predicting petrol shortages, Mike's father had decided they must leave their large house in Wilmslow and live closer to his work in Halifax. At the same time Ross Mackay arrived in London from Walton-on-the-Naze to find the capital 'amazingly empty'. Half a million people had been evacuated, and another half-million, like Gerald and Betty Hawker, had taken themselves off voluntarily. Posters dotting the capital showed a soldier in full combat gear talking to a small boy. 'Leave this to me, sonny,' said the caption. 'You should be out of London.'

As soon as Henderson had left the German Foreign Office, Paul Schmidt took the British ultimatum to the Chancellery. It was difficult to get through to Hitler's office: the room outside was packed with senior party officials and members of the Cabinet, all urgently demanding to know what had happened. In the past Schmidt had been in the habit of referring to international diplomats as his 'classroom'; now his only answer to the worried enquiries was, 'Classroom dismissed.'

At last he managed to push his way through. Inside the inner office Hitler sat at his desk; Ribbentrop was there too, standing silently, staring out of the window. Both looked expectantly at the interpreter when he came in. Schmidt stopped several feet short of the Führer's desk, took a deep breath and began to read. Ribbentrop resumed his stare out of the window; Hitler gazed fixedly at the top of his desk. When Schmidt had finished his translation, there was a long silence. Ribbentrop continued to look out of the window as if all this had nothing to do with him. Hitler sat immobile, silent and unmoving. Then with a savage glare the Führer turned abruptly towards his Foreign Minister, and in a voice which was a snarl, asked him the simplest and most difficult question. 'What now?'

Ribbentrop paused before quietly giving his answer. 'I assume that the French will hand in a similar ultimatum within the hour.'

As long ago as February, a Housing and Local Government Report had stated with gloomy frankness: 'In a country the size of England, there is, in the condition of modern war, no place of absolute safety.' Nevertheless evacuation of the urban centres was common sense, and heart-breaking as it was for parents to see their children tagged like parcels and crowded into trains, the nationwide programme had been phenomenally successful: in less than four days 1,473,391 evacuees, including escorts and teachers, had arrived in their reception areas, carried from 72 stations by 4000 special trains, without a single accident or casualty. The government paid their train fares, and, almost without realising it, British people undertook the greatest single migration of population in the history of their kingdom. For many city-born children it was their first sight of the countryside; for many of the country-dwellers it was their first contact with such children. 'FN' written on a child's documents meant 'few nits'; 'N' meant the child had some head-lice and 'V' meant they were visibly crawling. Many village shops ran out of dust combs, and even sheep-dip, and soon it seemed host families were trying to outdo each other with tales of pathetic ignorance and strange squalid habits. Derek Silver's editor entertained the office with the questions put to him by an East End boy who had never seen vegetables growing, and who thought cabbages, and then carrots, must be potatoes; stories were legion of children who would not eat unless they were allowed to sit, as they were accustomed to, on the floor, or who refused to sleep in beds. Much of it was true, as were many of the tales the other way round of grotesque exploitation of the evacuees by their hosts, and later the Prime Minister admitted that neither he nor his Cabinet colleagues had had any concept of the desperate conditions in urban working-class areas. Perhaps Silver was over-optimistic when, seeing the lawn of a mansion covered with evacuated children, he called evacuation 'democracy in action'; but he was certainly correct when he observed that 'whatever happens next, Britain will never be the same after this'. And it could bring great happiness, as one couple in Northampton testified:

We got our two little evacuees. We've always wanted children, and it's been our life's sorrow that they've been denied us. Now our home is alive for the first time. We've a boy and a girl, eight and six . . . they scream and race about the place, and yesterday, the little girl was sick on the drawing-room carpet, but that's what we've always wanted. Thank God for our little evacuees.

One person who had not left London, and did not, was Francis Vanek. After early Mass on the morning of Sunday 3 September, he was in Hampstead, preparing for a cycle club meeting. And one who had deliberately returned was David Howarth. On 1 September Richard Dimbleby had reached him with the long-expected phone call: would David care to come back from Ireland and go on 'a trip'? He certainly would. With a suitcase ready in the office, he gave his car to his secretary and left Ireland the same day, not even returning to the Porter Lodge. Now, in Broadcasting House in central London, simultaneously frightened and excited, he waited for eleven o'clock.

During the previous night Georges Bonnet, the French Foreign Minister, had made one last attempt to avoid the spread of war. Count Ciano was asleep when the imploring message was brought to him: could he not at least obtain a symbolic withdrawal of German forces from Poland? He did not even bother to tell Mussolini. Saying simply, 'Nothing can be done,' he threw the message in the waste-paper basket and went back to bed. 'This shows that France is moving towards the great test without enthusiasm, and full of uncertainty,' he wrote on Sunday morning. 'A people like the French, heroic in self-defence, do not care for foreign lands and for nations too far away.'

He could have added that though not entirely honourable, the central cause of French reluctance was understandable: if British and French declarations of war were followed by an immediate German attack, France would have to fight alone for some indeterminate, perhaps long, period before British forces could assist. Because of that hesitation, Ribbentrop's last prediction to Hitler (like so many of his other predictions) turned out wrong: the French ultimatum to Germany was not presented until more than three hours after the British one. Had the French General Staff had their way, it would have still included a forty-eight-hour deadline. As it was, Prime Minister Daladier had forced an earlier deadline, first to 5 a.m. on 4 September and then to 5 p.m. on the 3rd. But once Henderson had presented Britain's ultimatum, the questions of if and when the French one would come were academic. With or without them, the final countdown had begun. In the anteroom to Hitler's office, Goering heard Schmidt's news and turned pale. 'If we lose this war,' he said to the interpreter, 'then God have mercy on us!'

*

It was the busiest weekend John Landells had ever known. Since Friday morning the Creed machines in the office had been chattering out ticker-tape reports from Reuter's, and his paper, the *Shields Evening News*, churned out one special edition after another. The local sports programme continued, with the cricket season ending and the football season starting, but local news was thrust aside – it seemed unreal, and anyway no one could guess what next weekend might bring. Sunday presented a problem: weekday papers like his cost twopence, but Sunday ones cost fourpence. On this particular Sunday it was inconceivable they should not publish; but if they did so, at twice their normal price, how would that affect their sales? There was a short but lively argument before a solution was found which satisfied everybody in the office. On Sunday, 3 September 1939, there were three special editions of the *Shields Evening News*, sold at the usual weekly price of twopence, and every one was dated Saturday.

As far as the rest of Europe was concerned, it was definitely Sunday, and for the Revd Bob Leaney, vicar of Mountfield in Sussex, one of the busier days of the week; yet in contrast to the highly charged, hectic goings-on elsewhere, his morning was utterly placid. After an early cup of tea, he conducted Communion at 8 a.m., then returned home for breakfast. Around 10.30, leaving his wife Liz in the vicarage sitting-room, sewing and listening to the wireless, he went back to the church to make sure everything was ready for Matins at eleven. The inside of the building looked lovely, decked out with harvest festival flowers. Any chance visitor could only have admired the pretty displays, and wondered at this evidence of the villagers' depth of piety. In fact, from a population of about six hundred, Bob's congregation usually amounted to no more than thirty, and practically the whole of the harvest decorations were supplied by the squire. Privately Bob had to admit it was a bit of a sham, but he was not going to complain: one day he might persuade the villagers to contribute more, and in the meantime it was far better the church should be decorated than not, especially when the squire was such a regular attender. There he was now, coming to take his customary seat in the front pew, ready to read the lessons as he always did. The great clock on the tower ticked ponderously on towards eleven. The last notes of the summoning bells faded; then heavy and resonant, audible throughout the village, the clock struck the hour.

Ten minutes earlier Birger Dahlerus had made his last appeal, a frantic telephone call from Berlin to the British Foreign Office. With despairing, obsessive optimism, he still believed the situation could be saved. He had tried once already that morning, protesting then that with a bit of give and take everything could be arranged: the German government was anxious to satisfy the British, and willing to give assurances that the independence of Poland would not be violated. Somehow skating over in his mind the fact that this had already happened, he explained that German troops could not be expected to withdraw at once: 'Never in world history has an army withdrawn before negotiation.' In his final call, at ten minutes to eleven, he suggested that as a last resort Field Marshal Goering should fly over at once for discussions in London. It was preposterous. Cadogan's formal record of the conversation stated that Lord Halifax 'sent a reply to the effect that our position had been known to the German Government for some time, and we could not now delay our procedure'. In his own diary Sir Alexander was more succinct: 'Dahlerus rang up 10.50 . . . I said "Rats".'

In the Cabinet Room, set up for the broadcast, the BBC announcer Alvar Liddell was with the Prime Minister. Mr Chamberlain, he thought, looked 'crumpled, despondent and old'. By ten minutes past eleven no reply had come to London from Germany. At twelve minutes past, a definite message was received from the British Embassy in Berlin that no reply had even reached there; and at a quarter past precisely, the Prime Minister began the declaration of war: 'I am speaking to you from the Cabinet Room at Ten Downing Street . . .'

From thousands of wirelesses the dreadful words reverberated. 'This morning the British Ambassador in Berlin handed the German Government a final note, stating that, unless the British Government heard from them by eleven o'clock that they were prepared at once to withdraw their troops from Poland, a state of war would exist between us.'

In her drawing-room in the Yorkshire town of Rotherham, Dr Kennerley's wife Eleanor stood clutching their baby son. Her husband was with his TA regiment, the York and Lancaster, as far as she knew, somewhere in Norfolk. With eyes wide and heart pounding, alone with the infant, she listened in a paralysis of fear, completely unable to move.

'I have to tell you now that no such undertaking has been received, and that consequently this country is at war with Germany.'

In North Shields Lionel Tomlinson watched his mother's face go ashy white. Apparently unperturbed, his father sat puffing his pipe. They listened in silence, and Tomlinson knew that he and his brothers would have to go and fight.

'You can imagine what a bitter blow it is to me that all my long struggle to win peace has failed . . .'

In Mountfield Vicarage, Liz Leaney's sewing fell from her hands as she listened, feeling sick with shock. Bob, for a few minutes more of blessed sanctuary and ignorance, was in church and did not know, but he too would have to go to war.

'We have done all that any country could do to establish peace. The situation in which no word given by Germany's ruler could be trusted, and no people or country could feel themselves safe, has become intolerable . . .'

In Tunbridge Wells, sitting on the floor back to back with his girlfriend, Derek Silver listened, feeling strangely detached from reality – analytical, almost light-headed. It was such a lovely morning: blue sky, white clouds, green and beautiful garden. Compared to the words he was hearing his surroundings seemed incongruous, almost ridiculous, for invisibly, over it all, lay the actuality of war 'which we've so long regarded as the final horror'. In time he would grasp it, but he simply could not do so yet.

'We have resolved to finish it. It is the evil things we shall be fighting against – brute force, bad faith, injustice, oppression and persecution . . .'

In his temporary home in Middlesex, his father-in-law's boss's house, Donald Richardson listened and felt the same dream-like sense of separation from the actual world.

'. . . and against them I am certain that the right will prevail.'

Impossible to grasp, impossible to banish or cancel or undo, the speech ended and the National Anthem was played. Automatically scrambling to his feet, Richardson glanced outside and saw, on the golf links by the house, at least a dozen golfers carrying on with their games, oblivious of the reality he was being asked to accept. Somehow it seemed reassuring, quite in the tradition of Drake. The anthem ended; somebody switched off the wireless. There was a silence of about twenty seconds. 'Well,' said his father-in-law, 'now we're for it.' 'Now *someone's* for it, you mean,' said the owner of the house. That caused a laugh, and for a few minutes they felt cheerful again. And then the air raid sirens began.

The sirens were the first that Molly McAndrew knew of it. With a small group of friends and Ernie, her fiancé, she was happily bobbing around in *Monarch*, fishing idly, when the wailing from shore sprang up. 'My God!' said Ernie. 'They've landed!' With the clumsiness of haste and anxiety, he started the boat's engine, and as fast as possible, they motored towards the mouth of the Tyne.

In London Francis Vanek had had no more idea than Molly and Ernie of the imminence of war. Muttering in irritation and assuming that this was yet another exercise, he rode his bicycle into a school playground. It contained the nearest shelter he could see; and not until he was inside with other people did he learn that Great Britain was at war.

Oscar Baker and his sister Theresa learned it in St Philip Neri's church in Nottinghamshire, when Father McNicholas interrupted the service. Kit Dennis also learned it in her church in Devon, when the Revd Lucas told his flock; so too did Elspeth Harmes in Bradford, when the Revd Foster mounted the pulpit steps and, pacifist to the core, informed the congregation that the very gravest situation imaginable had come to pass. Declaring that all should pray for the earliest possible return to peace, he asked them to rise and join him in a hymn, 'Let there be light.' Looking up towards the choir stalls, sixteen-year-old Elspeth saw Eric Jones stand up and gazed at him as he did at her, and sang, though she felt her heart would break.

In Mountfield, the service of Communion proceeded without any interruption. Neither the people in church nor the Revd Bob Leaney had the faintest idea that anything untoward had happened. Around midday, after shaking hands with each of his outgoing parishioners – only two dozen, he noticed, with a collection of less than three pounds – Bob stood by the roadside with the squire, waiting for a coachload of evacuees that were supposed to be coming down from London.

Commander Egerton was in an exceedingly bad humour. 'Really, Vicar,' he exclaimed, 'it just isn't good enough. There are the Poles, who are meant to be our allies, being pounded by the Hun – for three days now – and here are we, who are meant to have guaranteed them; and what are we up to? Hmm? What's the Prime Minister about? What I'd like to know is, why on earth haven't we declared war?' Though he did not say it, it occurred to the Revd Leaney that Commander Egerton took it as a personal insult still to be at peace. 'What's the reason for it, eh?', Egerton continued. 'You're a man of the cloth. Can you see any sense in this at all? I'm damned if I can, none at all.'

To Leaney's relief, he suddenly heard the rumble of an engine and the toot of a horn. 'I'm sure you're right, Commander,' he said mildly. 'But I think these may be our evacuees arriving. Shall we be ready to welcome them?'

Grunting in dissatisfaction, the Commander gave a beaming smile.

It soon transpired that the air raid warning was a false alarm; but that did not change the new truth. 'All that beautiful Sunday,' wrote Ross Mackay, 'we were practically confined indoors.' Overhead hovered a host of barrage balloons. At last the time came when, if he were not to face the problems of driving in the blackout, he had to leave and head back for Walton-on-the-Naze. 'As my family were going to the south coast and I to the east, it was a sad farewell, for we could not tell whether we would be together again.'

From the Admiralty two short signals were sent in plain language to the British fleet. One was a statement of fact: 'Winston is back.' Instead of being a Minister without Portfolio, Churchill had entered the War Cabinet as First Lord of the Admiralty. Bearing no further comment or elaboration, the three words could be read either as a warning or a message of encouragement; Churchill himself chose to take them as the latter, and saw them as a personal compliment. The second message, an order, was even shorter, and had no ambiguity: 'Total Germany.' Among others who picked it up was the radio operator in Wilhelmshaven, the western headquarters of U-boat command. In minutes it was rushed to Captain Dönitz. He stared at the message in stunned, blank amazement, and his aides heard him whisper: '*Mein Gott! Also wieder Krieg gegen England!*' – 'My God! So it's war with England again!'

By the evening not only Britain but France too was formally at war with Germany. Despite the Pact of Steel, Italy had contrived to remain neutral and at peace; yet in his home, the Palazzo Chigi, Count Ciano was plunged in gloom. 'In what way can France and England bring help to Poland?' he wrote in his diary. 'And when Poland is liquidated, will they want to continue a conflict for which there is no longer any reason? The Duce does not believe so. He believes rather that after a short struggle peace will be restored before the clash, which in any case he considers impossible from a military point of view.'

However, Mussolini had not yet heard the speech Churchill had made that afternoon in London. The new First Lord was absolutely clear: 'This is not a question of fighting for Danzig or fighting for Poland,' he declared. 'We are fighting to save the whole world from the pestilence of Nazi tyranny, and in defence of all that is most sacred to man.'

Ciano had not heard the speech either. Nevertheless, sitting alone in Rome that night, he divined the future more accurately than his father-in-law had done. 'I am not a military man,' he wrote despondently. 'I do not know how the war may develop, but I know one thing – it *will* develop, and it will be long, uncertain and relentless. The participation of Great Britain makes this certain. England has made this declaration to Hitler. The war can end only with Hitler's elimination, or the defeat of Britain.'

About the same time as Count Ciano wrote his prophecy, John Landells was making his way home to Jarrow, worn out with the efforts of the day. Three special editions had been pumped out, and he had taken part in any and every job that needed doing. He had been copy boy, he had typed, he had even gone to get sandwiches. Physically exhausted, he was still mentally alert. What news, what news! The image of those specials being pasted up was as vivid as if it was still happening. The first had carried Britain's declaration, the second the text of a stirring speech by the king, and the third the news of France's declaration. His Majesty had called it 'perhaps the most fateful hour in our history'. *It certainly is in mine*, John thought. He had been very struck by something else the king had said: 'For the second time in the lives of most of us, we are at war.' It was the first time for John Landells.

Before reading the speech, he had never really considered how lucky he had been: born just a few months after the Armistice that ended the Great War with Germany, he had never until today known anything but peace.

Now, as his bus went bumping along through the darkening streets of South Shields, he looked out of its windows and watched the sun going down. It was the end of the first day of a new war with Germany. Staring at the dying light, he made a promise to himself: whenever it might come and wherever he might be, on the first day that peace returned, he would be alive and awake at dawn, and he would see the sun rise again.

Epilogue

Nowadays everyone knows what happened eventually; but at the time, Hitler's question to Ribbentrop – 'What now?' – was the only one that anyone anywhere could ask, and the only question that no one could answer. Day by day the impenetrable future became the dreadful past, part of the heritage of each nation and individual. Today we, the inheritors, know what happened next, and like unwise gods may choose to dispense judgment on those fallible people; and at the same time we make our own mistakes and grope blindly forward into our own future.

But what of their future, now the past? The fates of the public figures are well known: Chamberlain's unhappy death; Stalin's repulsive life; Churchill's defeat in the polls when peace was won; Hitler's cowardly suicide – the fulfilment of his promise to Germany that he would never witness the conquest of his nation; Mussolini's execution of his son-in-law Count Ciano, and his own execution at the hands of Italians, followed by hanging upside-down from a girder; Goering's suicide; the trials at Nuremburg, and the almost incomprehensible charge of six million humans going up literally in smoke from the chimneys of Treblinka, Belzec, Auschwitz. What an inheritance for the master race, or even for the human race. We may hope we would never have done it ourselves; we can never be certain.

The individual fates of many in this story must remain obscure. Those who wrote diaries for Mass-Observation (whose names have been changed here) may recognise themselves, and remember. Other witnesses continued to try their best, and for the most part succeeded. In March 1942 Oscar Baker joined the Merchant Navy, took part in Operation Torch and many convoys, including the delivery of Liberty ships. Chronic ill health contracted during Torch forced him to leave his post as a Master Mariner in 1953; nevertheless he fathered a happy family of six, and worked as a supply officer to the National Health Service until his retirement in 1984. Molly McAndrew married her sweetheart Ernie on 23 December 1939. In 1953, imbued with politics of the socialist tradition, she became a member of Wallsend council, and ten years later was the town's mayor. Later, in 1972, 'strangers' were voted on to the council, people from outside the locality with far-left militant views, and in 1980 Ernie decided to try and buy their council house. Molly took the application to the town hall. Then, while she and Ernie were on holiday, it was leaked (in her words) to leading councillors. When she and Ernie returned home, she was 'interrogated' by those councillors – who were later expelled from the Labour Party. But Ernie was never able to buy his council house. He was already ill, and his worries for her during this time precipitated a heart attack, from which he died on 8 July 1981, two months short of his sixty-fifth birthday. Molly left the Labour Party, and has twice been elected as an Independent Labour councillor. By 1988 she was the longest serving member with unbroken service on Wallsend council.

Kit Dennis, the farmer's daughter from Plympton in Devon, married her near neighbour Joseph Clifton. They had no children but prospered in other ways. Joseph's 127-acre farm, and his farmhouse with its leaky roof, were eventually sold for redevelopment; retiring to a centrally heated, fully carpeted modern house, they could only be amused when later generations yearned for the 'simple life'. Like them, Dorothy Williams, the South Wales schoolteacher whose spinster future seemed assured, never left her home district; but in June 1941 she too married, and was blessed with two children. Dreaming in Vacationland, USA, Barkeley Goodrich met, fell in love with and married Libby Tufts, the little girl from South Poland; they too produced a fine family, of some academic distinction. Claud Kennerley, the Yorkshire doctor, never properly recovered from the war: it temporarily destroyed his practice and permanently impaired his health. Having contracted an illness from treating members of the British Expeditionary Force, he was invalided out of the army late in 1942, and rebuilt his practice from scratch; but in 1972 he died of heart failure. In America Ernest Kroll went on, as his friends had predicted, to become a poet, and unexpectedly gained a most unusual distinction. Some lines of his were engraved in stone in Washington DC along with those of other poets, and he was the only living one. The authorities who had chosen his work were inexplicably under the impression that, like the others, he was dead too.

John Landells had foretold that his protégé Bill Armstrong would become a famous journalist, and he did. Landells himself survived to keep his private promise: after seeing military service in Europe, northern Africa, the Near East and the Mediterranean, he was in Brussels on VE day, and climbed to the roof of a high building to see the sunrise on the first day of peace in Europe. Thereafter he too returned to journalism, ending his career in 1984 as Chief Press Officer to British Shipbuilders. As an intellectual Christian, Bob Leaney found the ideal way of life once war was done, and became in time a Professor of Divinity. In Birmingham, alert to the huge inequities of the existing social system, Dr Haigh's later life followed a similar, though not identical, course, and he became a Professor of Social Medicine.

Niusia Zamecka, the ten-year-old Polish girl, spent four years in German-occupied Warsaw. From there, after the uprising in 1944, she was taken to prison in Germany. With the Allied victory she ended up recuperating in England, and there became Janine Phillips: she met and married an Englishman. The war separated Zofya Olscholwska from her husband Taddeus for five abominable years: although she was allowed to remain in Moniaki, the family home was taken over by the Germans for a command post, and from it – in a ghastly inversion of the biblical image – she could see 'a pillar of smoke by day, and a pillar of fire by night', unerasable plumes from the furnaces of Belzec extermination camp. Reunited after the war, the Olscholwskis also settled in England, and Taddeus lived until 1988.

Sandy Powell, the youthful, towering Marine, remained in the corps until 1953. His wartime record included Mediterranean, Atlantic and Russian convoys, 'D-Day and all that carry-on', and special work which remains secret. He was also in Malta, Palestine and Suez, and then worked for twenty-five years in the police force and a decade in charge of a centre for the elderly, handicapped and sick. By 1988 he was proud to say he had done thirty-five years' work for the community; and four of his eight children carry on the tradition as members of the Royal Navy, the Royal Marines, the WRNS and the police.

Lionel Tomlinson, the trawlerman, also did much wartime convoy work, and afterwards returned to fishing until 1965, when he took up the supply of oil rigs in Nigeria, Angola and the North Sea, prospering sufficiently to be able to retire at sixty-two to his home town. Mike Warbreck-Howell was delighted when the war came: he was able to leave Cambridge University and join the Fleet Air Arm as a pilot, which was more to his liking. John Scott, who had been an adolescent Communist in Birmingham, threw that off during the war and achieved respectability: he became a headmaster. He married Elspeth Harmes, who, despite her early departure from school, eventually graduated in theology, and whose childhood love for the choirboy Eric Jones turned into a fond memory. Charles King, the Australian Communist, found the Russian invasion of Finland too much to stomach. On writing an editorial condemning it, he was expelled from the party and returned to teaching and the study of poetry. Ironically, when he died in 1966, he was working on a history of the Communist Party in Australia.

Richard Richter, whose mother was imprisoned by the Gestapo in Vienna, achieved two of his wartime ambitions: he joined the British army, and as a member of its interrogation squad located the man who had 'shopped' his mother. The culprit was a rather pathetic clerk who was acting under considerable duress. Richter's interrogation work gave way after the war to a life in business, yet some things remained unfinished. In 1988 he still possessed, from his interrogations, first-hand evidence of a Nazi war criminal who was living unpunished and prosperous on the outskirts of Hamburg.

During the Second World War, Willie Smith, the Shetland fisherman, found new employment both in running the Foula mailboat and in fishing; his wife Lizzie, 'the Teacher', continued in her profession: and in the course of the war, on their tiny island, David Howarth met them and their three daughters, Stella, Nanette and Jessamine. His own pre-war BBC work changed, after some months as a war correspondent with Richard Dimbleby, to naval work, and as a member of the Special Operations Executive, based in those remote islands, he established a spy network that became known as the Shetland Bus. And he fell in love (though he had not expected it) not only with the islands and their people, with whom he lived and worked after the war as a boatbuilder, but also with Nanette Smith, though she was nearly fifteen years younger than him. They married, David changed his profession from boatbuilding to writing, and they had a family of three girls and a boy.

Francis Vanek, the cycling pilgrim, spent a large part of the war welding bridges. When it was over he was able to return to his real profession, at which he was far more skilled: the art of ladies' tailoring. He too married, in a match which has lasted, and fathered two daughters and a son; and has proved to be one of those who could only with the utmost reluctance consider retirement.

So, for better or worse, their lives panned out – a few of those millions who lived through August 1939. Fifty years later, the mood of the last four weeks of peace has become remote but is not forgotten. Memories remain, sometimes humorous, often painful and bitter, yet almost always astonishingly vivid. Now though, as it fades into history, and from history to legend, all that later generations can do is to try and imagine what it meant to be alive at the time, when the one real, living question in everyone's mind was unanswerable. Early in September 1939, the *Picture Post* asked that question of its readers: 'The war is on. How long will it last? What will it lead to? How much suffering will be undergone, how many lives will be lost, how many nights such as this will we go through before peace comes once more?'

Chronology

Wednesday, 2 August   After a lengthy debate the British House of Commons votes itself a summer holiday. The House will rise on Friday and will not expect to return until 21 October. In America, Albert Einstein writes a letter to President Roosevelt, warning him of the possibility that Nazi Germany might be attempting to build an atom bomb.

Thursday, 3   In the Free City of Danzig a dispute flares between Polish customs officials and members of the Nazi-dominated Senate. In Germany a detailed forecast of U-boat needs clearly does not anticipate an early war. In Moscow the German Ambassador, Count Werner von der Schulenberg, secretly meets Vyacheslav Molotov, Soviet Commissar for Foreign Affairs; and in London a similarly secret meeting takes place between Ambassador Herbert von Dirksen and Sir Horace Wilson, the Prime Minister's closest adviser.

Friday, 4   The 25th anniversary of Germany's invasion of Belgium and the declaration of war by Britain against Germany. In Danzig the customs dispute continues. In Britain the Bank Holiday weekend begins, and the Commons rise for the summer recess.

Saturday, 5   The first British transatlantic air mail service is inaugurated. A joint Anglo-French military delegation led by Admiral Sir Reginald Plunkett-Ernle-Erle-Drax and General Joseph Doumenc leaves Britain, travelling by sea to Leningrad, for discussions with Molotov. At Balmoral Castle in Scotland, two hundred boys are entertained to tea by the king and queen, while Albert Förster, Nazi Gauleiter of Danzig, flies to Berchtesgaden to confer with Adolf Hitler. The Danzig customs dispute is temporarily resolved, but its resolution is seen in other countries as a Nazi climb-down, infuriating Hitler.

Sunday, 6   The Feast of the Transfiguration. In Rome, fearing Germany will go to war with Poland, the Duce Benito Mussolini, and Count Galeazzo Ciano, his son-in-law and Foreign Minister, discuss possible ways to evade the terms of the Pact of Steel, signed with Germany on 23 May. The pact commits them to aiding Germany, but Italy is three years short of readiness for war.

Monday, 7   Bank Holiday Monday in England and Wales. Count Ciano asks to see Joachim von Ribbentrop, Hitler's Foreign Minister.

Tuesday, 8   Winston Churchill makes a fifteen-minute radio broadcast to America, warning of the increasingly serious threat of war in Europe and the likelihood of American involvement.

Wednesday, 9   At Weymouth, on the south coast of England, King George VI inspects the Reserve Fleet immediately prior to its mobilisation. Ambassador von Dirksen, preparing to depart on leave to Germany, visits the British Foreign Secretary, Lord Halifax. An official warning concerning the Polish attitude to Danzig is sent from Berlin to Warsaw, where it is viewed as an unwarranted interference in internal Polish affairs. Admiral Drax and his colleagues arrive in Leningrad late at night.

Thursday, 10   Night-time air war exercises are conducted over England on a larger scale than any since the Great War. Drax and the other delegates spend the day sightseeing in Leningrad, while in Berlin Julius Schnurre, head of the Economic Policy Department of the German Foreign Ministry, picks up discussions with Georgi Astakhov, Chargé d'Affaires of the Soviet Embassy, sounding out the possibility of a pact between Germany and Russia.

Friday, 11   The Anglo-French delegation finally arrives in Moscow. It is agreed to start talks next day. In Britain the Foreign Office learns that Germany will be in a state of complete military readiness on the 15th. While Gauleiter Förster warns Danzig Nazis to be prepared for anything, Karl Burckhardt, Commissioner of the League of Nations in Danzig, is summoned to see Hitler in Berchtesgaden. Ciano and Ribbentrop meet in Salzburg, and when Ciano asks Ribbentrop whether Germany wants the 'Polish Corridor' or Danzig, Ribbentrop replies, 'Not that any more. We want war.'

Saturday, 12   In Scotland the grouse-shooting season opens. In Moscow, the Anglo–French–Russian military talks begin. Ciano goes to Berchtesgaden to see Hitler, while Astakhov sends Schnurre new information from Moscow indicating Russian willingness to open political negotiations with Germany.

Sunday, 13   On holiday in Scotland, Neville Chamberlain, the British Prime Minister, complains of his poor luck at fishing. Ciano returns to Rome, disgusted at the attitudes of Ribbentrop and Hitler.

Monday, 14   Chamberlain and Halifax receive details of Ciano's meetings and consider the idea of sending a German-speaking Briton to negotiate directly with Hitler. Meanwhile in Moscow Ambassador von der Schulenberg receives instructions for a meeting with Molotov next day, and Marshal Klement Voroshilov, Commissar for Defence, puts his central question to the Anglo-French delegates: will the Red Army be allowed to march across Poland? Knowing it is almost impossible that the Poles will agree, Drax is unable to answer.

Tuesday, 15   The Feast of the Blessed Virgin Mary. Churchill begins a tour of the Maginot Line, France's main land defensive barrier against Germany. At last given permission by their political masters, the British Chiefs of Staff eagerly draft new instructions for Drax, while the Foreign Office and the Quai d'Orsay put pressure on Poland to allow Russian forces into Poland if necessary. In Moscow Molotov is highly interested in von der Schulenberg's proposals; von der Schulenberg in turn is surprised and pleased at the Russian's moderate conditions. Captain Karl Dönitz, head of the U-boat arm of the German Navy, is recalled unexpectedly early from leave. In Berlin, von Dirksen's own leave is uninterrupted: although he wishes to see Ribbentrop, the Nazi Foreign Minister will not receive him. Von Dirksen also discovers that the Italian Ambassador in Berlin, Bernardo Attolico, believes Germany is about to go to war with Poland, ignoring Britain's attitude. Von Dirksen is convinced Attolico is wrong.

Wednesday, 16   The British Deputy Chiefs of Staff report that 'it is perfectly clear that without early and effective Russian assistance, the Poles cannot hope to stand up to a German attack on land or in the air for more than a limited time'. Ribbentrop cables von der Schulenberg, telling him that all Molotov's conditions can be met. Captain Dönitz arrives at Kiel, the main U-boat base, and begins to implement plans for *Fall Weiss*, Case White, the projected attack on Poland.

Thursday, 17   In Moscow Molotov is highly gratified by the Germans' obvious haste to achieve a political agreement, and to Drax's outrage, Marshal Voroshilov – by now sure that neither the French nor the British mean business – dismisses their delegates for four days. For some time, American Intelligence has been far better informed than its British counterpart about developments between Berlin and Moscow, and now Sumner Welles, Under-Secretary of State, passes the information to British Ambassador Sir Ronald Lindsay. Lindsay immediately telegraphs London, confident his message will be in the Foreign Office first thing in the morning, London time. It is, but is not deciphered for four days. Meanwhile the British Ambassador in Warsaw, Sir Howard Kennard, fails to move Colonel Joseph Beck, the Polish Foreign Minister; and Hitler orders Admiral Canaris, the head of German Intelligence, to obtain Polish uniforms for a 'special SS operation'.

Friday, 18 Placards have been appearing in London with a simple but ambiguous question, 'What price Churchill?' Now *The Times* prints a letter signed by 375 academics urging the Prime Minister to include Churchill in his Cabinet. As the Foreign Office learns that a German attack on Poland is threatened to take place in two weeks' time, Sir Nevile Henderson, the British Ambassador in Berlin, begs Chamberlain to write personally to Hitler.

Saturday, 19 Henderson notes unhappily that while Churchill is inspecting the defences of France, Chamberlain is still fishing in Scotland. However, Lord Halifax and his advisers agree that the Prime Minister should be enabled to stay on holiday. Sending a telegram to Mussolini, who played a prominent part in the 'Munich agreement' of 1938, they begin to draft a letter for Chamberlain to send to Hitler. At the same time in Warsaw Colonel Beck replies to French pressure with '*un "non" catégorique*'; and after two further meetings with von der Schulenberg, Molotov suddenly produces a draft Russo-German pact and invites Ribbentrop to come to Moscow.

Sunday, 20 In the early hours of the morning an agreement is signed between Germany and Russia. Hitler, suspecting Molotov might cause delays in its ratification, sends a personal message to Stalin urging all speed. Lord Halifax telegrams Kennard in Warsaw, requesting him as urgently to try once more to gain Polish permission for Russian forces to enter their country. Churchill, resting at the château of a friend, paints a picture of the building and remarks that it will be the last picture he paints in peace.

Monday, 21 Chamberlain reaches London early in the morning, having travelled overnight from Scotland. British Intelligence suggests that Field Marshal Hermann Goering, founder of the Gestapo and head of the Luftwaffe, should come to London for discussions. But just as Drax and Doumenc decide to dispense with Polish permission and on the responsibility of their own governments allow Russian forces to enter Poland, Marshal Voroshilov – knowing of Ribbentrop's impending arrival – postpones indefinitely any continuation of the Anglo–French–Russian talks.

Tuesday, 22 Hints of a Russo-German Pact are everywhere. Chamberlain recalls Parliament for the 24th. *The Times* announces the massing of German troops on the Polish border. There are heavy losses of British gold reserves. The telegram from Ambassador Lindsay in Washington is finally deciphered, and Ambassador Kennard and his French counterpart Léon Noël try for one last time to make Colonel Beck change his mind. Sir William Seeds, British Ambassador in Moscow, accuses Molotov of negotiating in bad faith, and Chamberlain gives a fighting speech, to be broadcast by the BBC, saying it is unthinkable that Great Britain should not carry out its obligations to

Poland. Nevertheless Hitler addresses his generals, ordering them to be ready for war on the morning of the 26th.

Wednesday, 23   French citizens are advised to leave Paris. King George leaves Balmoral and returns to London. Churchill leaves France and also returns to London. A personal appeal from Chamberlain is delivered to Hitler at Berchtesgaden. Sir Percy Loraine, British Ambassador in Rome, is confident that the Italians will not fight, and Mussolini declares himself ready to mediate. At last Colonel Beck relents; but early in the evening Ribbentrop arrives in Moscow, and there, late at night, the Russo-German Pact is concluded.

Thursday, 24   Hitler has predicted that the Chamberlain government will fall; but it does not. While Marshal Voroshilov goes duck-shooting, in London Parliament reconvenes and immediately passes the Emergency Powers Act, which is given the Royal Assent the same day. The British Fleet is ordered to war stations. Goering has a meeting with Birger Dahlerus, a businessman from neutral Sweden, and proposes that Dahlerus, who has good connections in Britain, should act as a go-between. From Berlin Ambassador Henderson urges that Poland and Germany should re-establish contact, saying that it is the '*last* hope, if any, of peace: if there is a last hope'.

Friday, 25   For the first time in seven and a half years, the base rate of the Bank of England is increased, from 2 per cent to 4 per cent. The city of Coventry is bombed by IRA terrorists. Dahlerus arrives in London. Many border incidents take place in Poland, and a treaty of mutual assistance is formally signed between Poland and Great Britain. Ambassador Attolico tells Hitler that Italy will not support Germany without German help with the hardware of war. On hearing of this, Hitler cancels his invasion date, 0430 the following morning. To some it seems that war has been averted by a matter of hours; others are sure this is only a postponement.

Saturday, 26   In France, horses, cars and some property are requisitioned. The Pope issues a general appeal for peace. In Britain the football season opens, and from Italy Mussolini submits a preposterous list of Italian requirements to Ribbentrop. During the morning, Dahlerus sees Halifax again, flies back to Berlin with a letter for Goering, and returns to London later that afternoon. 'If things turn out badly,' Queen Elizabeth tells her lady-in-waiting, 'I must be with the King.' She goes to London – like many of their subjects, she prefers the idea of being bombed at home, if one must be bombed at all. Robert Coulondre, French Ambassador in Berlin, sees Hitler and appeals to him as one old soldier to another. When Coulondre cites the probable fate of women and children in any war, Hitler hesitates visibly, but

Ribbentrop strengthens him again. In the course of a Cabinet meeting in London, the Chiefs of Staff advise that the earliest possible date for any ultimatum to Germany is 1 September.

Sunday, 27   Ciano recommends British acceptance of Hitler's latest offer. The British Cabinet learns for the first time from Lord Halifax of 'Mr D', Birger Dahlerus, and his efforts. Colonel Beck agrees to consider an exchange of population between the predominantly German and predominantly Polish areas, and by midnight Dahlerus is back in Berlin.

Monday, 28   During the early hours Dahlerus meets both Goering and Sir George Ogilvie-Forbes, Counsellor of the British Embassy in Berlin, before breakfasting again with Goering. Colonel Beck refuses to go to Berlin, and Poland mobilises. Rationing is imposed in Germany, gold reaches £8 sterling an ounce; Chamberlain has another audience with the king, and Arthur Greenwood, Deputy Leader of the Opposition, visits No 10 four times. Colonel Beck at last accepts the principle of direct negotiations; but towards midnight he tells Ambassador Kennard that Polish mobilisation is proceeding.

Tuesday, 29   Ambassador Attolico suggests to Ribbentrop that a peace conference should be held; Ribbentrop rejects the idea with contempt. In the House of Commons Chamberlain makes a firm, uncompromising speech. Ambassadors Kennard and Noël persuade Colonel Beck to postpone any further mobilisation, and Hitler, angry at British interference, grudgingly accepts direct negotiations with Poland, but demands that a Polish plenipotentiary must arrive in Berlin by the end of the following day.

Wednesday, 30   There is sudden optimism on the London Stock Exchange; Hitler is said to have studied Chamberlain's speech with care. In Berlin, however, Ambassador Henderson is informed from Britain that Hitler's demand for the arrival of a Polish plenipotentiary that day is unreasonable. In Warsaw Beck tells Ambassador Kennard that Polish mobilisation will resume at midnight. Military guards are posted on all British railway stations; many D-notices are issued to newspapers, forbidding publication of specified aspects of news. Henderson and Ribbentrop meet again, and this time come close to blows: Ribbentrop 'gabbles through' Hitler's latest proposals and refuses to give Henderson a copy of the text.

Thursday, 31   During the night, Goering reads Hitler's new demands to Dahlerus, who telephones Ogilvie-Forbes at the British Embassy. Ambassador Henderson passes the information to Josef Lipski, the Polish Ambassador, and breakfasts with Ulrich von Hassell, an ex-diplomat and now a prominent anti-Nazi, before seeing Attolico. London children are evacuated from the capital, and Ciano calls Halifax to confirm that Italy will not fight either Britain or France. Nevertheless during the afternoon Hitler orders the SS as *agents-provocateurs* to attack a German radio transmitter near the Polish border, and issues 'Directive No 1 for the Conduct of the War'.

Friday, 1 September   Before dawn, German forces invade Poland. At 5.40 a.m. Berlin radio broadcasts Hitler's proclamation to his army; the invasion has been launched 'in order to put an end to this lunacy'. At 7.28 a.m. the British Foreign Office learns of the invasion. At 10 a.m. Hitler is driven through an abnormally silent Berlin to the Reichstag, from where he broadcasts the news to the world. At 2 p.m., while Colonel Beck formally breaks relations with Germany, British mobilisation starts. The House of Commons is summoned for six o'clock that evening, with all blackout curtains drawn; yet there is no immediate declaration of war against Germany. Instead, only a warning is sent to Berlin.

Saturday, 2   By 4.30 p.m. Poland has been at war for 36 hours, but no reply has been received in London from Berlin. In Cabinet, Neville Chamberlain reads out a message from the French government: they want 48 hours more delay. At 6 p.m. Halifax calls Ciano and Parliament meets 'in troubled silence'. At 7.30 p.m. a call is made from the Cabinet to Édouard Daladier, the French Prime Minister, resulting in their agreement to restate Britain's position to Germany, without a time limit. At 7.44 p.m. Chamberlain relays this to the House of Commons, where it is received as half-hearted: Arthur Greenwood demands 'no more devices'. By then, over 30 Polish towns and cities have been bombed with more than 1500 casualties of Polish women and children, while the IRA has launched a series of attacks on individual soldiers in the British Territorial Army. At 8.50 p.m. Ribbentrop informs Attolico that there will be no German withdrawal from Poland; at 9.30 p.m. Sir Percy Loraine calls London from Rome to say that Mussolini is abandoning his efforts for peace. Churchill, expecting at any minute to be invited to join the War Cabinet, has waited all day for a message from Chamberlain. A violent thunderstorm is raging over England, and a deputation from the House of Commons confronts Chamberlain demanding no further delay. 'Right, gentlemen,' the Prime Minister answers. 'This means war.' As he speaks, a great clap of thunder shakes the building. Nevertheless some people hope it may not yet be too late. Dr Fritz Hesse, Press Councillor to the German Embassy in London, comes to Sir Horace Wilson, Chamberlain's chief adviser, with an invitation from Ribbentrop for a secret meeting, 'heart to heart'. Wilson refuses, but repeats that if Germany withdraws from Poland, bygones will be bygones; and the French Foreign Minister, Georges Bonnet, contacts Ciano to try and arrange a symbolic German withdrawal. But Ciano, perhaps more realistic, ignores the message, throwing it in the waste-paper basket before returning to bed. Lord Halifax calls Paris to establish a time limit; and at 10.30 p.m. Chamberlain's peacetime Cabinet begins its final meeting. An absolute ultimatum will be sent to Germany.

Sunday, 3 At 9 a.m. the ultimatum is sent. It will expire in two hours. Worn out by the enormous efforts of the past few days, Paul Schmidt, Hitler's interpreter, oversleeps and arrives at the Foreign Office only just in time to slip in by a side door as Ambassador Henderson; enters from the front. Neither Ribbentrop nor Hitler will receive Henderson; the task is delegated to Schmidt. The brief meeting between interpreter and Ambassador is painful for both men, who have an honest respect for each other. Schmidt brings the ultimatum to Hitler and reads it slowly and carefully in English and German. Ribbentrop stares out of the window; Hitler turns to him with a savage glare and barks: 'What now?' His plans had been made in the belief, encouraged by Ribbentrop, that neither Britain nor France would fight. Now Ribbentrop predicts correctly that a French ultimatum will follow soon.

By 11 a.m. no reply has been received in London from Berlin. With great sadness and great determination Chamberlain broadcasts his tragic, historic declaration: 'I have to tell you now . . . that this country is at war with Germany.' People throughout the nation hear the message with shock and incredulity, mixed sometimes, now that there is a definite course of action to follow, with an odd sense of relief. The briefest of signals is sent to the Fleet, 'Total Germany'. Picked up in Wilhelmshaven, it is passed to Captain Dönitz, who reacts with despair and disbelief: 'My God! So it's war with England again . . .'

Newly reappointed as First Lord of the Admiralty, Churchill immediately states his fundamental policy: 'This is not a question of fighting for Danzig or fighting for Poland. We are fighting to save the whole world from the pestilence of Nazi tyranny, and in defence of all that is most sacred to man.' That evening, with most of Europe at war, Ciano writes a frank and accurate prophecy in his diary:

'I am not a military man. I do not know how the war may develop, but I know one thing – it *will* develop, and it will be long, uncertain and relentless. The participation of Great Britain makes this certain. England has made this declaration to Hitler. The war can end only with Hitler's elimination or the defeat of Britain.'

Notes on Sources

The majority of interviews with witnesses of August 1939 were conducted over the winter and spring of 1987–8 in a wide variety of locations and by correspondence. Some of the interviewees' names have been changed at their request, and to maintain a degree of privacy for them I do not feel I should specify precise dates and places. Moreover, since I have made use of the results in every chapter, it would be needlessly repetitive to include them again below; and for the same reasons I feel I should not make it explicit which of the unpublished diaries came from the Mass-Observation Archive. However the following notes on other source material may be useful.

Chapter 1   Take your gas mask with you
Churchill awakening: William Manchester, 'At home with Winston Churchill', *Illustrated London News* (May 1987); his letter to Wolmer: Martin Gilbert, *Winston S. Churchill* (hereafter *Companion*), V, *1936–39 Companion* (Heinemann, 1982), p. 1580. Parliamentary proceedings: *Hansard. Parliamentary Debates*, fifth series, vol. 350, cols. 2425–26 (hereafter *Hansard*). Paul Schmidt in Norderney: Paul Schmidt, *Hitler's Interpreter*, ed. R. H. C. Steed (Heinemann, 1951). Von Dirksen and Lord Kemsley: *Documents and Materials Relating to the Eve of the Second World War*, II, *1938–39* (hereafter *Dirksen Papers*), Ministry of Foreign Affairs of the USSR (Foreign Languages Publishing House, Moscow, 1948), pp. 113–15. Ronald Cartland in Parliament: *Hansard* vol. 350, col. 2495; and Harold Nicolson, *Diaries and Letters 1930–39*, ed. Nigel Nicolson (Collins, 1966), pp. 407–8. Background history of Poland: Norman Davies, *Heart of Europe: A Short History of Poland* (Clarendon Press, 1984); and O. Halecki, *A History of Poland*, rev. edn (Dent, 1955). Einstein and Szilard: Banesh Hoffman, with H. Dukas, *Albert Einstein: Creator and Rebel* (Hart-Davis, MacGibbon, 1973), pp. 204–8.

Chapter 2   The Earth's a good place
Fresdorf and Dönitz: Peter Padfield, *Dönitz – the Last Führer* (Panther, 1985), pp. 209–11. Cadogan: *The Diaries of Sir Alexander Cadogan 1938–45* ed. David Dilks (Cassell, 1971), pp. 168, 193, 237. Molotov and von der Schulenburg: Sidney Aster, *1939: The Making of the Second World War* (Deutsch, 1973) pp. 298–300. Wilson and von Dirksen: *Dirksen Papers*, pp. 116–25. Kubizek and Hitler: John Toland, *Adolf Hitler* (Doubleday, 1976), pp. 457, 534.

Chapter 3   The keys of peace and war
Mussolini's remarks on Nazism and Hitler: Toland, *Adolf Hitler*, pp. 326–7, 354–5. Ciano on Attolico: *Ciano's Diary 1939–43*, ed. M. Muggeridge (Doubleday, 1946), 3–4 August 1939. H. G. Wells on King George, royal visit to USA: Robert Kee, *The World We Left Behind* (Sphere, 1985), pp. 11, 252. Greenwood on Danzig: *Hansard*, vol. 350, col. 2430. Chodacki's confrontation with Danzig senate: Aster, *1939*, pp. 320–1.

Chapter 4   Holiday time, ladies and gentlemen!
Church services: Roman Catholic Missal for August 1939. Ciano and Mussolini: *Ciano's Diary*, 6–8 August 1939. Wilson and von Dirksen: *Dirksen Papers*, pp. 116–25. Cadogan's note: *Cadogan Diaries*, p. 193. Caribou flight, IRA suspects, Jewish refugees, air crash, Princess Elizabeth, Claude Viviers: in *South Wales Evening Post*, 8 August 1939. Churchill: Gilbert, *Companion*, p. 1583; and Charles Eades [Compiler], *The War Speeches of Winston Churchill*, vol. 1 (Cassell, 1951), pp. 102–5.

Chapter 5   Different worlds
Fleet inspection: *The Times*, 5 August 1939. Von Dirksen and Halifax: *Dirksen Papers*, pp. 126–32. Beck and Danzig dispute: Aster, *1939*, p. 321. Drax and Voroshilov: Aster, op. cit. p. 301. Wood and Churchill: Winston S. Churchill, *The Second World War, I, The Gathering Storm* (Cassell, 1948), pp. 183, 302. Schnurre and Astakhov: Aster, op. cit. pp. 296–300. Niusia Zamecka: Janine Phillips, *My Secret Diary* (Shepheard-Walwyn, 1982), pp. 34–5. Von Hassell: *The Von Hassell Diaries, 1938–44*, (Hamish Hamilton, 1948), p. 57. Förster: cited Kee, *The World We Left Behind*, p. 289. Ciano and Ribbentrop: *Ciano's Diary*, 11 August 1939. Hitler and Burckhardt: Toland, *Adolf Hitler*, p. 536.

Chapter 6   Can the Red Army march across Poland?
President and Mrs Roosevelt: J. P. Lash, *Eleanor and Franklin* (Deutsch, 1972), p. 582. Drax and Voroshilov: Aster, *1939*, pp. 301–2; Roger Parkinson, *Peace for our Time* (Hart-Davies, 1971), p. 173; A. P. Adamthwaite, *The Making of the Second World War* (Allen and Unwin, 1977), pp. 218–19. Ciano and Hitler: Toland, *Adolf Hitler*, p. 539; Schmidt, *Hitler's Interpreter*, pp. 132–3; *Ciano's Diary*, 12–14 August 1939. Cadogan: *Cadogan Diaries*, p. 195. Niusia: Phillips, *My Secret Diary*, pp. 11–12, 36. Chamberlain and Syers: Aster, op. cit. p.323. Von Hassell: *Von Hassell Diaries*, pp. 58–9. Schmidt: Schmidt, op. cit. p. 133.

Chapter 7   This is no time for half-measures
Von Dirksen and Attolico: *Dirksen Papers*, pp. 132–5. Dönitz: based on Padfield, *Dönitz*, pp. 170, 212; and others. Moscow talks: Aster, *1939*, pp. 304–10; Toland, *Adolf Hitler*, p. 540; Parkinson, *Peace for our Time*, pp. 174–5; *Cadogan Diaries*, pp. 195–6. Churchill: Gilbert, *Companion*, pp. 1588–9.

Chapter 8   In order to escape
Heydrich: Toland, *Adolf Hitler*, pp. 567–8; Parkinson, *Peace for our Time*, p. 171. Kennard, Moscow talks: Aster, *1939*, pp. 309–11; Lindsay, ibid.

pp. 314–17; and Parkinson, op. cit. p. 176. HMS *Formidable*: *South Wales Evening Post*, 17 August 1939. Ciano: *Ciano's Diary*, 17 August 1939.

Chapter 9 The present unusual situation

Cadogan: *Cadogan Diaries*, pp. 196, 207–8. King: Aster, *1939*, p. 317n; Noël, ibid. p. 311. Dönitz: Padfield, *Dönitz*, pp. 212-13, 220. Ciano: *Ciano's Diary*, 18 August 1939. Loraine, Beck, Henderson, Ribbentrop: cited Parkinson, *Peace for our Time*, pp. 176–7. Smigly-Rydz: cited Churchill, *The Gathering Storm*, p. 305. Henderson-Livesey, Churchill in Dreux: Gilbert, *Companion*, pp. 1590–1. Halifax *et al.* in FO, his letter to Chamberlain: *Cadogan Diaries*, pp. 197–9. Schulenburg and Molotov: Aster, op. cit. p.310; Parkinson, *Peace for our Time*, p. 178; William Shirer, *The Rise and Fall of the Third Reich* (BCA, 1968), pp. 637–8.

Chapter 10 I have them!

Hitler to Stalin: Aster, *1939*, p. 310; Parkinson, *Peace for our Time*, pp. 178–9. Ciano: *Ciano's Diary*, 19–21 August 1939. Halifax to Kennard: Aster, op. cit. p. 311; *Cadogan Diaries*, p. 199. Hitler's health: Shirer, *Third Reich*, p. 639. Dönitz: Padfield, *Dönitz*, pp. 212–13. Nicolson: *Diaries and Letters*, pp. 409–11. Stalin to Hitler: Shirer, op. cit. p. 640. Hitler's reaction: Toland, *Adolf Hitler*, p. 541. Maze on Churchill: Gilbert, *Companion*, p. 1591.

Chapter 11 The day is charged . . . and full of threats

Reactions to impending Pact: Churchill, *The Gathering Storm*, p. 307; Hore-Belisha, cited Parkinson, *Peace for our Time*, p. 179; Schmidt, *Hitler's Interpreter*, p. 134; 'Uncle Franz', Bernt Engelmann, *In Hitler's Germany* (Methuen, 1988), p. 149: *Von Hassell Diaries*, p. 62; Nicolson, *Diaries and Letters*, p. 411. The Berchtesgaden speech: Adamthwaite, *The Making of the Second World War*, pp. 219–21. Goering at Nuremburg and Town Clerk's warning: cited Parkinson, op. cit. p. 181. Churchill en route to and in Paris: Gilbert, *Companion*, pp. 1592–3. Speaker's recall: *House of Commons Journal*, vols. 194–5, Session 1938/40, p. 401. Cabinet meeting: Parkinson, op. cit. pp. 182–3; *Cadogan Diaries*, pp. 199–200. Preparations for Pact: Schmidt, op. cit. pp. 134–9. Voroshilov to Doumenc: Aster, *1939*, p. 312; Shirer, *Third Reich*, p. 651; Churchill, op. cit. pp. 305–6. Seeds to Molotov: cited Parkinson, op. cit. p. 183. Nicolson in Plymouth and London: Nicolson, op. cit. pp. 411–12. Kennedy and Halifax: Aster, op. cit. pp. 334–5. Ciano: *Ciano's Diary*, 23 August 1939. Niusia: Phillips, *My Secret Diary*, p. 42. Hitler to Chamberlain: N. Baynes (ed.), *Hitler's Speeches, April 1922–August 1939*, (II) OUP for RIIA, 1942, pp. 1682–5. Stalin to Ribbentrop: Aster, op. cit. p. 313. Halifax and Cadogan: *Cadogan's Diaries*, p. 200.

Chapter 12 Action will begin

King and Ciano: *Ciano's Diary*, 24 August 1939. Niusia: Phillips, *My Secret Diary*, pp. 42–3. Henderson to Halifax: Toland, *Adolf Hitler*, p. 550. Nicolson to Vita Sackville-West: Nicolson, *Diaries and Letters*, p. 413. Cadogan to

Halifax: *Cadogan Diaries*, pp. 200-1. Dahlerus and Goering: Aster, *1939*, pp. 339–40. Cazalet, Channon: Gilbert, *Companion*, pp. 1596–7. Commons vote: *House of Commons Journal*, p. 401. German return from Moscow: Schmidt, *Hitler's Interpreter*, pp. 139–41. Cadogan: *Cadogan Diaries*, pp. 200–1. Ciano: *Ciano's Diary*, 25 August 1939. Hitler's reaction to Chamberlain speech: Schmidt, op. cit. pp. 141-3; and to Anglo–Polish Treaty, ibid. p. 144; and with Coulondre, ibid. pp. 144–5; and with Attolico, ibid. pp. 145–6. I R A bombing: Kee, *The World We Left Behind*, pp. 300–1. 'Uncle Franz' and Hitler's cancellation: Engelmann, *In Hitler's Germany*, p. 150.

Chapter 13   To measure the unknowable
Seeds' reaction: Aster, *1939*, p. 319. Voroshilov to Drax: ibid. p. 313. Ciano: *Ciano's Diary*, 26 August 1939. *Von Hassell Diaries*, p. 63. Roberts: cited Richard Lamb, *The Ghosts of Peace 1935-1945* (Michael Russell, 1987), p. 112. Cadogan: *Cadogan Diaries*, p. 202. Radio team: Engelmann, *In Hitler's Germany*, p. 150. Ribbentrop and Attolico, and Hitler to Mussolini: Toland, *Adolf Hitler*, pp. 555–6. Cabinet and earliest possible ultimatum: Aster, op. cit. pp. 341–2; Parkinson, *Peace for our Time*, p. 190. Dahlerus and Hitler: Shirer, *Third Reich*, p. 691; Toland, op. cit. pp. 556–7; Padfield, *Dönitz*, p. 214.

Chapter 14   What's the use of worrying?
Strange man: Kee, *The World We Left Behind*, pp. 304–5. Von Hassell: *Von Hassell Diaries*, pp. 62, 64. Hitler to Daladier: Schmidt, *Hitler's Interpreter*, pp. 147–8; Toland, *Adolf Hitler*, p. 558. Dahlerus and Chamberlain: *Cadogan Diaries*, pp. 202–3; Toland, op. cit. p. 559; Parkinson, *Peace for our Time*, pp. 191–2; Aster, *1939*, pp. 343–4, 349. Ciano to Halifax and to Mussolini: *Ciano's Diary*, 27 August 1939; on British note, ibid. 28 August 1939. Oster: Shirer, *Third Reich*, p. 681. Nicolson: *Diaries and Letters*, p. 413. Henderson and Hitler: Aster, op. cit. pp. 350–1; Toland, op. cit. p. 560; Parkinson, op. cit. pp. 195–6; Schmidt, op. cit. p. 148.

Chapter 15   And still we wait from day to day
Cadogan *et al* in Park: *Cadogan Diaries*, p. 204; on plebiscite and Corbin, ibid. pp. 204–5. Nicolson: *Diaries and Letters*, pp. 414–15. Churchill on Eden: Churchill, *The Gathering Storm*, p. 201. Chamberlain's speech: *Hansard*, vol. 357, cols. 111–16. Niusia: Phillips, *My Secret Diary*, p. 46. Henderson and Hitler: *Cadogan Diaries*, p. 204; Schmidt, *Hitler's Interpreter*, pp. 148–9; Shirer, *Third Reich*, p. 699; Parkinson, *Peace for our Time*, pp. 198–9. Mrs Roosevelt: Lash, *Eleanor and Franklin*, p. 583. Ciano: *Ciano's Diary*, 29 August 1939. Kennard: Parkinson, op. cit. p. 200. Halder: Aster, *1939*, p. 365; Parkinson, op. cit. p. 201. Von Hassell: *Von Hassell Diaries*, p. 64.

Chapter 16   I hear the wings of the angel of peace
Ribbentrop and Henderson: Schmidt, *Hitler's Interpreter*, pp. 150–3; Aster, *1939*, p. 359; Parkinson, *Peace for our Time*, pp. 202–3. Dahlerus and Goering: Parkinson, op. cit. p. 204; Lamb, *The Ghosts of Peace*, p. 115; Shirer, *Third*

Reich, p. 705. Kennard and Lipski: Aster, op. cit. pp. 360–1; Shirer, op. cit. pp. 706–7; and Henderson: ibid. p. 708n. Ciano: *Ciano's Diary*, 31 August 1939. Henderson and Malhomme: Aster, op. cit. p. 361; and von Hassell: *Von Hassell Diaries*, pp. 67–8. Churchill: Churchill, *The Gathering Storm*, p. 313; Gilbert, *Companion*, p. 1601. Goering and von Hassell: *Von Hassell Diaries*, pp. 68–9; and tea-party: Parkinson, op. cit. p. 205; Shirer, op. cit. pp. 715–16. Henderson, Dahlerus, Lipski: Aster, op. cit, pp. 361–2; Parkinson, op. cit. p. 204; von Hassell, *Von Hassell Diaries*, pp. 69–70; Shirer, op. cit. pp. 710–11. Wilson and Dahlerus: Toland, *Adolf Hitler*, p. 566; Aster, op. cit. p. 363; Parkinson, op. cit. p. 204. Lipski and Beck: Aster, op. cit. p. 364; and Ribbentrop: Schmidt, op. cit. p. 154. Niusia: Phillips, *My Secret Diary*, pp. 46–7. Naujocks: Parkinson, op. cit. p. 205; Shirer, op. cit. pp. 718–19. 'Directive No. 1': ibid. pp. 712–13; *Hitler's War Directives 1939–45*, ed. H. R. Trevor-Roper (Sidgwick and Jackson, 1964), p. 3. Dönitz, and Hitler to Albrecht: Padfield, *Dönitz*, p. 215. Nicolson: *Diaries and Letters*, p. 416. Shirer: Shirer, op. cit. p. 704.

Chapter 17   Time limit?
Churchill to Ironside: Gilbert, *Companion*, p. 1602. Mrs Roosevelt: Lash, *Eleanor and Franklin*, p. 583. Hitler's speech in Opera House: Shirer, *Third Reich*, pp. 722–4. Reactions to it: ibid. p. 721; von Hassell, *Von Hassell Diaries*, p. 71; Engelmann, *In Hitler's Germany*, pp. 151–2. Niusia: Phillips, *My Secret Diary*, pp. 47–8. Hore-Belisha, Raczynski and Halifax: Aster, *1939*, pp. 368–9. Cadogan: *Cadogan Diaries*, pp. 211–13. Dahlerus and Hitler: Toland, *Adolf Hitler*, p. 571; and Cadogan: Aster, op. cit. p. 370; Shirer, op. cit. p. 726. French Parliament: Aster, op. cit. p. 372. British Parliament: ibid.; *Hansard*, vol. 351, cols. 126ff; Nicolson, *Diaries and Letters*, pp. 416–20; Aster, op. cit. pp. 378–80; Parkinson, *Peace for our Time*, pp. 214–15. Churchill to Chamberlain: Gilbert, *Companion*, pp. 1605–6. Halifax to Phipps: Parkinson, op. cit. p. 212. Italian intervention: *Ciano's Diary*, 2 September 1939. Bonnet and Halifax: Aster, op. cit. p. 375; and Beck, ibid. p. 376; Shirer, op. cit. p. 730n. 'Extremely difficult' Cabinet: Aster, op. cit. pp. 376–8; Parkinson, op. cit. pp. 213–14. Cabinet rebellion: Aster, op. cit. pp. 380–3, 385–7.

18   All that beautiful Sunday
Presentation of British ultimatum: Schmidt, *Hitler's Interpreter*, pp. 156–8; Shirer, *Third Reich*, pp. 739–40. Evacuation: Carlton Jackson, *Who Will Take Care of our Children?* (Methuen, 1985), pp. various. Ciano: *Ciano's Diary*, 3 September 1939. Dahlerus and Cadogan: *Cadogan Diaries*, pp. 212–13; Parkinson, *Peace for our Time* p. 218. Liddell on Chamberlain: Aster, *1939*, p. 389. Chamberlain's broadcast: ibid.; *Cadogan Diaries*, p. 213; Parkinson, op. cit. p. 218. Dönitz: Padfield, *Dönitz*, pp. 216–17. Churchill on Danzig: Eades, *Churchill*, pp. 106–7.

Epilogue
'The one real, living question': *Picture Post*, 16 September 1939, p. 30.

INDEX